THE *W*ING OF MADNESS

J'ai cultivé mon hystérie avec jouissance et terreur. Maintenant, j'ai toujours le vertige, et aujourd'hui, 23 janvier 1862, j'ai subi un singulier avertissement, j'ai senti passer sur moi le vent d'aile de l'imbécillité.

—Charles Baudelaire, *Mon coeur mis à nu, 87*

THE *W*ING OF MADNESS

THE LIFE AND WORK OF
R. D. LAING

DANIEL BURSTON

HARVARD UNIVERSITY PRESS

CAMBRIDGE, MASSACHUSETTS, AND LONDON, ENGLAND • 1996

Design by Marianne Perlak
Photograph on title page by Kirk Tougas

Library of Congress Cataloging–in–Publication Data

Burston, Daniel, 1954–
    The wing of madness : the life and work of R. D. Laing / Daniel
Burston.
        p.   cm.
    Includes bibliographical references and index.
    ISBN 0-674-95358-4 (alk. paper)
    1. Laing, R. D. (Ronald David), 1927–   2. Psychiatrists—
United States—Biography.   I. Title.
RC438.6.L34b87   1996
616.89'0092—dc20
[B]

95-53054

For my wife, Sharna

ACKNOWLEDGMENTS

There are several books in preparation or already published on R. D. Laing, written by former students, friends, and family members. Although I studied his work closely during my twenties and thirties, my personal contact with Laing was perfunctory. I cannot claim to be his pupil, nor can I write from an insider's perspective. Just before his death, though, we did exchange letters. On December 3, 1988, I wrote Laing in Austria to see what he thought of a plan of mine to do a historical monograph on Scotland's contributions to psychoanalysis, which would focus on the work of Ian Suttie, W. R. D. Fairbairn, John Sutherland, and Laing himself. He found the idea congenial and on January 1, 1989, wrote back to suggest a meeting that June in Vancouver, where he was running a week-long workshop with his friend and student, Andrew Feldmar.

As luck would have it, I was unable to meet Laing that spring and wanted to postpone our meeting to the following year. But it was not to be. On August 25, 1989, I got a note from Feldmar, saying that Laing had died two days before of a heart attack. Several months later, when Harvard University Press expressed interest in my projected study of Laing, I applied for grants that enabled me to travel to London, Glasgow, Edinburgh, and New York to speak with his family, friends, and associates. When face-to-face meetings proved impossible to arrange, I corresponded with many people in order to fill the gaps in my knowledge. But even now, after much work and reflection, many gaps and uncertainties remain.

From almost any point of view, and especially a biographical one, Ronald Laing is a formidable subject. A narrative account or reconstruction of a person's life is of necessity selective, and though objectivity is always a worthy goal, in matters like these, with a subject like Laing, complete objectivity is as elusive as the philosopher's stone. So a conscientious biographer will strive for balance and perspective, trying to reconcile the tales and impressions gleaned from his subject's friends, relatives, and associates with the available documentary evidence. Then a biographer is faced with the enormous task of reconciling stories that often sound as if they were about several different people, not just one individual. With Laing, this common problem assumed nightmarish proportions. Laing's kindness, generosity, courage, industry, and patience, and his egotism, sexism, and self-indulgence, his antic and sardonic humor, his boyish enthusiasms, his bottomless despair—all these traits were brought home to me in a panoply of recollections too rich to include in full.

Accordingly, and despite the invaluable assistance and insights afforded me by others, I must emphasize that the final responsibility for this portrait of Laing, and my analysis of his work, is mine and mine alone. I cannot possibly thank all my interlocutors with anything close to the generosity they have shown me, and so I resort to the rather cold expedient of listing them here in alphabetical order. Some are dead now, but to all of them my deepest thanks: Doris Nagel Baker, Joseph Berke, John Bowlby, Ted Carlson, Kay Carmichael, Ben Churchill, Leonard Davidson, James Davie, Andrew Feldmar, Lillian Fischer, Roland Forrester, Richard Gelfer, Alan Hall, James Hood, Ricki Hornstein, Edie Irwin, Douglas Kirsner, Ethel Laing, Peter Lomas, Leon Redler, Richard Rojcwicz, John and Flora Roy, Roberta Russell, Oliver Sacks, Louis Sass, Morton Schatzman, John and Phyllis Schimel, Mina Simyon, Anthony Storr, John Sutherland, James Templeton, Stephen Ticktin, Eric and Beulah Trist, Phyllis Webb, Wayne Whymark, and Earl Witenberg.

In addition to the ideas and information gathered from these people, I learned a good deal from Adrian Laing's *R. D. Laing: A Biography* and from Bob Mullan's *Mad To Be Normal: Conversations with R. D. Laing*.

Chapter 1 of my book is based in part on a presentation made to the History of Psychiatry Section at the Cornell University Medical Center, March 17, 1993. I am grateful to my friends and colleagues there for feedback and encouragement, particularly the late Eric Carlson. Chapter 9 stems from a paper delivered at the twelfth annual conference of the Simon Silverman Phenomenology Center at Duquesne University, March 11–12, 1994. I thank the Silverman Center's board and my colleagues at Duquesne for giving me the chance to plan and participate in the meeting.

Finally, I wish to extend very warm and special thanks to several interlocutors whose experience and advice were particularly helpful: Sidney Briskin, John Heaton, Theodor Itten, Loren Mosher, Charles Rycroft, Michael Thompson, and Marcelle Vincent. They may not agree with everything I say, but they broadened and transformed my view of Laing in many ways.

CONTENTS

1 BEGINNINGS 1

2 SCHOOLING 21

3 THE TAVISTOCK AND FAMILY RESEARCH 45

4 IN AND OUT OF KINGSLEY HALL 77

5 THE TURN TO MYSTICISM 93

6 BIRTH AND BEFORE 115

7 FADE TO BLACK 133

8 A TOPOGRAPHY OF BABEL 151

9 PHILOSOPHICAL ANTHROPOLOGY 175

10 THE CRITIQUE OF PSYCHOANALYSIS 197

11 PSYCHIATRY THEN AND NOW 235

NOTES 253

REFERENCES 259

INDEX 271

BEGINNINGS

Ronald David Laing was born on October 7, 1927, and died on August 23, 1989. He is buried in Glasgow Cathedral, and his portrait hangs in the National Portrait Gallery in Edinburgh. Laing was fiercely proud of his Scottish origins, and Scotland, on the whole, is proud of him. In the course of a colorful and turbulent life, Laing rose from somewhat unlikely beginnings to become the most controversial psychotherapist of the later twentieth century, with his books selling in the millions in more than twenty languages.

During the 1960s and 1970s Laing influenced many people in diverse disciplines and walks of life. He was committed to the idea that psychotic episodes involve a willful or involuntary repudiation of a socially adapted "false self" and could lead to a more integrated and authentic mode of personal existence. Rather than stop or contain the process, Laing wanted to facilitate it—free from the coercive sanctions that psychiatry imposes on regressive and irrational behavior. "Madness need not be all breakdown," he said. "It may also be breakthrough" (1970, p. 133).

Laing's forthright and articulate challenges to conventional wisdom about the origins, meaning, and treatment of mental disturbances elicited angry condemnation from the bastions of medical orthodoxy. And though his contributions to contemporary thought and modern psychiatry were profound, his craving for fame and his need to take the role of guru contributed to the decline of his reputation as a serious thinker. Now that he is dead, there is a real danger that his tarnished public image will detract from an ongoing discussion and evaluation of his work. That would be a tragic mistake.

Judging from anecdotes told by his friends, family, and colleagues, Laing was a study in sharp and bewildering contrasts. At different times and in different ways, he was by turns disciplined and debauched, self-effacing and arrogant, gentle and belligerent, shy and exhibitionist, empathic and self-centered, intensely emotional or profoundly cerebral. He had a rare sensitivity to those in acute mental distress, and an impish, ungovernable need to shock and offend those he considered dulled by convention. One of his associates, Leon Redler, remarks:

> Those of us who met Ronnie can testify that such meetings were fundamentally (and paradoxically) without supports, unpredictable, disturbing, heartening, inspiring, awe-ful and/or awful. There was enhanced possibility of what he and we once called "authentic meeting" . . .
>
> Ronnie had a quite an other effect on people, an effect coming, unpredictably, from elsewhere. Like the "pharmacon" in Plato's texts, it perhaps remains undecidable in any instance, whether this effect was remedy and/or poison. Or indeed, whether or not he was a *pharmakeus,* a kind of magician, a character no logic can confine within a non-contradictory definition. Or a *pharmakos,* a rascal, a contaminated and contaminating agent, to be expelled, in one way or another. (Redler, 1989)

Laing, we know, was nothing if not contradictory: an accomplished pianist, a precocious student of the classics, a rebel and a romantic, an iconoclast, psychoanalyst, philosopher, theologian, and drunk. In the process of living out these various roles, Laing had to show many different faces. So it is interesting to note that Laing often disparaged the idea that the individual possesses a core personality, a nucleus of personal attributes that remains relatively stable across time and different social contexts. In truth, Laing said, we all have as many selves or personalities as we have social contexts (1967a, pp. 82–83). Thus if we make a radical alteration in the person's social field, presumably a new "self" will put in an appearance—a view expressed earlier by William James, the dramatist Luigi Pirandello, the social psychologist George Herbert Mead, and more recently by the sociologist Erving Goffman, the psychologist Walter Mischel, and the philosopher Rom Harre.

It might be argued that Laing's social constructivism was totally at odds with his existentialist convictions. After all, his first book, *The Divided Self,* was predicated on the idea that everyone, sane or mad, possesses both a real and a false self (or selves). Ideally, Laing speculated, the sane person retains some ability for self-disclosure and communion with others, while the mad person desperately defends the real self from encroachment or dissolution by a flight into fantasy. Either way, sane or mad, the distinction between real and false selves was initially integral to Laing's interpretation of existential phenomenology.

Yet how can you posit a plurality of selves, as some constructivists do, and still maintain that one or another of them is more real or genuine than any other? From a purely constructivist standpoint, all "selves," as social artifacts, are equally real or equally false, depending on your point of view. The most that may be possible within an existentialist framework is to posit a plurality of false selves in contradistinction to one real self, however internally fragmented or contradictory that self may be.

But this issue aside, it may help to understand Laing if we consider the possibility that his assertions about context-dependent selves represent the fruits of introspection, as much as the disinterested observation of other people's behavior. Perhaps he sensed that deep down he had many characters, as Pirandello might have said, and this sensitized him to the inconsistencies of thought, feeling, and behavior elicited when people enter the different social worlds that comprise their existence. It may also account for the mercurial element in his personality. The anthropologist Joan Westcott, among others, likened him to the Trickster (Mezan, 1972, pp. 94–95), an archetypal figure in world mythology who deliberately transgresses social conventions and is able to assume animal forms or change its sex at will.

Mainstream psychoanalysis has yet to recognize the power and significance of the trickster motif. But Jungian psychology treats the trickster as a figure whose behavior in dreams and myths warrants close attention (Jung, 1954). On a positive and constructive plane, the trickster is an agent of change and renewal, who obliges us to relinquish our fictive self-image and beliefs by orchestrating a confrontation between the conscious personality and the side of our selves we prefer to disavow—in Jung's terminology, our "shadow side." Here the trickster is a relentless and often shocking truthteller, who gives voice to disturbing truths most of us repress. Thus the sudden appearance of the trickster figure in dreams may herald an episode of upheaval and constructive disillusionment—productive and memorable, though not always pleasant.

On a less constructive note, the appearance of the trickster in dreams may signify an arrest in development, since the trickster is an eternal adolescent whose antipathy to authority and convention renders it difficult or impossible for him to enter into the normal flow of life. This side of the trickster is more disturbing, since it harbors a potential for degeneration into fickle, exhibitionist, and sadistic behavior, with no way of outgrowing a somewhat childish attitude toward reality.

As an adult, then, R. D. Laing was a strangely powerful and not always constructive presence. He was capable of great warmth and sensitivity, but also took pleasure in upsetting people's perception of themselves and the world they live in. Doubtless there were some Socratic intentions behind Laing's therapeutic posturing. At other times, his trickster-like communications had more in common with a Marx Brothers routine, the problem being that others, including his closest friends, became the butt of his ridicule. In short, anger and contempt as well as a desire to emancipate or alert others to the truth were expressed in his protean personality and shifting therapeutic stratagems. Nothing conveys this more clearly than his mantra-like malediction from "The Bird of Paradise": "If I could turn you on, if I could drive you out of your wretched mind, if I could tell you, I would let you know."

Despite the dizzying proliferation of contradictions that emerges as one probes the effects of Laing's presence on others, it seems that there are several personal attributes that remained relatively constant, despite his shifting fortunes. From a very early age, Laing was driven by a deep desire to understand the various meanings and levels of human experience. He had an extremely low tolerance for sham and an uncanny ability to sense it in those around him. Despite the contradictions of his surface persona—and some glaring inaccuracies in his recollection of past events—Laing had a strong disposition to seek out the truth and a profound appreciation for the

unknown (and unknowable) depths of being that surround our isolated islands of consciousness—an epistemological humility and an
appreciation of the mysteries of human existence that is rare and re-
freshing in our scientistic culture.

As a consequence of all this, Laing also had an exquisite sensitivity to the demonic dimension of modern science, to the reifications
of medicine, psychiatry, and psychology, whose search for knowledge is often buttressed by the most appalling research practices. Indeed, a salient feature of Laing's critique of modern life is the
observation that the demonic side of science (which he depicted so
vividly) lies in its blind erosion of our sense of solidarity with one
another and with other species by rationalizing cruelty and indifference.

Another set of traits clustered in Laing's personality was loosely
tied with the first, to both good and bad effect. In his early adolescence, Laing relates (Mezan, 1976), he determined to become a
world-famous artist or intellectual, so that his thirst for knowledge
and the great energy he devoted to that goal were never completely
disentangled from his craving for fame and recognition. Laing's
driving ambition expressed itself in other ways as well. In later life
he was often given to intellectual one-upmanship and other kinds of
competitive self-assertiveness, which were antithetical to his emphasis on the importance of genuine meeting and communion.

Thus, despite his humane values and his antipathy to most standards of respectability, Laing was an ambitious and highly competitive man. He always admired people who stood at the top of their
class or field of endeavor, whether they were mathematicians, chess
players, or tennis pros, and no matter what their conduct was outside their specific areas of achievement—which, apart from its elitist
coloration, amounts to a kind of idolatry. And as more than one of
his friends noted, the fact that Laing died of a heart attack competing fiercely in a tennis match against a younger opponent comes as
no surprise.

This particular feature of Laing's character would not be noteworthy if it were not in such conflict with his stated values, and if it
did not play such a determining role in his life. On the one hand,
Laing's adolescent ambition, and his need to become a figure of
world-historical significance, drove him to prodigious intellectual effort and accomplishment. But it also gave his life an obsessiveness

that must have been difficult for him and for those close to him as well.

Another consequence of Laing's invidious passions is that they tended to corrode his capacity for trust, as ambition and competitiveness are wont to do. This was all the more unfortunate because the circumstances of his childhood had diminished his capacity for trust from the outset. Moreover, periods of tranquility were relatively few and far between in Laing's hectic life, and he probably would have benefited from being able to unburden himself to another human being without reservation. By most accounts, however, Laing could seldom open up to another person, since he thought no one was in step with him intellectually. (At any rate, that was his excuse.) Apart from the element of snobbishness involved, this attitude may have belied a deep fear of dependence, coupled with basic mistrust, that he carried with him throughout his adult life.

Another recurrent theme in Laing's life was a sense of personal disappointment. In the early 1960s, as his fame began to spread and his standard of living became more comfortable, Laing confided to Ben Churchill, a friend in broadcasting, that he felt ignored by the psychoanalytic community in Britain—as indeed he was. According to others who knew him then, he also expressed disappointment in his analyst, Charles Rycroft, and in his many associates at the Tavistock Clinic, most of whom liked and admired Laing tremendously, despite his perplexing ways.

In the late sixties, Laing started to become disenchanted with the Philadelphia Association, an organization he had co-founded to develop therapeutic communities. But it took him until 1983 to break completely with his colleagues (Cooper et al., 1989). Shortly before then, during the late 1970s, Laing experienced a number of convergent crises affecting his creativity and his financial solvency, as he tried to remold his public image as a psychotherapist, philosopher, and mystic into a more popular image as a kind of philosopher/poet/entertainer. Despite his earlier notoriety, however, the public was unsympathetic to his efforts, and he was frustrated by the failure of his literary, musical and theatrical endeavors. (This rendered him all the more vulnerable when his second marriage, to Jutta Werner, unraveled in 1981.)

Finally, in 1982, while lecturing at the Burgholzli Institute in

Zurich, Laing complained bitterly to Theodor Itten that he should
have been given the chair in psychiatry at Cambridge (currently held
by Martin Roth)—though he had already turned down the offer of a
professorship at Princeton University (Itten, 1992).

In short, for most of his professional life, Laing was beset by disappointment about something or other. If we examine the various
circumstances that vexed Laing, we can discern common threads
underlying his complaints: people did not understand or appreciate
him or were not on his intellectual level. Perhaps beneath his
rugged, independent exterior, Laing had a deep need for unconditional love and acceptance that was never met or even fully conscious, which led to many conflicts, crises, and felt betrayals.

Then again, Laing's complaints about the lack of recognition from
psychiatric colleagues points to a deep-seated ambiguity in his character that had torturous emotional repercussions: on the one hand, a
virulent contempt for conventional standards of respectability and,
on the other, a searing thirst for recognition. Leaving aside its patent
inconsistency (or indeed hypocrisy), this is a well-known recipe for
chronic malaise, and one wonders how often Laing was aware of it,
or if he even allowed himself to contemplate this painful ambivalence as a recurrent source of misery in his life. Though many have
disagreed with me on this point, I think that Laing was aware of
only one aspect of this internal contradiction at a time.

Judging from his memoirs and the testimony of friends and relatives, one has to imagine that Laing was an isolated and sad child, an
industrious and rebellious adolescent, and a gifted, iconoclastic
adult who distrusted authority and had a rare sympathy for the mad
and the oppressed. But he was also a troubled, often tormented
man, who in his own estimation suffered from severe bouts of depression and excessive drinking. And though he certainly worked
hard enough for it, fame did not bring him either happiness or stability. Indeed, many people have observed that it only intensified his
inner contradictions (for instance, James Hood, letter, *The Independent,* August 29, 1989; John Heaton, personal communication, June
1990; Phyllis Schimel, personal communication, June 7, 1991).

All that said, it bears remembering that in attempting to assess
ideas in substantive terms, they must stand or fall on their own merits. Although most of us stubbornly prefer to think otherwise, a the-

ory is no more likely to be true or useful if its author is sober, congenial, or saintly in personal conduct than it is if he (or she) is obviously unhappy or routinely transgresses convention.

It is a striking phenomenon. The educated public reads books about the creative geniuses of our century—Picasso, Stravinsky, Sartre, or Beckett, say—and discovers, to their horror and delight, that these men could be perfect scoundrels in dealing with their closest associates and with their spouses, children, or lovers. But no one declares that personal conduct or baser passions detract from the magnitude of their achievements. Similarly, nobody much cares if Albert Einstein kept a mistress or if Ludwig Wittgenstein was gay. (Nor should they.)

Rightly or wrongly, for better or worse, this is simply not the case in the mental health professions. In that sphere of endeavor, even well-educated people expect the reigning virtuosi to live exemplary or at least orderly lives. Without the appearance of normality, the faults and frailties of their idols begin to loom large in their imaginations, and they start to doubt the validity of their ideas. Thus, if someone had a secret history of drug use (such as Freud and cocaine in 1886–1895) or of psychotic interludes (such as Jung in 1914–1919), people will question their fitness to practice or to make pronouncements on the human mind.

Of course I am not denying that the public has a right to know the truth in such instances. But has it the right or, more important, the ability to judge such men? All too often, the views of pundits or the man in the street reflect repressed envy, or the dashed hopes of a former apostle, anxious to turn an old icon into a negative or inverted fetish on which they can now vent their spleen.

Still, with all the damning disclosures that have emerged of late, Freud and Jung continue to hold a firm place in posterity—and despite their secretiveness and their tendency to bully and manipulate their followers and to neglect their wives and children. By contrast, Laing's hold on posterity seems tenuous indeed. Despite the many criticisms of his life and work to be found in these pages, my thesis is that Laing's contribution to psychology and psychiatry—though different, of course, and distinctively his own—is possibly of the same order of magnitude as theirs, and that in the present climate of opinion, we must be very careful to assess his personal virtues and his intellectual merits on separate scales of value.

Those inclined to dismiss Laing because of his personal life may have difficulty with this book. My aim is to illuminate those aspects of Laing's life that have a direct bearing on the development of his work and, more important, to set his contribution to the human sciences within the history of ideas. Seen in this context and in historical perspective, the creative tensions in Laing's work are more likely to surface for inspection, and perhaps point the way for future theory and research.

Ronald David Laing was born at 21 Ardbeg Street in Glasgow, Scotland, on October 7, 1927. He was the only child of David Park McNair Laing and Amelia Elizabeth (nee Kirkwood), a quiet Presbyterian couple. Though situated in the middle-class district of Govanhill, the Laing flat was close to an impoverished district of Glasgow known as the Gorbals, where conditions of life were comparable to the terrifying squalor described in Manchester by Friedrich Engels in *The Conditions of the Working Class in England in 1844* and later by the novelist Jack London in *People of the Abyss* (1903).[1]

Young Ronald—named after Ronald Colman, the romantic actor—lacked for playmates and so he missed the kind of companionship most children need. Moreover, the Laing home was not always peaceful, and even when it was, there were complex tensions lurking beneath the surface. To begin with, the Laings and the Kirkwoods did not get along. David's younger sister, Ethel Laing, recalled that her parents heartily disapproved of Amelia, whom they thought an unsuitable match for a man of David's temperament. Amelia in turn, as Laing recalls, felt she had married beneath her station, and that her husband's lack of ambition was a kind of personal betrayal (Mullan, 1994, pp. 20–23).

Worse still, Ronald Laing had vivid memories of domestic violence dating back to infancy. Though David did not beat Amelia, confrontations with his own father, John, often erupted in brutal physical scenes in the parlor in the child's presence (for instance, Laing, 1976, pp. 4–5).[2] The fights between his father and grandfather had a profound effect. In middle age Laing often expressed a fear that he might perpetuate some of the same destructive interpersonal patterns with his own sons (1985, p. 104). He also feared that, like his father and his grandfather before him, he would suffer a late midlife crisis that would paralyse him emotionally and intellectually. (And so he did.) In any case, it is surely no accident that as an adult probing the causes of mental anguish, Laing came to emphasize the transpersonal and transgenerational character of many psychological disturbances.

Another noteworthy feature of Laing's childhood was the lack of affection between Ronald and his mother. Laing was born ten years after his parents married and, by their own peculiar account, long after they had ceased having sexual relations (Mullan, pp. 22–24). For reasons no one can fathom, Amelia managed to conceal her pregnancy from her entire family until the very day of delivery, suggesting that whatever maternal pride she might have felt was grotesquely overshadowed by prudery, shame, or a perverse need to keep others in the dark (A. Laing, p. 20). After his birth, Laing says, Amelia went into a precipitous decline, so that the infant had two rather negligent wet nurses minister to him before she felt fit (1976, p. 3). And two months after his birth, Amelia's father died, leaving her with a very complicated mourning process to deal with. The following year, David's mother died as well. Add to this familial anguish the deepening gloom that descended on Glasgow during the depression and World War II, and the opening chapters of Laing's childhood begin to look grim indeed.

All things considered, Ronald's relationship to his mother was the single most depressing factor in his early life. Without minimizing the suffering caused by their deepening estrangement, in his biography Adrian Laing suggests that the relationship between mother and son went awry "not because of the absence of love but because of the absence of genuine friendship" (p. 21). Other observers are less sanguine. As much as she disputed her nephew's recollections of early social isolation (see Mullan, p. 21), Ethel Laing did insist that Ronald's characterizations of his mother were true to character—that Amelia was not truthful and frequently made up stories to foment trouble between her husband and his friends. In addition, Ethel said, Amelia was inclined to intense envy and jealousy, had extravagant suspicions of others' motives, and liked to indulge in character assassination.

Years later, Laing recalled, Amelia was scandalized upon seeing the word "fuck" in his *Politics of Experience;* she started the habit of sticking pins into an effigy of her son, called a "Ronald doll," with the express intention of inducing a heart attack (Clare, 1985). Whether this gesture was intended as an act of magical retribution, like voodoo, or just as a joke—which seems doubtful—the malevolence expressed in such bizarre behavior is palpable.

Then as now, vehement displays of hatred would not be tolerated toward young children, so Amelia's anger took more indirect forms. For example, when Ronald was five, he became very fond of a little wooden horse. Although such an attachment was quite normal, Amelia had the toy burned, saying that the boy was getting too attached to it (Laing, 1985). She immediately replaced Ronald's beloved toy with a shiny new pedal car. But Ethel Laing, who witnessed this event, felt that the real purpose of the exercise was not to gratify wee Ronnie with a better toy but to part him forcefully from what he loved. Her heart went out to him. As a result, evidently, a few weeks later Amelia forbade unsupervised visits between Ronald and his aunt on the grounds that he was becoming too attached to *her*. These were not isolated instances. Many years later, when Laing returned from army service, he discovered that Amelia had burned all his school and university papers, and that the baby grand piano he had learned music on was gone. Though she refused to explain things to Laing directly, Amelia told Laing's daughter, Susan, that she had taken an ax to the piano so that Ronald would not sell it (Mullan, p. 55).

To explain this last instance of hostile behavior, some have suggested that Amelia was utterly unsentimental about the past and unusually averse to clutter. Perhaps. But Laing's music was rooted in a deep bond with his father, and in attacking that link—bodily, as it were—Amelia was being more than merely thoughtless. Reading Laing's memoirs, listening to his aunt and to others who knew or met Amelia, one gets the distinct impression that from the outset, on some very deep level, Laing was not a wanted child. At the same time apparently, Amelia felt constrained to behave in ways that conformed to prevailing cultural expectations of what a mother *should* feel toward her offspring. While sending Ronald tacit messages that she did not want him or respect his needs and feelings—burning his favorite toy, exiling his favorite aunt—she also had to disavow the real content of these communications, disguising them as love. Moreover, to live up to her image of what a mother should be in her own mind, she not only had to deceive herself about her real feelings and intentions, but had to make her son, her spouse, and all concerned experience the ostensible meaning behind her hostile outbursts as the real ones, which required the others to disavow their experience of what was really happening, and so on. Laing later termed such a process within families *mystification.*

Was Amelia mad? Laing waffled on the question. He emphatically denied that she was mad in terms of clinical psychiatric classifications but freely acknowledged that, even before he was born, she was mad "in a sense" and that throughout his childhood this intelligent, vigorous, and beautiful woman was extremely withdrawn, ambivalent, and schizoid (Mullan, pp. 61–64). But according to Joseph Schorstein, a neurologist who mentored Laing in his mid-twenties, Amelia Laing was not merely schizoid but psychotic. This view is shared by Richard Gelfer, a schoolmate of Laing's who trained as a psychiatrist and introduced him to LSD. Gelfer notes that, as Laing himself recalled, on the rare occasions when Amelia traveled downtown with the boy, she took lengthy and elaborate detours around certain districts of Glasgow in order to avoid the malign influence of people living there who were hostile to her. The pinpricking of a voodoo doll fits the same pattern, as did her habit of burning most of the trash inside their flat, lest the neighbors discover what was in it.

Whatever diagnostic label one might affix to Amelia's odd behavior, one can only suppose that the tensions and perplexities generated by his mother's behavior could have driven a weaker or less self-possessed child over the edge or into severe developmental arrest. So it is no fluke that Laing's first book, *The Divided Self,* thematized the problems of "ontological insecurity" experienced by people whose needs, feelings, and experiences are consistently nullified in early childhood. Nor is it a coincidence that in *The Facts of Life,* some seventeen years later, Laing speculated that most infants are actually unwanted.

In the current climate of opinion, such descriptions of mother-child interactions tend to elicit the charge of "mother bashing." Granted, there are such tendencies in the literature, which feminist criticism calls attention to and which Laing himself cautioned against back in 1960. Still, if Laing's memory of his mother can be more or less trusted, as Aunt Ethel believed, Amelia's behavior warrants this kind of description. Although we should avoid scapegoating mothers who are trapped in loveless marriages, we must remember that, like men, women are also capable of severe cruelty toward their offspring. When this happens, the only argument in their defense is that they were victimized in turn—a point made eloquently by Alice Miller (1986), whose work Laing admired, and before her by David Bakan (1971) and by Laing himself (1969).

Accordingly, and since the data seem to support the inference, I would venture to speculate that Amelia Kirkwood was also unwanted—by her father at least. A woman's lingering and bitter hatred toward her own father can make life impossible for her little boy, and there is no reason to suppose that Amelia and Ronald were an exception to this general rule. As Laing confided to Morton Schatzman (1989), among others, Amelia often insisted that Ronald took after her own father—an attribution Laing deeply resented. Though it cannot be proven, it is likely that Amelia displaced some of her animosity toward her father onto her son and that, even as a youngster, Ronald Laing was being called to account for another's misdeeds.[3]

In such difficult circumstances, it seems likely that Laing devoted considerable mental energy to holding his own against his mother, and that this process in turn fostered a certain precocity in his intellectual development. This is shown by a vignette toward the end of Laing's second book, *Self and Others,* which he later acknowledged as autobiographical. In it, a boy of seven was accused by his father of having stolen his pen. The boy protested his innocence but was not believed. The mother intervened by telling the father that the boy had already confessed the theft to her—possibly to save him from further punishment. The boy continued to protest his innocence, however, and was thrashed twice over for being a liar and a thief. Since both parents now behaved as if he had stolen the pen and confessed, the boy began to doubt his own recollection of events and wasn't even sure whether he had done the deed or not, confessed or not. But soon the mother found the missing pen and privately acknowledged to her son that she knew he was falsely accused—though significantly she never mentioned this fact to his father, who evidently continued to believe the worst. Instead of asking the boy's forgiveness, however, she demanded it, by saying, "Come and kiss your Mummy and make it up." As Laing recalled, at this point the boy's temptation to embrace his mother was almost overpowering. Yet he felt that doing so would be "twisted," and he resisted his desire, standing silently until his mother gave up and left the room. In his own words:

> The room seemed to spin. The longing was unbearable, but suddenly, everything was different, yet the same. He saw the room and himself for the first time. The longing to cling had gone. He had somehow broken into a new region. He was alone. Could this woman be connected to him? As a man, he thought this incident crucial to his life; a deliverance, but not without a price to pay. (1961, pp. 163–164)

Pondering this experience from an adult vantagepoint, Laing came up with no less than thirteen possible metameanings or tacit communications underlying Amelia's demand that he forgive her after she discovered her mistake. But, curiously, one thing that never occurred to Laing was the clear implication that Amelia felt she had to be trusted as the final authority on who or what he was (or did)—that his own opinions were distinctly secondary, while those of his father were altogether irrelevant. If this kind of communication between mother and son was habitual, perhaps the only way Laing could maintain a solid sense of identity was by clinging to an attitude of quiet defiance and seeking occasional support from his father.

A revealing anecdote along these lines comes from Laing's adolescence. Until the age of fourteen or fifteen, Ronald was forbidden to lock the bathroom door, so that his mother could come in to scrub his back as he was bathing—a circumstance he found increasingly embarrassing. One day Ronald locked the door, which precipitated a frightful outburst that went on for some time, until his father intervened forcefully by dragging Amelia away from the bathroom door, threatening to create an even more embarrassing commotion unless Amelia settled down and left Ronald in peace. Laing was grateful to his father for coming to his aid (1985, pp. 74–75). On Amelia's side, however, this episode proved to be a major turning point in her feelings for her son. As she later confided to Susan Laing, she became convinced of Ronald's "wickedness" from that point on.

Meanwhile, however, the younger Ronald Laing could not always rely on his father's support and had to suppress or sublimate his rebellious impulses. In view of his constricted surroundings, his rebelliousness initially took a cerebral and introverted turn:

For as early as I remember I never took my self to *be* what people called me. That at least was crystal clear to me. Whatever, whoever I may be is not to be confused with the names people give *to* me, or how they *describe* me, or what they *call* me. I am not my name.

Who or what I am as far as they are they are concerned, is not necessarily, or thereby, *me,* as far as I am concerned.

I am presumably what they are describing, but not their description . . . what they say I am is their map of me.

And what I call myself is, presumably, my map of me (1976, p. 4)

Laing's insistence that his essential self was never what others imagined him to be is eloquent testimony to the lack of empathy, bonding, and connectedness in his early familial environment, and of a need to maintain a sense of selfhood in opposition to all these shifting perceptions and definitions of him. His later contempt for respectability and his delight in shocking people probably had their roots in the feelings he suppressed for the sake of his own survival in early life. In this way Laing's childhood experiences lay the foundation for what might be termed an "oppositional identity," a sense of selfhood rooted in the defiance of authority, coupled curiously, in later life, with empathy for the mad—a measure, some say, of his unconscious identification with Amelia and his childish desire to "cure" her.

Another noteworthy feature of Laing's familial environment was the prudery and repression around sexual topics evidenced by his parents. The lovelessness that surrounded him was embodied in the family's sleeping arrangements. The Laing home was a large three-room flat. Ronald and his mother slept in one room (on separate beds), while his father slept in another room. This arrangement lasted until Laing reached puberty. By his own account, Laing did not learn the proverbial facts of life until he was almost sixteen, when he bought a book on venereal disease. He resorted to that expedient because he couldn't go to his father, who insisted that he couldn't understand how Ronald was conceived, since he and Amelia had long since stopped having physical relations (1976, p. 8).

Of course many marriages survive the disappearance of sexual passion, particularly with advancing age or if both partners agree to satisfy their desires elsewhere without rancor and not to hurt their children in the process. Such arrangements were actually more common when the stigma associated with divorce was still prevalent and intense. But this was not the case in the Laing household. David Laing was a vigorous but thoroughly traditional man who would not contemplate extramarital involvements, and Amelia was averse to physical intimacy of any kind. So his parents' declaration that they had abjured sexual intercourse long before he was born—which qualifies them as odd, by any reasonable standard—was probably the first family myth that Laing encountered. Later on, as a clinician and family theorist, he would say that such myths are ubiquitous and that the structure of the family, or any social group, is based on shared fantasy systems, pervasive fictions that construct a sense of individual and group identity.

More to the point, though, this shared delusion (or barefaced lie) must have generated serious doubts in young Ronald about the real identity of his biological father. Most parents don't lie about such straightforward matters, so why should his? Were they covering something up? If not, why all the fuss? If Laing had any such anxieties, he never, to my knowledge, shared them publicly. Perhaps the only hint he dropped in his published work is in *The Facts of Life* (1976, p. 8), where he says: "But there is a birthmark on his [father's] right knee and one on mine. A fact against immaculate conception." It would have been more fitting in this context if Laing had said "immaculate deception," since his parents' need for prevarication and self-deception in regard to sexual matters was clearly quite extreme.

Laing's relationship to his father was more positive, on balance, than his relationship to his mother. He referred to his father as "one of the purest spirits I have ever come across" (1985, p. 103), while his characterizations of his mother are consistently unflattering. Significantly, John Laing, David's father, was a Spencerian, an evolutionist, an atheist, and an alcoholic. As Ethel Laing recalled, her brother David never forgave John for turning their mother into a nervous wreck. Despite all the fights with his father, David Laing's hero was Mahatma Gandhi, which is doubly interesting in view of his military career as an engineer in the tank corps and the air force. This preceded his employment as an electrical engineer for the city of Glasgow, where he remained for the duration of Ronald's childhood and the rest of his working life.

Though his father meted out corporal punishment occasionally, Ronald trusted him more than he did his mother. Eyewitnesses report that during Ronald's teens and early twenties, David Laing welcomed his son's friends into their home with warmth and generosity, engaging them in musical pastimes and sing-alongs, with Ronald at the piano. (Amelia, by contrast, made herself scarce or was openly unfriendly to Ronald's friends.) As is often the case between fathers and sons, however, it wasn't all smooth sailing. The tensions that lingered from Ronald's childhood, when his father was less reliable, erupted in intense theological debates between father and son. Leaving aside what it says about Glaswegian culture and family life, I think this fact is significant because like Carl Jung—another psychiatrist who rose to prominence from a troubled childhood—Ronald doubted the sincerity of his father's religious convictions. Indeed at one point he accused him of being an atheist—or of being like John Laing, or "Old Pa," whom David despised.

Although the storms of theological controversy eventually blew over, it is interesting that when Ronald entered medical school, David Laing suffered a nervous breakdown of almost three months' duration, and problems of religious belief—or the lack of them—surfaced once more. David was about to succeed his immediate superior, a man named Inglis, who was up for retirement. But he thought Inglis was conspiring to block the appointment and bring his career to an humiliating halt, on the grounds that he, David Laing, was an atheist. As Laing gently suggested to his father that his fears were groundless, or at the very least excessive, and that Inglis was merely a symbol of "Old Pa." In due course, David recovered, got the desired promotion, and indeed another before he finally retired (1985, pp. 102–103).

In any case, in view of his home environment, and the relative absence of playmates in early childhood, it is hardly surprising that Ronald was an introverted child and sought solace in books and music, which existed in abundant supply in his home. Moreover, the Laing flat stood opposite a public library, where Ronald spent many happy hours reading. Ethel Laing recalled that her brother David, though very clever, was profoundly ashamed that he never went to the university, because of his own father's boozing and spendthrift ways. And David refused to familiarize his son with the tools of his trade. This helped to ensure that Ronald did not sully his hands with manual or technical labor and jeopardize his future as an intellectual.

One pleasant feature of the Laing home was that there was always music. David was the principal baritone for the Glasgow University chapel choir, and one of the high points of his life was when he was accompanied by Albert Schweitzer at the organ. David's musical talent facilitated his social life too, since he and Amelia would organize frequent musical gatherings where, as Laing recalled, singing was at a premium and serious talk on any subject was discouraged (1985, pp. 65–71).

In later life, Laing boasted that even before his birth he "heard" his father sing the baritone parts of the church repertoire and "the usual repertoire of a professional baritone with a penchant for Italian opera and Victorian ballads" (p. 66). No doubt this is a reasonably good description of the sounds that enveloped him as a growing boy. Evidently David Laing was professional but for one failing: he was frequently moved by the music he produced and often faltered or wept during his own performances. How this affected Ronald is uncertain, but the adult Laing would experience considerable difficulty controlling his feelings in public concerts when affecting music was played. Moreover, like his father, he achieved a professional level of competence in music without pursuing it as a career, receiving a licentiate from the Royal Academy of Music at age sixteen.

But even music, which fostered a kinder, more elevated emotional atmosphere, became fraught with conflict in the Laing home. Once, for example, when Laing was young, Amelia broke up a budding musical friendship between her husband and a handicapped pianist known to us only as Gladys (1985, pp. 72–74). And though it became a source of solace for him in later life, at a very early age Ronald was expected to practice several hours a day on the piano. On a radio program entitled "The Lies of Love," which aired on a Canadian Broadcasting Corporation series on May 18, 1989, four months before he died, Laing remembered:

> As a boy, I was particularly imbued with Chopin. I just couldn't imagine what life could have been like before Chopin. My music teacher was a woman [Julia Ommer] who'd been trained at the Berlin Academy and classical piano playing. In fact, she almost literally fainted on one occasion when I proposed to play for her "Rhapsody in Blue." Just staggered, you know . . .

I was never allowed . . . to hear a single note of jazz properly speaking. Gershwin was just on this side of the tracks and Cole Porter and popular songs were tolerated on the radio when they had them, but as soon as the Blues or Louis Armstrong came on the radio, the radio was immediately turned off. So I actually never heard this stuff until I was 16, and taking all of my courage in my proverbial hands, I went into a music shop and got into a booth and played (I think) some Bessy Smith and Louis Armstrong to myself on the earphones. It was absolutely amazing . . .

Laing later made up for his adolescent deprivation by befriending Oscar Peterson and other jazz musicians. And according to Ricci Horenstein—a former neighbor, a performer, and a piano teacher— Laing could improvise "like an angel" for hours on end. For white middle-class youth on both sides of the Atlantic, African-American music has always been attractive as a form of protest and for its open avowal of the artist's sadness, exaltation, irreverence, and, last but not least, sexual concerns. Yet Laing's interest in jazz did not diminish his affection for classical music, and he expanded his classical repertoire over the years.

To summarize Laing's childhood, one would have to say that it was often oppressive, particularly earlier on. Still, in all fairness to Laing's troubled parents, they did do everything to ensure that young Ronald received the kind of education they never had, a fact he seldom acknowledged aloud. The common denominator for David and Amelia—perhaps the one thing that held them together—was their ambition for their son to become an accomplished scientist or man of letters. But ambition is a double-edged sword. In Laing's case it led to prodigious intellectual accomplishment, which brought him fame and riches (for a while) and enriched the world he lived in. It also seemed to be a substitute for the unconditional love that Laing never had, and it continued to feed the passions that caused so much suffering for both him and those around him. Throughout his life Laing was torn between his craving for success and his humanistic values, between his public and private selves. The resulting disharmony fed his anger, aggression, and discontent. Nor could he ever get over his youthful oppositionalism, though he did try to channel it productively, by championing the cause of the mad.

2

SCHOOLING

Laing's account of his early education at the Cuthbertson Street School and Hutcheson's Boys Grammar School is a little puzzling. On the one hand, he assures us that "I had none of the bad experiences that mar so many people's lives. I savored the company of most of my schoolmates . . . I was never brutalized, humiliated, degraded, savaged, raped, beaten up, bullied, and I never did anything like that to anybody else" (1985, p. 57). On the other hand, he goes on to describe the many beatings he received from teachers for rebellious and high-spirited behavior, which he relinquished reluctantly at thirteen—not from any scruples or a desire to please, but simply to avoid further pain. Many of his "partners in crime" were also high achievers, scholastically speaking, and so it would be invidious to construe his acting up as symptomatic of a problem with authority. It was an integral part of the grade-school ethos. Moreover, as Laing tells it, the beatings he got at school were less severe than those he got from his father. Indeed it was only when the vice-principal at Hutcheson's—known as "the Beak"—threatened to tell David about Ronald's infractions that he was finally intimidated into good behavior (Laing, 1985, p. 59).

Judging on performance alone, one would be inclined to say that the young Laing's greatest strength—apart from music—was in the classics. When he graduated high school, his tutor informed him that he had achieved a comfortable M.A. level in Greek and Latin, and in this he scored well above his classmates (Laing, 1985; Templeton, 1990). His weakness was math. Like the youthful Jung, Ronald was unconvinced that numbers are real entities, and not imaginary or invented. Like Jung, Laing found many of the axioms underlying simple arithmetic and geometrical operations quite arbitrary and paradoxical, and he experienced enormous relief as an adult on discovering that his youthful misgivings had a basis in fact. In his words:

> I could not understand how the distance between two infinitely divisible points could be said to be the same as the distance between any two points. Worse still I could not understand what a number was. What is a number? I kept on trying to imagine what a number was but there are unimaginable numbers. And so on. It was a terrible nightmare. (1985, pp. 60–61)

In retrospect, it is may be that Laing's mathematical paralysis contributed to his eventual choice of vocation: any branch of science that required advanced mathematical skills was out of the question. Medicine and psychiatry, by contrast, were areas outside classical scholarship where he stood a chance of making a contribution, and perhaps, indeed, of really understanding the bewildering psychological processes going on inside of and all around him. In an interview with Peter Mezan in 1972, he described his early intellectual trajectory:

> By the time I was about fourteen I knew that I was really only interested in psychology, philosophy and theology. I suppose I was in love with knowledge. I was reading Plato then for the first time and realized that this love of knowledge could be a means of liberating the soul. I guess at the time it took the form of a sort of Neoplatonic Christianity. Then I went to University, which I found largely to be a waste of time. Most teachers seemed to me to be ridiculous—that someone should think to tell me how to write, or even who was a good writer and who wasn't . . . I decided to do medicine because it would give me access to birth and death. For some reason I wanted that. And I also had some sense of myself as a physician. (Mezan, 1972, p. 165)

It is interesting to note the different emphasis in this first sketch of his early intellectual development and his later, more detailed dis-

cussion in *Wisdom, Madness and Folly* (1985). His remarks to Mezan
implied that the same thirst for knowledge that drew him to Plato,
Plotinus, and other mystics later propelled him toward medicine
and the mysteries of birth and death. In short, they hint at the possibility that his immersion in Neoplatonic Christianity remained a hidden but nonetheless integral dimension in his pursuit of secular
knowledge, if in a sublimated form. (And on some level, as we shall
see, it was.)

In 1985, by contrast, Laing neglected to mention his early mystical
leanings but noted that, during this period of his life, he came into
conflict with the evangelical Christianity that was prevalent in Glasgow (pp. 84–85). One of his school chums, James Templeton—now
a psychoanalyst living in Largs—recalls these events with particular
vividness:

> At an early age we both became involved in the Scripture Union, an
> evangelical movement, which held meetings throughout the year and
> ran summer camps in Pertshire which Ronnie and I attended and at
> which we were both duly "saved" and "saw the light" . . . When we
> were about 15 and beginning to have our doubts about all this evangel-
> ical stuff, we received a circular from the Scripture Union which
> pointed out that during the past year there had been something like
> 345 indecent portrayals of women in the cinema. Ronnie and I decided
> that we were missing out on the really important things in life and we
> resigned from the Scripture Union. Later he became a fairly ardent
> atheist and would pour scorn in a humorous manner on those who
> might believe in some personalized kind of god. (Templeton, 1990)

Predictably enough, Ronald's attempts to get his adolescent priori-
ties straight met with stiff opposition. Michel John, the evangelist
who "saved" him—referred to as the Boss by Ronald and his
friends—did his best to keep him in the fold, to no avail (A. Laing
p. 31). In a heated exchange, at age sixteen, Ronald even remarked to
the Boss that Buddha was more mature than Jesus—an assertion
that sparked anxiety on his behalf among the faithful.

While doubtless intended to assert his intellectual autonomy, and
to express his disappointment with the Boss, and all he stood for,
Laing's reference to the Buddha was no mere provocation. Like the
young Erich Fromm, in his mid-teens Laing started to develop an
interest in eastern religions, which soon branched out to include

Hinduism and Taoism. In later life, Laing would become thoroughly familiar with the works of Hindu sages like Sri Sankaracharya and Nagarjuna, with various Pali and Tibetan sutras, as well as with the burgeoning literature on Zen. If nothing else, this early interest in oriental religion attested to a continuing need on Laing's part for spiritual solace, even though (or precisely because) his faith in a personal God had vanished.

In the meantime, Laing's budding fascination with Asian wisdom did not detract from his other reading. At age fifteen he was already dipping into the works of celebrated skeptics: Epictetus, Montaigne, Voltaire, Marx, Nietzsche—and Freud. Clearly young Ronald Laing was consumed with curiosity about the sources of human belief and suffering, and his thinking patterns were not shaped by any particular desire to conform to prevailing cultural norms or expectations. He wanted to figure things out for himself and reveled in a profusion of ideas, resenting anyone who tried to interfere by supplying the "right" answers, which would presumably bring all the excitement to a halt. Despite his curiosity and openness to different points of view, then, he was not what one would call an impressionable young man.

Apart from the mystical leanings, his growing sense of himself as a writer, and the turn toward eastern religion, another important element in Laing's adolescence and early adulthood was the escalating threat of nuclear war. With dire warnings from Einstein, Bertrand Russell, and Robert Oppenheimer circulating freely in the press, and the cold war heating up week by week, Laing's fears were not irrational. A good part of Laing's generation—and not just nihilists and naysayers—believed that the long-range chances for species survival were slim and that our collective extinction would be a terrifying ordeal.

In any case, rational or not, visions of planetary death and devastation haunted him as he grew to manhood, and probably strengthened pre-existing tendencies to nihilism and despair—tendencies clearly expressed in *The Politics of Experience* (1967). Arguably, he never entirely overcame them, despite the "upbeat" periods in his life when these feelings and fantasies were in abeyance.

Having graduated from Hutcheson's school near the top of his class, Laing entered the University of Glasgow in 1945 to study medicine. He continued to live at home throughout his university days—

which only contributed to the deepening and ultimately irreversible deterioration in his relationship with his mother (A. Laing, 1994, p. 36). Laing did the customary year of physics, chemistry, and biology, followed by a year of anatomy, physiology, and embryology. These years of theoretical preparation were followed by three years of practical training in pathology, obstetrics, gynecology and anesthetics. Decades later, in "The Bird of Paradise" (1967), and *The Facts of Life* (1976), Laing published some gruesome recollections from this period, when he was called on to deliver babies and perform various surgical procedures in ugly circumstances.

But Laing's university years were not all storm and stress. Despite the difficult environment at home, he developed a diverse and exciting social life outside it. James Hood recalls:

> To his medical peer group in Glasgow Laing showed himself an extraordinarily gifted musician, scholar and discussant. He formed a Socratic club; most afternoons he played jazz, classical and improvised piano music in the student union. He talked and listened. He introduced us to psychoanalysis. In a population still heavily influenced by puritan values, and highly respectable civic expectations, his behavioral example and the range of his mind were exhilarating. (1989)

By most accounts, Laing's closest friend at the university was Douglas Hutchison, whom he was paired with for clinical training in his third year. They probably met first through the Glasgow University Mountaineering Club, whose members were mostly medical students like Laing and Hood. Another friend and drinking companion in those days was John Duffy. Unlike Laing, Hutchison and Hood, Duffy was at the Royal College of Science and Technology, but despite his technical bent, was a frequent participant at the meetings of the Socratic Club, which Laing organized as a forum for free discussion. A colorful character, Duffy was probably Laing's closest friend after Hutchison died in 1959. When I met with him in June 1990, he spoke with pride of his role in helping Laing to extricate himself from his familial environment and to overcome his naiveté and awkwardness with women.

Another close friend and drinking companion, though no climbing enthusiast, was Leonard Davidson, also a medical student at the time. Like Duffy, Davidson liked Ronald's father but thought Amelia a baneful influence and the relationship between David and

Amelia extremely odd, even by depression-era Glaswegian standards. When I spoke with him in 1990, Davidson insisted that many of Laing's ideas derived from his efforts to come to grips with the bizarre complexities of their union.

Two other members of Laing's circle were Aaron Esterson and Richard Gelfer, who now live in London. Esterson was never as close to Laing personally as Hutchison, Duffy, and Davidson but, as an existential phenomenologist, shared more of his intellectual passions and was destined to play a important role in Laing's life in the late fifties and early sixties, when they collaborated on family research. Gelfer, another psychiatrist, was a peripheral presence in Laing's professional life, though Gelfer's analyst, Marion Milner, was one of Laing's clinical supervisors in London from 1957 to 1960, and Gelfer roomed with Laing and his first family during those years. Laing and Gelfer also shared an interest in psychosis and the therapeutic potential of psychedelic drugs.

Another friend of Laing's, a classicist known to us only as George-Paul (Mullan, 1995, p. 29), introduced Laing to a young French-woman studying English there, named Marcelle Vincent. Despite a strong initial attraction, at her insistence they did not become lovers until Laing visited her in Paris a year later.[1] Laing asked her to marry him, and she refused, he said, because she had no intention of being an army wife. For her part, Marcelle says, she was daunted by the mercurial element in his character and his tendency toward nihilism and despair. She was prone to depression herself and feared that they might intensify one another's malaise. Laing was deeply disappointed.

In the midst of all this courting, mountain climbing, piano playing, debating, and drinking, Laing's studies continued apace. During his second year, he became interested in embryology and hypnotism. To study mass hypnosis, he attended Billy Graham's revival meetings in Glasgow and once more felt a yearning to embrace Christianity, despite his intellectual misgivings. He also attended seances and had compelling, inexplicable experiences that convinced him of the existence of telepathy.

Laing was also dabbling in radical politics and once addressed a Communist Party meeting in Glasgow on Marx, Engels, Bukharin, and Trotsky. He continued to read voraciously in philosophy, working his way systematically through Nietzsche, Husserl, Heidegger,

Sartre, Merleau-Ponty, and Wittgenstein, dazzling his friends with the breadth of his philosophical reflections.

Leaving aside Laing's obvious need to embrace, explore and ultimately reject the dogmatic certainties of his elders—religious, scientific, and political—what comes through in his own colorful recollections from this period is his thirst to live life directly, to discover and distill his own convictions in the crucible of experience and independent inquiry. This combination of traits and passions—his openness, self-reliance, and curiosity—contributed considerably to his later creativity as a theorist. Meanwhile, however, despite his brilliance as a musician, philosopher, and bon vivant—or because of them—Laing failed his qualifying exams, which caused considerable embarrassment, especially for Amelia. As Laing later recalled, he was so angry at his parents' attitude that he left 21 Ardbeg Street abruptly and seldom stepped inside their home again (Mullan, pp. 46–47). Unlike his parents, Laing felt that the responsibility for his failure did not rest entirely on his own shoulders. In *Wisdom, Madness and Folly* he remarked:

> I've often wondered whether my failure might have had something to do with our Final Year Dinner, when, sitting with the professors at the top of the table, as an after dinner speaker, I drank too much whiskey, claret and port, and expressed far too candidly what I felt about a few things in medicine. (1985, p. 107)

Perhaps there is a grain of truth in this. As Adrian Laing points out, the after-dinner speech was a provocative rant on the "syphilization of society" (p. 42). Then again, in view of his active social life, his omnivorous reading, and his extracurricular activities, it seems possible that he simply never devoted enough time to his regular studies. John Roy, a contemporary of Laing's and a member of the Socratic Club, notes that Glasgow University during the 1940s and 1950s was a pretty wild place, even by contemporary standards, and that outspoken challenges to authority and convention were not at all unusual (Roy, 1991). Leonard Davidson also expressed strong doubts about the truth of Laing's conjecture. Indeed, the consensus among his contemporaries seems to be that Laing drew an unwarranted connection between the two events—his drunken speechifying and his subsequent failure—in order to save face and to shift the blame for his setback.

In any case, Laing's failure to qualify was temporary. During the six-month interval between his public insouciance and his next try at the exams, he worked as a half-paid, full-time intern in the psychiatric unit of Stobhill Hospital in Glasgow, which was run by Hunter Gillis, an ardent Kraepelinian who stressed the physical origins of mental illness. This was his first formal apprenticeship in psychiatry. As Laing later recalled, he was particularly impressed by one Dr. Mackenzie, who "had a way" in dealing with the many cases of "involutional melancholia" among elderly male patients. Most of these men had strong Calvinist beliefs and were brought in by exasperated relatives at their wits' end. As they approached death, Laing recalled, these elderly men increasingly suffered paroxysms of self-loathing and self-pity, complaining volubly to anyone who would listen about the damnation that awaited them for their sins. Nothing could deter them or relieve their despair.

From a therapeutic standpoint, these patients posed a formidable problem, since the Calvinist creed itself reinforced their fears and any attempt to pry them loose from these obsessive ruminations could be misinterpreted as a challenge to their faith and, indeed, to their identity. Dr. Mackenzie circumvented the problem: he simulated the effects of hellfire by injecting 10 cubic centimeters of turpentine into the patients' buttocks. This induced a brief but raging fever and swollen buttocks that burned painfully for several days. As he explained to Laing, this technique forced the patients to "shut up and count their blessings," and since none of them ever returned or complained, he claimed a remission rate of 100 percent, a discharge rate of 100 percent, and a relapse rate of zero (Laing, 1976, p. 91).

Though his experience at Stobhill was not particularly edifying, Laing was not that interested in the exigencies of treatment anyway. He was probably just going through the motions, still caught up in his theoretical-metaphysical conundrums. During this transitional period, he said,

> I became completely focused on the central nervous system. How does the brain produce the mind? Or is it the other way around? Or are both questions so stupid they should be dropped immediately? If I went in for neurology I would have a chance of becoming clinically scientific about an area that I could not stop thinking about, even agonizing over, very unscientifically. So when I graduated . . . I took a

job . . . as an internist in a neurosurgical unit, skipping the usual two post-graduate years of internships in general medicine and surgery. (Laing, 1985, pp. 108–109)

Laing graduated from medical school in 1951 at the age of twenty-four. The next phase of his career was at the Glasgow and Western Scotland neurosurgical unit at Killearn, near Loch Lomond. His teachers there were Sloane Robertson, Alisdair Paterson, and Joseph Schorstein, three of the best neurosurgeons in Great Britain. Robertson had a splendid reputation, but he performed lobotomies routinely, which Laing abhorred. Paterson was a more positive influence. He scorned Laing's metaphysical vapors but strongly encouraged him to go into research, especially after Laing fainted twice in the operating theater. Schorstein had similar hopes for Laing but, unlike the other two surgeons, actively encouraged Laing's intellectual pursuits. Laing's description of their first encounter is quite memorable:

> At three o'clock in the morning in the changing room after one operating session that had been going on for hours, Joe Schorstein decided to check me out. He proceeded to grill me from Heraclitus and, in between, Kant, Hegel, Nietzsche, Husserl, Heidegger, in very specific detail. The interrogation went on for two hours before Joe was "convinced." Then began a real argument that went on for another two hours. No one, before or since, has put me through such a grinder.
>
> After that night Joe adopted me as his pupil; he became my spiritual father, neurological and intellectual mentor, and guide to European literature. (1985, pp. 112–113)

Who exactly was Joe Schorstein? The son of a Hassidic rabbi from a village near Vienna, he was seventeen years older than Laing. Joe's father was no ordinary rabbi: he held a doctorate in philosophy from Heidelberg and once punished his ten-year-old son by assigning Kant's *Critique of Pure Reason* to be read and reported on in detail three months hence. At sixteen, Joe rebelled, became a communist, and fled to Prague, where he started his studies in medicine. Sometime in the 1930s, the impending Nazi storm prompted Schorstein to flee to London and then to Manchester, where he studied neurology under Jeffrey Jefferson. Soon Schorstein joined the British army and became chief of a neurosurgical unit, journeying from El Alamein in North Africa, to Italy, and back to his native Austria by the end of the war. Laing recalls:

> He was the first older, fully educated European intellectual I had come to know. He seemed to be the incarnation of all the positions of the European consciousness; Hassidism, Marxism, science and nihilism. He believed in the Crucifixion, but could not believe in the Resurrection . . . He had to varying degrees knowledge of Greek, Latin, Hebrew, Czech, French, Italian, English, German and for all I know, bits of Bulgarian and Portuguese too.
>
> He was also very cultivated musically. He sang Hassidic and Central European songs, many of which I first heard from him. I can still surprise a central European Jew by coming out with one of them. "How did you come across that one?" (p. 114)

Though Laing admired several men who served as some sort of mentor or model for him, his relationship with Schorstein was unique: he was the only one Laing ever called a "spiritual father." It is not hard to see why. Laing's sheltered beginnings, and his early immersion in books and music, had not given him much scope to experience life, and for all his audacity and breadth of mind, and his revelries at the university, he was acutely aware of that fact. Schorstein was a man of action and experience who was more than his match in philosophy and who could also share his musical interests. He was an energetic, demanding, generous man with an irrepressible, often sarcastic sense of humor.

But, in addition to all of this, Joe Schorstein was also a very private and tormented soul. Laing comments that Schorstein "believed in the Crucifixion, but could not believe in the Resurrection." Unless these were Schorstein's own words, this is a strange figure of speech to use with reference to the son of a rabbi. One wonders if the imagery is related to a story Laing liked to tell about an unnamed colleague from Vienna. Just before World War I, this man's mother, then in her forties, was diagnosed as suffering from nerves. Loathe to see Freud, whose reputation was "iffy," she consulted the celebrated neurologist Julius von Wagner-Jauregg, who decided she was suffering from general paresis, or tertiary syphilis. Because this woman was an orthodox Jew of the upper-middle class, the diagnosis caused considerable anguish. But it was not disputed, since it came from such an eminent authority. The poor woman dutifully took the prescribed treatment, which was a dose of malaria, and died as a result. After her body had been slivered into microscopic specimens for scientific study, no evidence of syphilis was found (Evans, 1976, pp. 17–18). Crucifixion of a kind, but no resurrection.

Though Laing never said so, it is likely that this story is about Schorstein's own family. Strangely enough, the horrendous experience did not deter Schorstein from becoming a neurologist himself. Indeed, it may have contributed to his resolve, despite the visceral antipathy he had to the widespread dehumanization of medicine. In any case, the fact remains that when Laing decided to abandon neurology for psychiatry some time later, Schorstein vigorously attempted to dissuade him.

Army service was obligatory for able-bodied men of eighteen and over, and Laing entered the army very reluctantly. He had hoped that his widely acknowledged talents would get him a special dispensation to pursue his studies (1985, p. 117); in due course, he could join Marcelle in Montmartre—she was now more optimistic about their relationship—and spend a year or two studying with Karl Jaspers in Basel (Vincent, 1993). Had all this come to pass, it would have probably altered the course of his life. For all we know, had the army agreed, Laing might have settled in Europe and taken up a different career.

To the distress of both Vincent and Laing, the authorities were intractable. Though it doubtless resonated with earlier experiences of loss and disappointment, it was Laing's first adult experience with this kind of heartache—the feeling that the world itself conspires to obstruct the fulfillment of one's deepest wishes and desires. As a result, it seems, his state of mind at this time oscillated between cautious optimism and bitter despair. While working at the British Army psychiatry unit of the Royal Victoria Hospital at Netley, Laing wrote a long letter to Marcelle, dated October 1, 1951, about the Sartrean "freedom" to choose between madness and suicide. He notes:

> Perhaps now that recovery is taking place to some extent in Europe, the suffering of the war, which was experienced more intensely . . .
> there . . . is finding expression in philosophy and poetry which, if it is

more bitter than ours, is more keenly felt—and for that reason, like a fierce wind in the face, more abundantly alive if one has the strength to bear it. (Courtesy Marcelle Vincent)

From this letter and others like it, we can see that during the early 1950s, Laing's primary intellectual commitment was moving in the direction of existentialism. Still he was not neglecting other perspectives on mental disorder. Around 1951 Laing became interested in schizophrenia and read widely in American psychoanalytic theory: Margaret Sechehaye, Frieda Fromm-Reichman and Harry Stack Sullivan, whom he greatly admired (Mullan, 1995). Although Laing's first clinical paper, "An Instance of Ganser Syndrome" (1953), made few references either to American psychiatry or to existential thought, it did show a very good grasp of Freudian and Kleinian theory. One wonders whether this was a deliberate move.

In any case, while Laing's apprenticeship gave him much food for thought, it posed challenges of another kind. As time passed, he became increasingly disgusted with the comas and shocks he was obliged to administer at the Netley hospital. Despite occasional "successes" with these methods and the great enthusiasm of his colleagues, he doubted whether the artificial administration of an insulin coma or an epileptic seizure could really benefit someone who was already psychologically distressed or deranged, and he was shaken by the occasional deaths that occurred during or after these risky undertakings.[2] On top of all this, Laing learned that beatings of patients by the custodial staff were common, and that the percentage of cases discharged or returned to barracks had far more to do with the fluctuating manpower and morale objectives of his superiors, and little to do with the needs of individual patients.

Another striking feature of the psychiatric unit at Netley, where Laing worked in 1951–52, was the ban on any spontaneous communication between patients and staff, or even between patients and other patients. In Laing's account,

> the staff . . . had strict orders not to talk to the patients or to encourage the patients to talk to them, or to each other, or to themselves, or at all. No patient was expected to speak to a member of the staff unless spoken to. Talking between patients was observed, reported and broken up. You must not let a schizophrenic talk to you. It aggravates the psychotic process. It is like promoting a haemorrhage or

giving a laxative to someone with diarrhea. It inflames the brain and
fans the psychosis. As in bone fractures, so in fractured minds: immo-
bilization is the answer. No communication is better than any for the
period of treatment. (1985, p. 123)

Needless to say, Laing had doubts that "fractured minds" could
ever mend in such dehumanizing circumstances. The suppression of
all spontaneous communication and the tendency to construe it as a
sign of illness—rather than of health or a striving away from isolation—may have been influenced by the fact that this was an army,
and not a civilian hospital. Still, it doesn't require genius to realize
that for frightened and disoriented men an authoritarian stricture
against spontaneous communication, coupled with a demand to
speak only when ordered to, is bound to engender willful silence
and oppositionalism, thereby manufacturing some of the very symptoms the injunction is allegedly designed to treat. This in turn has
the effect of rendering it impossible—from a medical standpoint—
to differentiate between features of the patient's behavior that are
directly related to current circumstances and those that are engendered by the underlying disturbance.

As a young, inexperienced doctor, Laing kept silent. But in defiance of the spirit of his unit's ordinances, and without actually
breaking the rules, Laing managed to develop rapport with some of
the patients, by sitting quietly with them in their padded cells, a
move construed by his superiors as dedicated research. And in a
sense it was. Laing was anxious to discover how these miserable,
frightened, and deeply confused people experienced the world, and
how they would respond given the chance to communicate freely.
One of the hallmarks of Laing's approach was that he never demanded anything from patients, either silence or speech, and that he
did not interrogate them as a conventional psychiatrist would have.
On the contrary, he maintained a relaxed, nonthreatening posture in
their presence and allowed them to open up their thoughts, feelings,
and fantasies at their own pace. This afforded the framework
needed to explore undisclosed features of the patients' experiences,
and it furnished the case material for *The Divided Self* and *Self and
Others*.

Though profoundly disenchanted with prevailing treatment methods, Laing became increasingly absorbed in problems of differential

diagnosis. In his words, he "developed an intense desire to ferret out the differences between deception, malingering, self-deception (hysteria), neurosis and psychosis, functional and organic" (1985, p. 133). And despite his sympathy for the mad, Laing had none for malingerers. His interest in these problems was probably a saving grace. Ideologically, it enabled him to stay within the fold and, in practical terms, to coordinate his own research interests with those of his employer. The Korean War was underway, and the army had a powerful interest in determining whether a soldier was ill or unbalanced or just shirking his duty. Indeed, they seemed to arrange things so that would-be malingerers would be deterred by the brutality of the treatment afforded to those deemed ill. Or so it seemed to Laing.

Unlike most of his colleagues, however, Laing had no interest in seeing real madmen returned to active service. Despite the occasional faker, most of the patients Laing saw were too shattered to manage the rigors of war, regardless of the etiology of their particular problems. Still he was regularly called upon to determine whether someone was "fit to stand," ready to be disciplined or court-martialed, and if not, why not. Judging from his recollections in *Wisdom, Madness and Folly,* the behavioral anomalies among soldiers referred to him for assessment were mind-boggling. Despite his best efforts at methodical scrutiny and analysis, Laing discovered that it is often impossible to determine with anything approaching certainty whether symptoms like mutism and deafness—which were very common—were hysterical or schizophrenic, organic or functional, genuine or faked. In many instances, one could only offer a best guess that, for good or ill, had to pass for truth.

After a year at Netley, Laing was promoted to the rank of captain and placed in charge of the Catterick Military Hospital in Yorkshire. While still stationed at Netley, he had met an attractive nurse named Anne Hearne, who was originally from Devon. In *Wisdom, Madness and Folly* Laing described her as "the most emotionally honest person I know"; in view of the value he placed on honesty, this is no small commendation. Not much is known about their courtship, but when Anne informed him that she was pregnant, Laing thought they should get married, despite his lingering attachment to Marcelle Vincent. The wedding took place in Richmond, North Yorkshire, on October 11, 1952, and after a few more months at Catterick, the

couple returned to Glasgow, where they bought a flat with the help 35
of Anne's parents.

SCHOOLING

Laing left the army in 1953. He was a changed man, somewhat
poorer in illusions and much clearer about what army psychiatry
was all about. As he put it:

> When I came out of the British Army . . . I had learned what was
> expected of a psychiatrist in the Army. It was much more than the
> exercise of a straightforward clinical, medical judgement, and in the
> treatment of patients, something very different from ordinary straight-
> forward medicine and surgery. The decisions I had been called upon
> to make, and the commands to which I had had to respond, entailed
> all sorts of man management, administration, organizational institu-
> tional power and structure, that had nothing to do with medicine.
> (1985, p. 147)

Laing's new civilian posting was as a junior hospital medical officer
at Gartnavel and later as a registrar at the Southern General Hospital, which brought some welcome changes and new opportunities
for observation and experiment. During this time, Laing worked
under Angus MacNiven, an eccentric, deeply humane psychiatrist
who was vigorously opposed to electroshock therapy and, unlike his
counterparts in the army, was well known for conversing with his
patients. MacNiven's superior was Ferguson Rodger, who was more
ambitious and keen on developing innovative treatment methods.

Laing's first patients had all been men, but now he was assigned
to the women's wing of the hospital. Army psychiatry had demanded rapid treatment or discharge to civilian facilities and made
no provision for long-term custodial care. Now Laing had the
chance to observe and interact with people who had been confined
to hospital for years. As Laing recalled in an interview almost two
decades later, the impact of class was also much heavier here than it
had been in the army.

> It wasn't such a bad place in many ways—it was full of eccentrics, and
> the patients were allowed to be far more eccentric than you'll find
> nowadays in modern mental hospitals, where they won't put up with
> it. People developed relatively whole lives for themselves inside it—
> mainly the wealthy ones, who were fee payers and lived in what were

called "Gentlemen's West" and "Ladies West." On the other side, for non-fee payers, were "Men's East" and "Women's East," which is were I worked. The fee payers had rooms coming off a central dayroom fitted out like a Victorian conservatory, with palms and aspidistra and armchairs. For the non-fee payers there was no dayroom—it was crammed with beds packed tightly together side by side, so you had to climb over the end to get into bed . . . On the intractable ward there were about sixty women. They were allowed no personal possessions of any kind—no underwear, no stockings, no cosmetics, no books . . . Baths were on order—about once a week you'd be stripped, put in a bath, scrubbed very hard, dried and put back in your dress, a clean one, if you were lucky . . . You hardly ever saw a doctor—except for the six-month physical examination required by law, to check for body ulcers, and so on . . . Many patients had been there for six years or more in no other context than their beds and the small yard attached to the ward. (Mezan, 1972, p. 168)

Unlike the vast majority of his colleagues, whose presence on their wards was fleeting at best, Laing did not avoid his patients. On the contrary, he decided to live with the patients for varying periods of time, totaling more than two months altogether. During his first night on the ward, he was assaulted by several women, who tried to remove his trousers. In due course, they got used to his presence, and things slowly returned to normal. And "normal," as Laing recalled, was not what you might expect:

My psychiatric presuppositions had prepared me for the autism of my patients. For the most part, they all seemed to be living in their own worlds. This was true in a sense but as time went on I realized it was only one side of the coin. There were a few patients with whom one did not need to speak schizophrenese. (1985, p. 151)

Among these there were women who, despite occasional bouts of craziness, understood their fellow inmates' moods and behavior far better than any of the attending psychiatrists or nurses, and who were only too happy to share their insights with him in their lucid intervals.

Laing began to wonder how much of the autistic self-absorption he saw might stem from environmental factors. The ward was terribly overcrowded, the nurses surly and overworked, and the patients had nothing to do. Also he noted that patients would conduct themselves in a somewhat quiet, reclusive fashion most of the time. But the imminent arrival of the doctor on the ward quickly triggered their most florid symptoms—"muttering, walking up and down, or crouching in a corner, or whatever their numbers happened to be" (Mezan, p. 168). Was this behavior contrived for the doctors' benefit? Was it a product of fear and anxiety, or a parody of the role that patients were expected to play? Or all of the above?

Sometime in 1953 Laing asked his superiors to provide him with a bright, spacious, and comfortably furnished room, and to allow twelve of the most intractable chronic patients to stay there from nine to five, Monday through Friday, for an extended period. Thanks to MacNiven's support, the experiment was reluctantly allowed. The patients were provided with magazines, materials for knitting, rugmaking, and other pastimes; unlike their counterparts, the control group, they were allowed to have underwear, stockings, and regular shoes, and to have their hair done.

Furthermore, in the dayroom—or the Rumpus Room, as it came to be called—the ratio of staff to patients was radically altered. Two nurses supervised the twelve patients and gave them individualized attention whenever possible. In this new, relaxed environment, the nurses had much less need for their customary vigilance, and patients had less need or desire to act out. Indeed, to their surprise, the nurses became fond of the women in their care and concerned for their welfare, which occasioned angry accusations of unprofessional conduct from their more overworked colleagues.

Finally, after several months and much administrative angst, a gas oven and stove were installed so that patients could make their own tea and biscuits. One day a doctor, Ian Cameron—later the director at Chestnut Lodge—brought a tray of buns the women had made under the nurses' watchful eyes into the psychiatrists' lounge. Most of the psychiatrists refused to touch them. For Laing this illustrated the total breakdown in human solidarity that so often occurs in mental hospitals:

> This incident convinced me of something. Who was crazier? Staff or
> patients? Excommunication runs deep. A companion means, literally,
> one with whom one shares bread. Companionship between staff and
> patients had broken down. The psychiatrists were afraid of catching

schizophrenia. Who knows? It might be contagious, like herpes, through the mucus membranes. (1985, p. 154)

Behavior like this is reminiscent of attitudes toward leprosy or, today, AIDS. It is as if the diagnosis of schizophrenia conferred mysterious powers to damage or derange other people through physical contagion—a belief for which there is no anecdotal, never mind empirical, evidence (as there was for leprosy, say) but which was obviously widespread.[3]

Leaving his colleagues' behavior aside for a moment, the results of the experiment as originally planned are worth noting. After eighteen months in their new environment, all twelve subjects were so dramatically improved that they were discharged (Cameron, Laing, and McGhie, 1955). One year later, without exception, they were all back again. Most of Laing's colleagues argued that this corroborated the theory that schizophrenia is an insidious and incurable disease; improvements are only temporary. Laing argued that, if patients always returned, it was because there was something radically wrong with the social contexts "out there." And if they left the hospital to return to their families of origin—as most did—perhaps the families were the source of the problem. Perhaps they wanted to come back, or get themselves put back, because they experienced more genuine friendship from fellow inmates than from the so-called normal people in the outside world.

Laing's position did not please his colleagues. And in retrospect, he thought, this episode intensified his growing estrangement from the psychiatric profession. At Netley Laing had already begun to wonder whether the traditional link between neurology and psychiatry were not in fact forced or arbitrary. He had no doubt that damaged or disordered brains could lead to deranged minds, with corollary disturbances in interpersonal relationships. He had seen too many brain-damaged people to doubt this. But he was also aware that in many cases severe neurological disorders could affect specific sensory organs or body systems without having a harmful effect on the ability to relate, and that brains, once damaged, could often compensate for severe systemic defects and restore more or less normal functioning, at all levels.

So what is the connection between the brain, the mind, and the personality? Laing resolved to study the interpersonal processes that accompany recovery from severe brain injury. One illuminating vignette (around 1953) concerns a fifteen-year-old girl named "Nan," who sustained severe head injuries and lay comatose for months before giving any signs of awareness. The puzzle in this case concerned the vivid alterations in her personality and style of interpersonal relatedness before and after the accident. Her "premorbid personality" was described as dutiful and conscientious—a girl who readily helped mother clean house and tend four younger siblings. After her convalescence, Nan was described by everyone, including her parents, as a coquette: an impish, flirtatious, and fun-loving girl who liked to make jokes and clever conversation, but had no taste for housework and quickly lost her temper if she did not get her way.

What happened in the intervening period to effect this radical transformation? Laing describes her slow, arduous recovery. Nan's first movements were limited and, to the neurologists on staff, appeared to be no more than involuntary contractions of certain muscle groups, around her eyes, forehead, and mouth. To the neurological specialists, Nan's first movements as she emerged from coma were wholly *reflexive* and indicated no specific intentions or a personal "presence" behind the actions. But to the nurses and relatives around her, Nan's first movements appeared to be expressive or *communicative* gestures, not mere reflex actions. As a reward for communicating—or trying to, as they thought—they would stroke her hair or skin. They frequently put sweets in her mouth and would interpret any instance of Nan's opening her mouth to be a tacit request for sweets.

Nan's post-traumatic smiles and verbal communications were singularly confused and inappropriate at first, indicating to the neurologists that she had no grasp of what was going on or what words and facial gestures mean. But her trial-and-error efforts were construed by everyone else as deliberate humor; they became the occasion for considerable mirth, for which Nan in turn was rewarded with more sweets and caresses. Soon she acquired a reputation around the ward as a real comedian who made light of her handicaps, which presumably attested to her pluck and spirit, her desire to please, and so on.

Leaving the doctors out of the picture, the one consistent thread in the behavior of those who comprised Nan's new environment was that they attributed a measure of meaning and intentionality to her behavior before there actually was any. Moreover, the kinds of meanings and intentions so attributed had a dramatic impact on who she subsequently became. Laing concluded:

> The new "Nan" began as a construction of the others. "She" was the significance of, the meaning of, "she" was what they made of the openings and shuttings of her eyes, contractions of her facial muscles . . . uncoordinated jerks of her hand. These contractions and jerks were read as attempts at gestures and expressions when neurologically they were still read as involuntary. The assimilation of these neurologically non-personal movements into a personal form seemed crucial for the formation of the new personality. They were endowed with meaning before they had a meaning in themselves . . .
>
> As her verbal ability developed Nan accepted and tried to fill out the role of playing to the gallery, and saw herself as a bit of a wit, which she had never been before.
>
> Such reactions to . . . others [became] fixed, indeed rigid, autonomous established traits of a post-traumatic personality . . . She learned to build on this foundation other complementary patterns of behavior that, as it were, "fitted in" with the original basis . . . If at first she was almost passively inducted into a role provided and defined by others, she quickly became adept at using the "new" personality they gave her to manipulate them. Her relationships to others became more *dialectic*. This process continued until she had a sufficiently stable and adequate set of patterns through which to interact with others and through which she could maintain a personal and social equilibrium between her impaired functions and the demands and expectations of others. Thus was formed her post-traumatic personality. (1985a, pp. 162–164)

Cases like these led Laing to ask: "when does a body become a person? How can we answer that question? When and how did a 'he' a 'she,' a 'you' re-emerge? . . . I wanted to approach this moment in terms of a possible interpersonal neurology." After 1955, Laing reluctantly dropped his ambition of coordinating neurology and interpersonal processes. Still it is interesting to note that even at this early stage, existential-phenomenological themes and preoccupations—such as the irreducible role of intentionality and created meaning in human psychology and the constitution of the "I" in the interpersonal field—were already in evidence.

Admittedly it is risky to search for tenable homologies between normal ontogenetic development in the infant and the emergence of a post-traumatic personality in a brain-damaged teenager. But it may also be instructive, and Laing obviously thought there were parallels worth exploring. Extrapolating by analogy from his experience with Nan, Laing later speculated that personality traits are constructed in an interpersonal field, where essentially involuntary (reflex) movements and sounds are absorbed in a world of meanings and intentions created *for* the developing (or recovering) organism by others, notably by the primary caregivers (Laing, 1961, 1968). The role of individuals in constructing or defining their own identity consists in their taking on the roles scripted for them, so to speak, and developing complementary strategies and styles of interaction (as the environment permits) into a well-orchestrated repertoire of behavioral schemas—"numbers"—to meet their own needs and objectives. The ingenuity and skill with which they do this, presumably, is the true measure of their intentions and of their personal agency, but these need not be visible to or intuitively grasped by "others," who only see their outward effect. For Laing, we are seldom identical with the parts we play or the faces we present to the world. To borrow Erving Goffman's term, the presentation of self, either conscious or unconscious, is often an *instrumental* undertaking, a performance of sorts, although the specific purposes it serves may be hateful, loving, or selfish.

Laing applied the same logic to clinical psychopathology. The difference between normal people, neurotics, and the mad, however, is that for neurotic and mad people, disturbances in the interpersonal field, and the constraints put on their self-development, render their connection to the roles thrust on them more problematic, so that the effective integration of an "adapted" persona becomes difficult or impossible (Laing, 1964, 1967). For the person suffering a mental breakdown, the interactive repertoires they have learned or acquired, while quite adaptive in environmental terms, have ceased to be effective vehicles for the purposes of the real self, which is progressively estranged from the surface persona and frequently threatened by it as well. This burgeoning conflict between surface and depth leads to the collapse of the externally adapted persona, and then to an attempt to heal the split through regression to the chronological age before the split between the inner and outer selves became so serious. In this healing process—which Laing termed *metanoia*—a new personality may emerge: one that is oriented to external reality but anchored in the real self as well (1967).

Meanwhile, despite the disappointments of his experiment Laing's work at Gartnavel did not go unnoticed. Ferguson Rodger was quite impressed and brought him to the attention of J. D. Sutherland who, from 1947 to 1968, was the medical director of the Tavistock Clinic in London. Sutherland, who had trained with W.R.D. Fairbairn, was also the editor of the *International Journal of Psychoanalysis* and later the *British Journal of Medical Psychology*. Sutherland admired what he saw of *The Divided Self,* which in manuscript was well underway. Together with John Bowlby and Charles Rycroft, Sutherland helped to get Laing, his wife, and four children to London in 1956. In doing this, these senior psychiatrists were launching a program to bring talented young doctors to London for analytic training, in the hope of effecting a more equitable distribution of analytic expertise throughout the United Kingdom (Sutherland, 1990; Rycroft, 1990). Training for the out-of-towners was paid for by the National Health Service, and they supported themselves by working as registrars at the Tavistock Clinic. So Laing was trained on public funds, along with his friend and fellow Glaswegian David Sherret, who now practices in Toronto, and Harwant Gill, who was analyzed by Rycroft under a version of the same scheme.

Apart from his promise as a writer and a clinician, what commended Laing most to Sutherland and the others was the Rumpus Room experiment, which Bowlby in particular found intriguing. In the mid-eighties, almost two decades after Laing's departure from the Tavistock, Eric Trist extracted a promise from Laing that he would rewrite the original *Lancet* article about the experiment for the second volume of his Tavistock anthology, *The Social Engagement of Social Science* (Trist and Murray, 1987.) In a telephone conversation in 1990, Trist expressed profound regret over the fact that Laing's unexpected death had prevented him from fulfilling his promise, despite the fact that the experiment had preceded Laing's tenure at the Tavistock by two years. From this we can surmise that some of Laing's ideas were admired by his colleagues well before he came on board and long after they parted company.

Another factor in his favor was that Laing was not yet considered a radical, a maverick, or a troublemaker in professional circles. Though he dabbled in radical politics and had a reputation for being ambitious and a seasoned drinker and partygoer, he was perceived as a clinical conservative (Mullan, p. 107). In those days, remember, promoters of lobotomy and electroshock were commonly construed as innovators and radicals, and opposition to lobotomy and electroshock was only found among men in their sixties and seventies, such as MacNiven, or among characters like Schorstein, whose numbers were steadily dwindling. That made Laing seem something of an anachronism, rather than the radical or visionary he was later made out to be.

3

THE *T*AVISTOCK AND
FAMILY RESEARCH

The first years in London were difficult for Laing, personally and professionally. His fourth child, Paul, was born shortly after the family's arrival, and his wife Anne, who was already burdened with domestic cares, had no friends or relatives there and was more isolated than she had been in Glasgow. While she toiled over five young children, growing more dissatisfied with each passing year, Laing led a hectic professional life five full days a week, devoting most of his evenings to writing *The Divided Self.*

Laing's work life was not always gratifying either. In view of his deepening disenchantment with mainstream psychiatry, one might have expected him to welcome the move to the Tavistock. As he later confided to Bob Mullan, however:

> What I didn't bank on, what I hadn't realized was that Tavistock was an exclusively *out-patient* organization. All my work had been done in hospitals, and this was to be the first time since I had left school that I worked outside of a hospital and clinical context. These were ordinary people who lived in Hampstead and all very white and middle class . . . From very early on I felt . . . I had really fucked myself up there. I was shunted into doing this out-patient work, seeing people in an office, of a kind that, compared to the extremity of distress that I'd seen in the army—and neurology and Gartnavel and the department of psychiatry—this wasn't what I wanted to be doing. There was no

integration of this with the body and disturbances of the body, just all sitting and talking, and that's where I felt I went down the drain in my career.

I had to do something about this and make the best of it . . . the Tavistock Clinic was lost in a miasma of human relations and the Tavistock Institute seemed to be lackeys of business organizations and were doing things like studying what sort of lavatory paper to market—whether people wanted to have rough grain paper or whether it was to clean you or soothe you. (1995, p. 149)

In addition to being ill at ease with the Tavistock as a whole, Laing had strong differences in scientific and political matters with John Bowlby, who was to become the chief administrator there. According to Laing, Bowlby thought that

a sane society depended on the sanity of its members which was very much likely to be affected by a wholesome early life and a wholesome relationship with the mothering or caretaking person. If there were enough people, a critical mass in society that held it together that had that chance . . . society could be saved . . .

If there are enough good people bred. Enough "vitamins." That was Bowlby's disastrous comparison of maternal affection being equated with a critical period of being fed a vitamin, and if you didn't get the vitamin then you were lost and gone forever statistically. It's such a terrible condemnation for someone who's had a lousy childhood . . . Also completely unscientific. (p. 156)

Bowlby, in turn, had serious misgivings about Laing's immersion in continental philosophy, suggesting, for one thing, that he drop the terms existential, phenomenological, and ontological from *The Divided Self*. Bowlby thought that ethology, and not philosophy, was the best idiom for communicating with fellow scientists. He had no idea how offensive this suggestion was to Laing. By the time I interviewed Bowlby in London in June 1990, he did know, but still felt that existential phenomenology was too muddled and misguided to matter. He even suggested that the personal and professional tragedies that plagued Laing toward the end of his life were actually a vindication of his theories. But he was quick to acknowledge that Laing's "real" work had a profound impact on him and his colleagues.

In the meantime, at the Institute of Psycho-Analysis things seemed promising at first. Laing missed the connection between neurology and in-patient psychiatry here too, but felt nonetheless that he was training with the best and brightest of his generation, all of them attending seminars led by W. R. Bion, Melanie Klein, D. W. Winnicott, and Paula Heimann. The problem was that there was so little dialogue between teachers and students, and some of his preceptors approached their work in a spirit of indoctrination rather than of free inquiry (Mullan, pp. 149–150).

One revealing anecdote, from Laing's second or third year, concerns Herbert Rosenfeld, who was conducting a seminar on transference psychosis. Rosenfeld had a psychotic patient who dreamed of two vertical cliff faces standing opposite one another. A mechanical bird emerged from one cliff face, said "Cuckoo!" three times and disappeared, to be followed immediately by an identical performance on the other cliff. According to Rosenfeld, this dream image depicted the structural split in the patient's mind. With humor unintended (so he said), Laing suggested that the dream might represent the patient's perception of the therapeutic dialogue. Punning aside, where more orthodox theorists interpreted symbols in terms of intrapsychic structures or processes, Laing, after Sullivan, was construing them in interpersonal terms. Rosenfeld sat silently and made no comment. Whether he sensed a tacit criticism of his clinical skill or merely disapproved of the theoretical framework Laing was invoking, he took the remark amiss, and Laing, feeling the anger, decided not to attend the seminar again (Mullan, p. 287). This decision would cause him trouble later. To get the unfolding situation into proper perspective, however, a digression on the history and politics of the institute is in order.

Well before Laing's arrival, the Institute of Psycho-Analysis in London was riven by the theoretical disputes of two rival factions: that of Anna Freud, Freud's daughter, and that of Melanie Klein, who had been analyzed by Sandor Ferenczi and Karl Abraham. After a rather shaky start in Budapest and Berlin, Klein came to London in 1926, encouraged by James and Alix Strachey and by Freud's opportunistic lieutenant, Ernest Jones (Grosskurth, 1986). At that time Jones and Abraham were engaged in a bitter power struggle with two of Freud's intimates, Ferenczi and Otto Rank (Fromm, 1959; Grosskurth, 1991). Rank was particularly vulnerable to attack because he lacked medical credentials (as did Anna Freud). Throughout the 1920s Freud was furious at Jones for opposing him on the issue of lay analysis and allying himself with the Americans. So Jones used his advocacy of Klein to buttress his claim to support lay analysis, but promptly withdrew his support when it no longer suited his purposes (Grosskurth, 1986).

As a result of Jones's power plays and equivocations, Freud and his daughter distrusted Klein, whose ideas on the origins of the superego and the Oedipus complex differed dramatically from theirs. In addition, Klein's approach to child analysis was more radical than Anna Freud's pedagogic orientation. From the moment the Freuds fled the Nazis and arrived in London—and indeed for some years before—the battle between Anna Freud and Melanie Klein had been joined, with Ernest Jones acting as a far from disinterested mediator. Oddly enough, though Klein hailed from Vienna and trained in Europe, her therapeutic approach was referred to as "the English school." Since the Freudians and the Kleinians could not get along, this led to a split at the institute in 1946, which was cleverly arranged by Sylvia Payne (Fuller, 1985), who had studied with Hans Sachs and leaned toward Klein earlier. Henceforth the Kleinians were known as the A Group, Anna Freud's as the B Group, while those in neither camp joined the Middle Group, which was technically a subsection of the A Group. The Middle Group attracted many practitioners who were fed up with the dogmatism of the Kleinian and Freudian factions, and the authoritarian fashion in which training was conducted to ensure doctrinal purity. They tried to avoid the sectarian controversies that split the rest of the institute and made no attempt to enforce uniformity among themselves. In this group were Michael Balint (Ferenczi's pupil, friend, and literary executor) and his wife Alice, John Sutherland, John Bowlby, and D. W. Winnicott (an analysand of James Strachey's), and Charles Rycroft and Marion Milner (both analysands of Sylvia Payne's).

Though they welcomed defectors from Anna Freud's faction, the dominant intellectual influences on the Middle Group were Ferenczi and Klein. Ferenczi's influence, mediated through the Balints, was less open because of the stigma attached to Ferenczi's ideas by

Freud and Ernest Jones. Nor did Klein's dislike of Ferenczi help his reputation. But the Middle Group incorporated some of his ideas by a kind of osmosis, and in a positive fashion. Klein's impact was more overt, but often expressed in the rejection as well as the acceptance of her ideas. Among the more controversial Kleinian shibboleths was her notion of the death instinct, which she adapted from Freud to suit her own theory of infantile development.

While the Middle Group acquired a reputation for theoretical independence, some of the earliest criticism of Klein came not from London but, curiously enough, from Scotland. The first frontal attack was launched by the Glasgow psychiatrist Ian Suttie, author of *The Origins of Love and Hate* (1935). Klein had speculated that the death instinct is operative from birth and that infantile anxiety is the by-product of the projection of malicious impulses onto external objects, resulting in the splitting of the ego and internalized object relations. In short, in Klein's estimation, the newborn is paranoid and only acquires a sociable disposition when it acquires a capacity for remorse and relinquishes its harmful fantasies (Segal, 1973).

Suttie, who was a Ferenczi enthusiast and an early figure at the Tavistock Clinic, believed that the opposite is true—sociability is innate, and malignant aggression is a secondary phenomenon, a product of environmental deficiencies that warp normal development. Another Scotsman who criticized Klein along these lines was Sutherland's teacher, W.R.D. Fairbairn. Unlike Suttie, however, Fairbairn commended Klein's ideas about internalized object relations, and he developed a novel notion of the schizoid personality that became highly influential, rivaling Klein's. While recognizing the ubiquity of splitting and schizoid processes, and stressing their primacy over oedipal phenomena, Fairbairn also stressed the primacy of sociability over destructive drives in infancy, maintaining that what Klein regarded as the normal situation in infancy could only be the product of severe parental neglect or hostility, and not of endogenous drives and processes (Fairbairn, 1954).

Though he never cited Suttie and seldom cited Fairbairn, Laing was aware of their views, and he too rejected the death instinct. Curiously, however, he did not champion the innate sociability or object-seeking propensity of the newborn, but echoed Gregory Bateson's objection that the whole notion of the death instinct was based on an obsolete biological orientation that viewed the human organism as a closed energy system (Bateson and Reusch, 1951; Grosskurth, 1986). Significantly, John Bowlby concurred with Laing on this issue. In fact, Bowlby's attempt to effect a synthesis between ethology and psychoanalysis—later known as attachment theory— was predicated on precisely this point.

Although he was anxious to establish the originality of his own views, Laing shared one feature with his Scottish compatriots: an attitude of independence toward Freud and Klein. This commended him to most members of the Middle Group but estranged him from the other two. Klein, for all her faults, was an original, even though she perversely insisted that her theoretical innovations were the logical or necessary extensions of Freud's work. No number of denials or protests from Sigmund and Anna, to the effect that her "Freud piety" was mistaken or misplaced, clouded her conviction on this score. Despite novel departures in theory, however, Klein was every bit as demanding, doctrinaire, and manipulative of her students as Freud was of his, and in this sense at least she was thoroughly Freudian.

In any case, for a multitude of reasons, Laing lacked Klein's odd veneration for Freud and came to resent her authoritarian manner toward analytic candidates, whom she treated as potential converts, enemies, or pawns in the institutional power struggle. In 1957, when Laing asked Klein to be his clinical supervisor, she refused, on the grounds that Laing's analyst, Charles Rycroft, had not himself been properly analyzed—an oblique slur on Sylvia Payne, Rycroft's analyst. Still, as Laing confessed to Phyllis Grosskurth, he did admire certain things about Klein. He abhorred her "adamantine dogmatism," her haughty, self-centered behavior, and her gaudy appearance. But he regarded her as "someone of calibre, not *trivial*," and admired her bravery in the face of scorn and rejection (Grosskurth, pp. 446–448).

After one year in analysis with Rycroft and the usual course work at the institute, Laing approached Winnicott and Milner to serve as his clinical supervisors. Milner found Laing an engaging and promising young man. As she later remarked in her report to the Training Committee (1960), Laing was always "a pleasure to work with because I never feel he is distorting the material to make it fit into a preconceived theory or formula, he never gives ready-made or cliched interpretations." Furthermore, she continued, "I feel he will always be able to learn, and to learn quickly, from his patients." Reading between the lines, one gets the impression that the traits Milner valued in Laing were not common among analytic candidates at the time—indeed, that most trainees did try to fit their case material into preconceived theoretical schemata and thus had difficulty in learning from patients.

Laing's relationship with Winnicott was also predominantly positive, at least initially. Judging from their correspondence—which, though meager, is instructive—it was based on a strong sense of affinity and mutual respect, although Winnicott, like Bowlby, lacked sympathy for and familiarity with existentialism. On April 4, 1958, Laing wrote to Winnicott asking him to read his manuscript for *The Divided Self*, which, Laing said, was inspired by Winnicott's ideas. He agreed, and Laing mailed the manuscript on May 30. On June 28 Winnicott responded:

> Yesterday I had my first chance to read your Ms., which I insulted by getting through it in two hours. You will understand from this that I did not do it justice. After reading it I tried to ring you because I was so excited. I suppose my excitement had to do with the fact that you make so much use of the sort of things I think important . . .
>
> It is possible that in your build-up at the beginning you are talking to yourself quite a bit. This may be a good way of starting a book but I did not really get interested until I was a third of the way through. I hope the book gets published soon and that from there you may get on to making a more concise theoretical statement.
>
> Incidentally, I learned something from your book, which is always exciting; something you said about being watched in paranoid states made me see that one of my patients is being watched by a projection of her true self. This is something I had not thought of, and it helps me considerably.
>
> Thank you very much for letting me see the Ms.
>
> I look forward to reading the book. (1960)

Judging from subsequent events, Laing took Winnicott's encouragement to heart. Richard Gelfer, boarding with the Laing family at the time, remembers Laing devoting every spare evening to the completion of the manuscript, with no time for his wife and children. By

1959, even Laing's instructors were complaining about his frequent absences from their lectures, which he attempted to justify by his need to finish the book.

Whether Laing's work on *The Divided Self* was the primary reason for his frequent absences from the institute may be doubted. Other factors were probably involved. Laing's childhood experience and adolescent precocity predisposed him to distrust authority and to pursue his own path. In his late teens and twenties, Laing had trouble at the university because he thought he had arrived there as an intellectual in his own right. Finally, as Charles Rycroft remarked in his letter to the Training Committee, there was something in Laing's personality which polarized people's feelings about him in a definitively positive or negative direction. Perhaps Laing sensed that some of his instructors did not like him, and he simply preferred to stay away from the institute.

Whatever his motives, Laing's lack of attendance precipitated a move in the spring of 1960 to postpone his qualification and to hold him back a year. Moreover, the documentary evidence suggests that the effort to postpone his qualification was seen by some as merely the first installment in a longer-range plan to keep him disqualified altogether.

Though it was probably initiated by Rosenfeld, the disciplinary action was strongly supported by the training secretary, Frances (Fanny) Wride, and by I. Hellman, who met and corresponded with Laing. The opposition of Laing's analyst and clinical supervisors to the plan was unanimous. In their letters to the training committee, Milner, Rycroft, and Winnicott all argued that requiring Laing to repeat a year of coursework and supervision would be extremely counterproductive. In a report dated May 1960, Milner suggested that such a move would

> reflect on the psychoanalytic society, by suggesting that we are incapable of being flexible enough to meet the needs of a specially brilliant student; in this case a man who, during the time he missed most of his seminars, was deeply preoccupied with the creative work of planning an independent research and getting financial support for it. (Courtesy Marion Milner)

In an unusually blunt letter, written a few weeks later, Charles Rycroft, who had preceded Wride as the training secretary, cautioned her and the committee against acting in a way which makes it appear that it values conformity more than it does intelligence and originality. Dr. Laing is by far the most intelligent candidate I have yet had in analysis or supervision and has more than an average feel for the unconscious, and he thinks for himself. When one considers that one of the major problems encountered by the Society is that so many candidates are passive, anaclitic, ocnophilic types, I should have thought that it should be the policy of the Training Committee to adopt a liberal approach towards the occasional student who shows originality and drive, especially when, as in the present case, the student already has a measure of achievement behind him and enjoys the confidence of those best placed to judge the quality of his work. (Courtesy Charles Rycroft)

In his letter to Wride, Winnicott took a slightly different approach:

if there is nothing in this man that will make him want to go on developing, no amount of prolongation of the teacher-student relationship will have any effect. In my personal opinion it is likely (though I have not talked this over with Dr. Rycroft) that Dr. Laing needs freedom from the student position in order to make the next step in his personal analysis, and it is this and not the teaching trick that will produce the result. (1960)

The cumulative impression these letters convey is that Milner, Rycroft, and Winnicott believed that Laing was not being penalized for nonattendance but for his originality and independence, and that the disciplinary initiative reflected more on the institute than it did on him. Furthermore, in view of Milner's and Rycroft's frequent references to Laing's industry and initiative, one can only wonder whether an element of collective envy sparked these proceedings. After all, Laing's work in progress showed great promise, and he took far more freedom in thought and deed than his instructors would have allowed themselves at his age or in his position.

In any case, thanks to Milner, Rycroft, and Winnicott, the Training Committee eventually backed down, and Laing graduated on schedule in 1960. Now a qualified psychoanalyst, he began to supplement his income as a researcher at the Tavistock with an increasingly busy private practice at 21 Wimpole Street. But Laing did not use his graduation as an opportunity to continue in his personal analysis, as Winnicott had hoped he would. On the contrary, he complained bitterly about his analysis, telling Ben Churchill, John Heaton, and almost anyone who would listen that he thought his training had been of little value and he would have to unlearn most of it. Laing's copious complaints eventually reached Rycroft, who had made no secret of his fondness for Laing and his wife Anne, and who was taken aback by the vehemence of Laing's feelings. What could account for it?

A number of factors could have been in play. To begin with, despite his chosen vocation and the traits his teachers commended in him, Laing was probably unable to avail himself of the benefits of psychotherapy with any competent practitioner at any point in his adult life. Part of this came from his arrogant notion that because no one was more intelligent or skilled than he, no one was competent to take him on. And apart from temperamental resistances, several troubling events occurred, which would doubtless have interfered with the most resolute attempt to explore early childhood issues as his analysis drew to a close.

First, on January 5, 1959, Laing's closest friend, Douglas Hutchison, fell 3,000 feet to his death from Ben More in northern Scotland during a climb. Though reported as a tragic accident, rumor has it that it was a suicide. In any case, accident or otherwise, Laing was shattered. He wept uncontrollably at Hutchison's memorial service—so much so that Tom Freeman, a local psychoanalyst, thought his behavior a scandal and publicly questioned his manliness (James Davie, personal communication, 1991). For the last year of his analysis, then, it is safe to assume that Laing was in mourning over the loss of a dear friend.

To complicate matters, Laing's relationship with Anne was steadily deteriorating and would continue to do so for the next several years. All in all, the last year of Laing's analysis must have been a hellish time—Douglas dead, Anne sullen and estranged, and his future as an analyst hanging in the balance. As a result of all these pressures, by late 1960 Ronald Laing was very ill. Adrian Laing reports that he nearly died. No diagnosis seemed to fit: some symptoms suggested a glandular fever, and for a time several doctors speculated that he might have cancer (A. Laing, 1994, p. 67). Given Laing's fondness for the ideas of Georg Groddeck (see Chapter 10), it seems likely that Laing himself believed that his illness had a strong psychosomatic inflection, though whether he shared this with his analyst is anyone's guess.

Either way the fact remains that people coping with deep and lingering grief, career uncertainty, marital strife, and undiagnosable ailments of the flesh are not generally noted for generosity of spirit or balance in their dealings with others. No wonder that his analysis ended on a somewhat sour note, as far as Laing was concerned.

Another factor influencing Laing's attitude toward his analyst was that Rycroft was not intransigent enough in his struggle against medical and analytic orthodoxy. As his letter about Laing attests, in 1960 Rycroft was appalled at the dogmatism and conformity in analytic circles. But he steadfastly avoided controversy and remained a member of the society until 1978, when he quietly allowed his membership to lapse (Fuller, 1985). Laing, by contrast, left the society in anger at an early point in his career. Instead of forging ahead in the analytic tradition, as Rycroft did, he set out on an independent path, occupying a position on the margins of psychoanalysis that I have referred to elsewhere as the dissident fringe (Burston, 1991).

If we examine the politics of psychoanalysis in broad historical perspective, it becomes apparent that major analytic theorists can be classified according to their emotional relationship to Freud and his ideas, no matter what of the specific content or merit of their theoretical positions. The orthodox, now a dwindling minority, adhere to classical Freudian theory with minor deviations, revering Freud with an attitude bordering on religious piety. At the opposite extreme are the dissident fringe, practitioners once involved in the analytic movement who divest themselves of their reverence for Freud piety as a result of bitter disappointment, or to follow their own creative muse, or both.

In between these poles are two other groups, the crypto-revisionists and the loyal opposition. The loyal opposition makes a candid avowal of its theoretical differences with Freud on many salient points, but some Freud piety remains. By contrast, the crypto-revisionists try to make radical departures from Freudian doctrine seem like logical extensions of Freud's thought and method. They often curry favor with the orthodox and profess loyalty to Freud, while attempting to redefine the boundaries of orthodoxy altogether. In effect, they are like religious reformers who legitimate new ethical or cosmological conceptions by attributing them to a more ancient source, resulting in a creative misreading of the original texts and a change (for good or ill) on the tradition as a whole.

In terms of this typology, we could map the English scene in 1960 in the following way. Melanie Klein was a crypto-revisionist, albeit a genuinely creative one. Despite her contributions to ego psychology, Anna Freud was primarily the faithful guardian of late Freudian orthodoxy, and the Middle Group comprised the loyal opposition, making no claims to orthodoxy of either kind. The dissident fringe, to which Laing belonged, included people like Ian Suttie, the later John Bowlby and one or two other notable figures, all of whom relied on Freud when necessary but who tried to reorient their work when Freud wouldn't carry them where they wanted to go.

What bearing does this typology have on the relationship between Laing and his analyst? When examined chronologically, the works of Charles Rycroft describe a slow but steady trajectory away from the sectarian squabbles and tunnel vision of Freud and Klein. In the late fifties and early sixties, Rycroft's perceptiveness and originality were still operating inside the framework of relatively orthodox assumptions. But by 1968, when he published *A Critical Dictionary of Psychoanalysis,* his revisionist intentions became explicit. Since then, Rycroft has occupied a position analogous to that of Erich Fromm in America: a member of the loyal opposition with strong affinities to the dissident fringe, who has endured marginalization for not paying lip service to orthodox shibboleths while enjoying considerable recognition outside mainstream psychoanalysis.

In 1977, when Laing's fame was beginning to wane and Rycroft's was beginning to grow, they met by chance in a shop one summer afternoon and spent the evening together talking over drinks. On this occasion, Laing thanked Rycroft for not turning his analysis into the usual course of Freudian indoctrination. And in 1985, in an even more generous frame of mind, Laing wrote a glowing review of Rycroft's *The Innocence of Dreams* (1981). By that time, of course, Rycroft had allowed his membership in the British Psycho-Analytic Institute to lapse and had changed his theoretical orientation in a way that Laing found quite congenial.

But from 1956 to 1960, while Laing was in analysis, Rycroft's theoretical views were still relatively orthodox, despite his distaste for compliant and doctrinaire candidates. Laing was moving rapidly toward the dissident fringe, propelled by the oppositional identity acquired in childhood and by his commitment to existential phenomenology, which compelled skepticism on important doctrinal issues. (More on this in later chapters.) So Laing probably felt that Rycroft's posture toward the analytic establishment was too accommodating. In any case, and in addition to everything else, one suspects that Laing's behavior toward Rycroft was affected by his complex ambivalence for psychoanalysis as a whole.[1]

Leaving his own analysis aside, another factor that may have alienated Laing from Institutional psychoanalysis was his openness to Jungian ideas. Laing was first exposed to Jung through his friend Karl Abenheimer in Glasgow, and the first documented episode of contact with a Jungian society dates to July of 1960, when he skipped one of his analytic seminars to lecture to the Society for Analytical Psychology on his emerging theory of schizoid states. I suspect that news of the lecture was greeted rather coldly at the institute.

Though anathema to orthodox Freudians, Jung's influence in Britain was strong. Jung lectured at the Tavistock in 1935, and at least one of the senior faculty there, Eric Graham Howe, was an admirer. Howe joined the Tavistock in 1928 and was the author, among other books, of *Motives and Mechanisms of the Mind* (1930), *The War Dance: A Study in the Psychology of War* (1939), *Mysterious Marriage* (1942) and *Cure or Heal?* (1965), to which Laing wrote a warm introduction. Howe's father was a bishop, and he himself tried to synthesize Christianity and Buddhism, and was a friend of Krishnamurti, D. T. Suzuki, Niyanaponika Mahathera, and Alan Watts—men who played a significant role in bringing eastern philosophy and spiritual practices to the west. Laing met Howe at John Heaton's home in 1960, and they became good friends. In 1962 Howe was instrumental in securing the directorship of the Langham Clinic for Laing (Cooper et al., 1989).

In a letter to Winnicott, dated October 31, 1962, Laing explained that the Langham Clinic (on Queen Anne Street, in central London, which crosses Harley Street) was formerly the Open Way Clinic, under the directorship of Alfred Torrie. It offered psychotherapy at reduced rates for people unable to afford private fees and was staffed by eight part-time therapists, three of whom were candidates at the Institute of Psycho-Analysis. Roland Forrester, a Toronto-based psychoanalyst, was one of these candidates, and he remembers Laing as a brisk but accessible administrator who was committed to creating a clinic that would bring Jungian and psychoanalytically oriented practitioners together under one roof.

By 1962, Laing had achieved considerable success. His first book, *The Divided Self*, although not a runaway bestseller, was doing well and brought the attention of many thoughtful people to its author, despite withering reviews from the Freudian establishment (Brierley, 1961; Freeman, 1961). *Self and Others* appeared in 1961 and, though less popular, helped to consolidate Laing's reputation as a serious thinker in the existential tradition.

The Divided Self, which is Laing's most popular and widely acclaimed book, addressed the problems of what he called ontological insecurity and the accompanying fears and fantasies of engulfment, implosion, and petrification that beset schizoid individuals, whose characteristic conflicts and defenses Laing attempted to trace back to profound interpersonal disjunctures in the first year or two of development. In this book, disturbed interpersonal relationships are seen as both the cause and the consequence of the internal or intrapsychic processes that characterize the psychotic individual. But despite the adverse impact of others on mental equilibrium and self-image, Laing, like Sartre, construed the mad (or nearly mad) person as an active agent in the creation and perpetuation of his own misery, who must choose, finally, to abandon his schizoid isolation in favor of authentic relatedness to others in order to regain his sanity.

In *Self and Others* Laing dropped his emphasis on the inner world of the schizophrenic and focused primarily on the interpersonal processes that accompany madness, the so-called social fantasy systems. The promising developmental hypotheses he raised in connection with the schizoid personality in *The Divided Self* were abandoned, and the notion of ontological security was only mentioned in passing. Despite some thematic inconsistencies between the earlier book and its ostensible sequel, which I explore in detail in Chapter 10, *Self and Others* contains many reflections that prefigure Laing's later theory of interpersonal defenses.

In addition to these authorial achievements, in 1962 Laing had a thriving private practice and was the director of the Langham Clinic. He was also the principal investigator of the Schizophrenia and Family Research Unit at the Tavistock, where with Aaron Esterson he was conducting research for *Sanity, Madness and the Family*

(1964). To familiarize Laing with the growing research on the families of schizophrenics, the Tavistock sent him to the United States to meet the luminaries in the field, including Gregory Bateson, Ray Birdwhistell, Don Jackson, Roger Shapiro, Albert Scheflen, Ross Speck, Lyman Wynne, and Erving Goffman. By his own reckoning, his meetings with Bateson, Jackson, and Speck were probably the most useful for his future development. He gave a striking account of his meeting with Goffman to Richard Simon, a writer for the *Family Therapist Networker:*

> Although we had never met or seen photos of one another we recognized each other immediately. He was fibrillating and twitching and carrying on like a very frisky dog—very vibrant, very conscious, very alert. He wasn't particularly frightened of me . . . but was maintaining a sort of courageous terror in the face of the horror that was his central vision of things and his despair at not making any difference to it. With Goffman there was no consolation in the possibility of transcendence. It was as if he was saying "It might be all right for God in his heaven, but it is not all right for me." (Simon, 1983, p. 60)

The phrase "courageous terror" also sums up Schorstein's experience of the human condition, which Laing shared to a large extent.

Though the psychedelic era was still several years away, Laing had been dabbling with drugs for some time. In 1960 Richard Gelfer acquired some LSD for experimental purposes and, at Laing's request, gave him a sizable dose. Having already tried it himself, Gelfer expected to see some strange and disoriented behavior, and he offered to stay with Laing for the duration of his "trip." Laing graciously declined the offer and retired to his bedroom for six hours, after which he quietly opened the door and went about his business (Gelfer, 1992). Though uneventful in its externals, Laing's first trip had a profound effect, and he started to experiment with LSD as a psychotherapeutic agent at 21 Wimpole Street. Some of his patients derived little tangible benefit from their acid trips, and others found it an aversive and unproductive experience. But some credit their LSD sessions with helping them to achieve dramatic breakthroughs and are grateful to this day for having used it under Laing's guidance (for instance, Ram Dass, the former Richard Alpert, in Mezan, 1972, pp. 97, 160).

Though Laing's LSD experiments may sound radical, we should remember that, at this particular moment in history, similar experiments were taking place around the world. Stanislav Grof, a Czech psychiatrist, and Timothy Leary and Richard Alpert of Harvard University were among those whose writings on the subject were well known by the end of the decade. On the Canadian prairie, Humphrey Osmond and Abraham Hoffer experimented liberally with LSD, while another Scottish psychiatrist, Ewan Cameron, used it extensively in his CIA-funded experiments at the Allan Memorial Hospital in Montreal. As a past president of the American and Canadian Psychiatric Associations and founder of the World Psychiatric Association, Cameron had an international reputation and was as respectable and "scientific" as Laing was radical and mystical (Collins, 1988).

My point is that, in the early sixties, LSD was being hailed by reputable researchers with widely discrepant agendas as a promising therapeutic and research tool. Laing's case was neither isolated nor as reckless as others (A. Laing, 1994, chap. 11). Nevertheless, Laing's use of psychedelics cost him credibility as the years went on. His Tavistock colleagues were dismayed. Bowlby often told him that he was ruining a splendid scientific career. In December 1965, Howe, who thoroughly disapproved of drugs, demanded Laing's resignation from the directorship of the Langham Clinic, ending what had been a sustaining friendship for them both. And in 1976 a former friend and patient, Clancy Sigal, published a fictionalized memoir, *Zone of Interior,* which chronicles Laing's use of LSD in terms that are both funny and frightening. Sigal's caricature of Laing—in the fictional person of Dr. Willie Last—may be tainted by personal animosity. But it raises serious questions about Laing's attitudes toward his own body and mind at the time. Even allowing for satirical overkill, one gets the distinct impression that, like many drug users, Laing cherished a fantasy of invulnerability to the cumulative effects of LSD. Indeed, Sigal's pseudonym, Willie Last, sounds suspiciously like a question, "Will he last?"

But unlike most drug users, as Sigal (among others) attests, Laing was not leading a frivolous or merely self-indulgent life. On the contrary. While Laing experimented with LSD, both on himself and his patients, he continued to work hard and to extend his growing network of friends and co-workers. Many, though not all, were psychiatrists or former patients, who banded together in 1963 to create an informal association known to insiders as the Brotherhood. Apart from Sigal himself, one important player in this evolving drama was Aaron Esterson, who had joined Laing in London in 1958, when Laing was learning about Bateson's double-bind theory of schizophrenia.

Another important figure in Laing's social and professional world was David Cooper, a psychiatrist from Cape Town, South Africa, whom Laing first met in 1958 at the Belmont Hospital. Unlike Laing—who was short, slender, and a stylish dresser—Cooper was a large man with an expansive temperament who cared little about his appearance. Like Laing, though, he was keenly sensitive to the lack of human connection in mental hospitals; many features of the professional role he saw as a kind of violence against the mad, confirming their powerlessness. In 1962 Cooper started an experiment in breaking down patient-professional barriers and fostering the patient's autonomy at Villa 21, a unit in Shenley Hospital in St. Albans, London—an experiment that continued until 1965 (Cooper, et al., 1989). Though he never actually set foot in the unit, Laing took it as a model for the therapeutic community at Kingsley Hall.

One of the salient things about David Cooper was his emphasis on the links between psychological healing, individual empowerment, and the creation of community, ideas advanced by the psychiatric survivor and self-help movements of today—sometimes to the point of utter banality. But when Cooper first addressed these issues, he expressed them in such fresh and arresting language that people invariably took note, whether they agreed or not (Cooper, 1967). Laing and Cooper also shared an involvement in existential phenomenology and Marxism. As it turned out, Cooper's Marxism intensified and Laing's vanished toward the end of the decade, and this created friction. But in 1963 they still saw eye to eye sufficiently to collaborate on a book, *Reason and Violence: A Decade of Sartre's Philosophy* (1964), which was written—after months of informal dialogue—in three weeks of intensive, nonstop writing. Many specialists still regard it as a splendid elucidation, and Sartre evidently thought so too. He wrote a glowing foreword to their book:

Like you, I believe that one cannot understand psychological disturbances from the outside, on the basis of a positivistic determinism, or reconstruct them with a combination of concepts that remain outside the illness as lived and experienced. I also believe that one cannot study, let alone cure, a neurosis without a fundamental respect for the person of the patient, without a constant effort to grasp the basic situation and relive it, without an attempt to rediscover the response of the person to that situation, and—like you, I think—I regard mental illness as the "way out" that the free organism, in its total unity, invents in order to live through an intolerable situation. For this reason, I place the highest value on your researches . . . and I am convinced that your efforts will bring closer the day when psychiatry will, at last, become a truly human psychiatry. (Laing and Cooper, 1964, p. 6)

It was Laing, not Cooper, who tried to create "a truly human psychiatry." A few years after Sartre expressed these thoughts, Cooper rejected psychiatry altogether, arguing that it is an oppressive institution used to buttress international imperialism (1968). His views on the family were equally uncompromising (1971). As we shall see later, Laing's views on psychiatry and the family were more complex. Still in 1968, in the preface to a popular paperback he edited, Cooper coined the term "anti-psychiatry" to describe the orientation shared by him and Laing. Despite Laing's frequent repudiation of the term, it was a label that stuck to them both. Laing never fully forgave Cooper for this presumption.

But in 1963, despite his growing reputation, Laing was getting restive. His efforts to enlighten his Tavistock colleagues about the fruitfulness of existential phenomenology for clinical practice and research seemed to be falling on deaf ears. Moreover, having launched a formidable research program, he now wanted to put his theories into practice and start an experimental community for schizophrenics. We can see this in his review of Harry Stack Sullivan's *Schizophrenia as a Human Process* in the *International Journal of Psycho-Analysis* (Laing, 1963b). Laing gave Sullivan a ringing endorsement for trying to understand schizophrenia in interpersonal and familial terms. He punctuated his praise with muted expressions of dismay for the rest of the psychiatric profession:

So many reports of the so-called mechanisms . . . supposed to characterize schizophrenics in particular are not descriptions of what "goes on" in the patient, but descriptions of events in the psychiatrist's or analyst's mind which are the ghostly double of what he thinks is going on somewhere "in" the other person. The scientific paper in which is reported what Freud or Federn said about narcissistic neurosis or ego boundaries, then what Peter or Paul had to say, followed by what the author has to say, in agreement or disagreement, with or without emendations, supported by that extraordinary postdictive horoscope known as a "clinical" history, and a few sentences more or less imperfectly remembered, purporting to have been uttered by this or that patient in God knows what context, but clearly confirming the author's theory, tells us little except what that particular writer is selectively aware of, and to those of his readers who are selectively attentive to other aspects, it reveals of course plainly enough to *them* what he selectively does *not* notice. (p. 377)

Laing goes on to note that Sullivan's work at the Shepard-Pratt Hospital in Baltimore

showed plainly that very rarely need a person remain mad for more than a few months, given an ordinary good enough environment, to borrow Winnicott's expression. This requires a small homogeneous unit, nurses or social therapists selected on the basis of their ability to interact non-destructively with schizophrenics, the elimination of what Goffman has recently called the degradation ceremonials and subsequent profanations and humiliations of and to the self, that the person is subject to at the inception of his career as a mental hospital patient, and subsequently . . .

Reading these articles by Sullivan written thirty to forty years ago is a somewhat depressing experience. They are altogether more contemporary than they should be. What were brave and sometimes reckless dicta then should have become hypotheses, long since confirmed or disconfirmed. Instead, most of the issues are still open, most of the work that Sullivan's vision demanded is still not done. Perhaps there is still time. (p. 378)

Judging from his subsequent actions, if not from his actual words, Laing evidently thought that there was still time. Later that year, on December 18, 1963, he sent a brochure to Winnicott in which he and Aaron Esterson outlined their plans for something they called the London Centre for the Study and Treatment of Schizophrenia. Here Laing and Esterson declared categorically that the person labeled schizophrenic is not suffering from any kind of organic or neurological disorder, but is someone whose life has gone "radically wrong" in ways that are intelligible if one studies the patterns of communication and relationship in his family. Furthermore, his madness, far from being a disease in the ordinary sense, is actually an attempt at self-healing that, if properly guided, would lead to the eventual restoration of his sanity. Allowing the process to unfold naturally is not something that ordinary mental hospitals are designed for, and so an alternative is needed. Ideally, these sanctuaries should be staffed by people who understand the kinds of intra- and interpersonal processes that engender madness. Laing and Esterson went on to describe the specific features of the facility they envisioned, which never materialized. But the brochure does shed light on Laing's aspirations for the Philadelphia Association two years later.

On December 23, 1963, Winnicott wrote back to applaud Laing's project. It is not difficult to see why: Laing's therapeutic agenda for schizophrenics, which he termed "the way of dissolution and renewal," was partly inspired by Winnicott, and it may have had a stimulating effect on him in turn. Having been asked to explain the sudden onset of psychosis in many apparently normal people, Winnicott wrote (to Nicholas Latimer, January 2, 1964) that one must take into account

> the division of the personality into what I call the true and false selves. Normally, this is no more that saying that . . . one is not always saying what one thinks, and that it pays to put forward a self for social acceptance that is not what one really is at heart.
>
> Many people do not find this easy. They find it dishonest to be acceptable socially . . .
>
> More ill people find all this a major problem. They live a life that is perhaps successful and socialized, even particularly well socialized. But they gradually feel more and more dishonest, or less and less real. Eventually, (not really knowing what they are doing at all), they switch over to living from the true self . . . and this means an abandonment of all that has been built up on a basis of the false self.[2]

Despite his apparent enthusiasm for the program, Winnicott never joined Laing's network of supporters. Laing's drug use may have been a factor in this decision. In any case, over the next few years Winnicott declined many invitations to attend fundraisers and social gatherings sponsored by the Philadelphia Association or Kingsley Hall, always citing other commitments or his role as president of the Psycho-Analytic Society (Mullan, p. 191). Another reason for Winnicott's reluctance may be that, on paper, Laing's schizophrenia center promised to be a sensible and dignified treatment facility, which would presumably maintain clear lines of demarcation between those needing and those offering remedial interventions. But from its inception Kingsley Hall was a something of a scandal, because the usual professional roles and patient expectations were turned upside down. So perhaps Winnicott adopted a wait-and-see attitude at first and then decided to steer clear of the whole scene, while maintaining a friendly but distant posture with Laing in correspondence.

Despite the noteworthy lack of support from Bowlby, Winnicott and other erstwhile supporters, and the eroding esteem of E. G. Howe, in 1964 Laing was hitting his stride professionally. In terms of family and domestic life, however, it was a terrible year. His relationship with Anne was now so bad that he seldom came home. And when he did come back for brief visits, as Adrian Laing recalls, they fought so fiercely that their neighbors asked the authorities to intervene.

As his marriage was unraveling, Laing, Cooper, and Esterson—whose marriages were also in trouble—planned their first therapeutic community in the Brotherhood's informal meetings, and Laing began to familiarize his growing readership with his theory of madness as an "inner journey," a voyage of self-recovery and reintegration, which he later called *metanoia,* a term used in the Greek New Testament for atonement. This idea, which became Laing's stock in trade, first appeared in a book review for the *International Journal of Psycho-Analysis,* in which Laing attacked Karl Jaspers' classic *General Psychopathology* (1963). Significantly, the basic idea behind Laing's theory of madness as metanoia was adumbrated by an anonymous patient cited in Jaspers' book, who gave an extraordinary account of his psychosis:

I believe I caused the illness myself. In my attempt to penetrate the other world I met its natural guardians, the embodiments of my own weaknesses and faults. I first thought these demons were lowly inhabitants of the other world who could play me like a ball because I went into those regions unprepared and lost my way. I later thought they were split off parts of my own mind [passions] which existed near me in free space and thrived on my feelings. I believed everyone else had these too but did not perceive them, thanks to the protective and successful deceit of the feeling of personal existence. I thought the latter was an artefact of memory, thought complexes, etc., a doll that was nice enough to look at from outside but nothing real inside it.

In my case the personal self had grown porous because of my dimmed consciousness. Through it I wanted to bring myself closer to the higher sources of life. I should have prepared myself for this over a longer period by invoking in my omission a "higher" impersonal self, since "nectar" is not for mortal lips. It acted destructively on the animal-human self and split it up in to parts . . .

Then came illumination. I fasted and so penetrated into the true nature of my seducers . . .

A larger and more comprehensive self emerged and I could abandon the previous personality with its entire entourage . . . A new life began for me, and from now on I felt different from other people. A self that consisted of conventional lies, shams, self-deceptions, memory images, a self like that of other people, grew in me again, but behind and above it stood a greater and more comprehensive self which impressed me with something of what is eternal, unchangeable, immortal and inviolable, and which ever since that time has been my protector and refuge. I believe it would be good for many if they were acquainted with such a higher self and that there are people who have attained this goal in fact by kinder means. (Jaspers, pp. 417–418)

Commenting on his patient's narrative, Jaspers urged the reader "not to take this merely as a jumble of chaotic contents. Mind and spirit are present in the morbid psychic life as well as in the healthy." Yet Jaspers cautioned that "interpretations of this sort must be divested of any causal importance." Laing objected vigorously:

This patient's experiences . . . are in no way alien to me. The inner world reaches through domains of experience (imagination, reverie, dreams, fantasy, visions . . .) into realms that we are *only beginning* to discover. It seems as reasonable to me that a man should wish to climb the Mystic Mountain as Mount Everest. It is as understandable that a man should undertake a journey into his own mind, and get confused

and lost, as that he should discover a new ocean or explore a new
continent.

I wish to state that I hope if I ever lose my way in my travels on the same path as this patient, I have the courage to endure, the luck to get back and the grace to express myself with such lucidity, insight and humility. (1964b, p. 3)

Another major development in 1964 was the publication of *Sanity, Madness and the Family*, with Aaron Esterson. Of all Laing's books, this is the one that John Bowlby admired most. It contains no mention of madness as an attempt at self-cure, an idea Bowlby found contrived and misguided. Though he regarded *Sanity, Madness and the Family* as the single most important book on families published in this century, Bowlby also complained that Laing and Esterson should have published their studies of normal families and that, by not doing so, they missed a golden opportunity to galvanize the field of family studies (Bowlby, 1992).

Others would also criticize Laing and Esterson for not writing up their research on normal families (for instance, Mishler, 1973; Freidenberg, 1973). But, for many, this book was more than enough. *Sanity, Madness and the Family* was a forthright challenge to mainstream psychiatric views of schizophrenia and ignited fierce controversies that would follow Laing for the rest of his life. In their introduction Laing and Esterson challenged biological psychiatry to come up with a cogent account of this mysterious illness:

Psychiatrists have struggled for years to discover what those people who are so diagnosed have or have not in common with each other. The results so far are inconclusive.

No generally agreed upon objective clinical criteria for the diagnosis of "schizophrenia" have been discovered.

No consistency in pre-psychotic personality, course, duration, outcome, has been discovered.

Every conceivable view is held by authoritative people as to whether "schizophrenia" is a disease or a group of diseases; whether identifiable organic pathology has been, or can be expected to be found.

There are no pathological anatomical findings *post mortem*. There are no structural changes noted in the course of the "illness." There are no physiological-pathological changes that can be correlated with these illnesses. There is no general acceptance that any form of treatment is of proven value, except perhaps sustained careful interpersonal relations and tranquillization. "Schizophrenia" runs in families, but observes no genetically clear law. It appears to usually have no adverse effect on physical health, and given proper care by others it does not cause death or foreshorten life. It occurs in every constitutional type. It is not associated with any other known physical malfunctions . . .

That the diagnosed patient is suffering from a pathological process is either a fact, a hypothesis, an assumption or a judgement.

To regard it as a fact is unequivocally false. To regard it as a hypothesis is legitimate. It is unnecessary to make the assumption or to pass the judgement.

The judgement that the diagnosed patient is behaving in a biologically dysfunctional (hence pathological) way is, we believe, premature, and one that we shall hold in parenthesis. (p. 19)

Today, of course, advances in neurology and scientific instrumentation tend to support the belief that people diagnosed as schizophrenic often suffer from some sort of brain defect—though whether these neuropathologies are the cause or the effect of the condition and iatrogenic effects is seldom entirely clear. Besides, many abnormalities found in the brains of diagnosed schizophrenics, such as enlarged brain ventricles, damaged or inactivate right hemispheres, impaired limbic systems, undersized frontal lobes, and so on, could be the unintended consequence of years of electroshock and neuroleptic treatment (Breggin, 1991; Sass, 1992).

Many of these neuropathologies are also found in people suffering from affective disorders, alcoholism, and other kinds of problems. They are found too in people whose behavior is normal, from a purely symptomatic point of view (Sass, 1992, appendix). As a result of the indeterminate state of the evidence, even ardent exponents of the neurobiological explanation concede that not even one variety of schizophrenic disturbance has been adequately defined and accounted for (Muselam, 1990).

In retrospect, what is most astonishing about *Sanity, Madness and the Family* is its cogency. In 1964, the state of research into schizophrenia was just as appalling as Laing and Esterson described it. After decades of research, biological psychiatry had gone nowhere. So the time was ripe for another approach.

In order to appreciate what was so distinctive about Laing's and Esterson's work, it is important to remember that research into the families of schizophrenics had been confined largely to doing interviews with family members individually, taking oral histories from each, and then trying to generate some overarching biological and/or psychogenetic appraisal by blending the individual narratives and the impressions they made on the researchers. By contrast, Bateson and his colleagues held the controversial view that the confusion and distress of the schizophrenic patient is not a product of organic disorder or individual psychopathology, but of disordered or disturbing communication patterns within the family as a whole. They took the unprecedented step of supplementing individual interviews by observing the families of schizophrenics interacting in unison over extended periods of time, arguing that the way family members behave individually with a clinician, or what they say in a one-to-one interview, is not necessarily indicative of what they do in their natural setting.

Laing and Esterson went a step further, taking their interviews right into patients' homes whenever they could. And from Sartre they took the distinction between "praxis" and "process" that runs throughout the book:

> Events, occurrences, happenings may be deeds done by doers, or they may be the outcome of a continuous series of operations that have no agent as their author. In the first case we shall speak of events as the outcome of praxis; in the second, the outcome of process.
>
> When what is going on in any human group can be traced to what the agents are doing, it will be termed praxis. When what goes on in a group may not be intended by anyone, it will be termed process. No one may even realize what's happening. But what happens in a group will be intelligible if one can retrace the steps from what is going on (process) to who is doing what (praxis). (p. 22)

In order to convert the anonymous group process into an intelligible expression of concerted individual practices, Laing and Esterson developed a new method, called social phenomenology, in which they could ideally study (1) each person in the family, (2) relations among all persons in the family and (3) the family as a whole or, as they would say, as a system. By their own reckoning, they did not fully achieve this objective, focused as they were on the identified patient and her position in the family.

To qualify for this study, their identified patients had to fit the following profile. They had to be women, between the ages of fifteen and forty, who had been diagnosed as schizophrenic by at least two senior psychiatrists. The women had to be of normal intelligence and free of such organic conditions as brain injury or epilepsy; they couldn't have had brain surgery of any kind and no more than 50 electroshocks in the year prior to the investigation (and no more than 150 electroshocks altogether). Finally, they had to have at least one living parent, although no other strictures about family composition were imposed. They could be living with their families or on their own. Either way, the first step Laing and Esterson took was to ask the patient if they could bring her relatives into the research. If the patient agreed, they would contact her parents, who invariably offered to cooperate. Then they met the parents, singly and together, with and without the patient present, and conducted a lengthy series of interviews in the patient's home. All the interviews were taped, and transcripts were made.

Though Laing and Esterson describe only eleven families in *Sanity, Madness and the Family,* their study encompassed more than one hundred. Despite the impressive size of their sample, there was nothing pressured or hurried about the procedure: Laing and Esterson knew the families they reported on for three years before they began to write up their findings.

Though Laing and Esterson were working as a team, they couldn't do all their interviews together. Laing, the senior researcher, spent many hours interviewing family members, but Esterson spent far more. Interviewing was only the first step. As Sidney Briskin recalls,

> the three of us used to meet every Tuesday evening to listen to the taped interviews for the book. We would then act out the different family roles, switching around until it was felt that we had got a better understanding of what was going on and what was significant in the interview. Sometimes the recorded verbal exchanges were far from clear, such as a mother and a daughter both speaking at the same time. We would play that bit over and over again, sometimes for hours until some sort of clarity had been reached. These meetings often went on

well into the early hours of the next day. Nothing, but nothing, was taken for granted. (Briskin, 1993)

Though Laing was trained as an analyst, neither he nor Esterson made any interpretations during these interviews, and they were very sparing in their use of analytic formulations to interpret the data afterward. They thought it would detract from the purity of the study and undercut its major goal, which was to demonstrate that the symptoms of schizophrenia have a high degree of social intelligibility, once the group process is methodically sorted out in individual practice. Moreover, from an empirical standpoint, they noted, making analytic interpretations would create insurmountable problems of reliability, since other observers might draw different conclusions about unconscious dynamics or dismiss them altogether as mere conjecture.

What Laing and Esterson really wanted to demonstrate was the usefulness of a method that deliberately refrains from making inferences about unconscious experiences or desires. Social phenomenology would focus instead on what is actually present to the conscious awareness of family members, in order to discern and describe the overt experiential disjunctions that exist within the family system, and then to explain their impact on the various people in the nexus. Although they, as researchers, would often "totalize" a family's testimony differently than the family members themselves would, their observations were based strictly on what family members actually said and did, not on what they might have been thinking, feeling, or intending beneath the threshold of consciousness.

Though Laing and Esterson did not rehearse all of the earlier arguments from *The Divided Self* and *Self and Others,* they made it abundantly clear that viewing people called schizophrenic through the lens of neuropathology robs their experience and behavior of its social context, which in turn renders it more difficult for the person who is so labeled to get a grip on reality and go on with process of living. And this in its turn can have profound biochemical effects, which might be mistaken for the cause of the disorder. In other words, Laing and Esterson were suggesting that the pathological signs of schizophrenia may be the result of prolonged anxiety and confusion, not the other way around, and that standard psychiatric procedure could only intensify them.

Pressing even further, Laing and Esterson rejected the idea that individual distress is a product of collective psychopathology, arguing that the very idea of family pathology is an unwarranted extension to the group of a medical metaphor whose usefulness, even for the individual, is dubious at best. Rather than clarifying matters in terms of process and praxis—determining who is doing or saying what, and to whom and why and with what results—the term "family psychopathology" conveys the misleading impression that the family is an organism, or a unit, as it is sometimes called. Borrowing from Sartre, Laing preferred to define the family as a series, or a multiplicity, of individuals whose actions and interactions are often opaque to themselves. Accordingly, Laing and Esterson declared:

> Neither organic pathology, nor psychopathology, nor for that matter group pathology is assumed to be (or not to be) in evidence. This issue is simply bracketed off. Whenever we use such judgmental clinical terminology outside the clinical section at the beginning of each chapters, the reader should bear in mind the parenthesis or suspension of judgement that all such terms are placed in parentheses. (p. 19)

That said, of course, neither Laing nor Esterson doubted that people deemed schizophrenic are miserable, confused, and tormented. Nor is there a trace anywhere in this book of a tendency to idealize the mad, which Laing was so often accused of in later years. Laing and Esterson evidently hoped to invent a new vocabulary, a way of seeing these people phenomenologically.

Looking back on this period in the early 1980s, Laing recalled that in order to test their surmises about communicational patterns in the families of schizophrenics, he and his colleagues—Esterson, Briskin, and Joan Cunnold—conducted a study of "normal" families, which was never published. He said he lacked the mathematical sophistication needed to explicate the data (Evans, 1976). Furthermore, he noted,

> although we were interested in contrasting the two different sorts of families, we were very scrupulous in not framing the question in the form of "Is the family a causative agent in the generation of schizophrenia?" Instead the schema of the project was this: "Given that these people X have a diagnosed schizophrenic in their family and these people Y do not, is there a difference one can make out in the

variables of their family?" To answer the question we did things like
trying to identify double binds, paradoxes and tangential communications from tape-recorded interviews. We had a lot of trouble getting
reliability in the measures, but eventually we convinced ourselves that
there was a lot more of that sort of communication going on when
there was a diagnosed schizophrenic in the family. (Simon, 1983, p. 26)

In short, after hundreds of hours of painstaking research and observation, Laing and his colleagues came to the somewhat disappointing conclusion that the patterns of disordered communication
they observed in the families of schizophrenics were often present in
normal families as well. But families with schizophrenic members
evinced far *more* of this kind of thing, and families where disordered
communication was rare showed no incidences of schizophrenia.
Apparently, then, mystification, double binds, and so on, are a necessary but not a sufficient condition of schizophrenic disturbances.
It may be that, in order to result in a schizophrenic breakdown, the
density of concurrent experiential disjunctures within the family has
to exceed a certain critical threshold, which would be impossible to
quantify, and may vary from case to case. Or it may be that other un-
specified factors are involved.

Many critics of *Sanity, Madness and the Family* echoed Bowlby's
complaint that Laing should have followed through with the research on normal families. And some have voiced the suspicion that
Laing was deterred by the prospect of having to take the biological
dimension of madness more seriously than he did (Friedenberg,
1973; Mishler, 1973). If pressed, I think, Laing might have replied
that even if normal families evince the same sorts of communicational deviance and experiential disjunction that families of schizophrenics do, they differ because they make no attempt to isolate the
disturbed person in the labyrinth of confusion and despair that typically besets the schizophrenic; they either allow or encourage her to
seek corrective mediation elsewhere, and to define her identity outside the family.

But this still does not explain Laing's failure to publish his study
of normal families. Briskin suggested to me that the study of normal
families—which had considerable merit, in his opinion—was never
published because it fell victim to the deepening rift between Laing
and Esterson. One reason was that Esterson felt he got insufficient

credit for the work he did. Esterson remarked to Adrian Laing that he did almost all of the interviews and that Laing's contribution was purely literary (A. Laing, p. 78). Laing, in turn, charged that Esterson did not write a single line of the book (Mullan, p. 279). But whatever the case, the fact remains that Laing never replied to his critics convincingly. He did say that his work with the families of schizophrenics was exhausting and time-consuming, and that the prospect of doing further meticulous studies of this kind was unpalatable. He added that

> interviewing the normal families was a more gruelling experience than speaking with the families of schizophrenics. They were just so dead and stifling and, at the same time, it was very hard to describe what the deadening was. So it was difficult to say what the difference between the two was except that in the normal family nobody cracked up. (Simon, p. 26)

Now what of Laing's own family? Did his feelings toward the families he and his associates interviewed reflect his own family situation at the time? Laing denied it categorically. But he openly admitted that the time and energy devoted to finishing *Sanity, Madness and the Family* caused an even greater deterioration in his marriage, so that by late 1963 all semblance of normality had vanished from the Laing household. Rather than face the barrage of anger and recrimination that awaited him at home, Laing did most of his writing at his office and spent most of his leisure time going to clubs and hobnobbing with musicians and people from television and film. He had an open affair with a newspaper columnist, Sally Vincent, a friend of Ben Churchill's former wife (Churchill, 1994). Then he proposed once more to Marcelle Vincent, who was visiting London at the time. Again Marcelle declined, and shortly afterward Laing met Jutta Werner, a young singer and graphic artist. In 1965, after several more months of intolerable strain, Laing's marriage to Anne was finally over. As he later said to Roberta Russell:

> I was living with my first wife Anne and we had five children ranging from about three to nine . . . I couldn't stand her at all, and I was very sorry for her, but . . . that didn't make matters better. It became obvious that the whole arrangement was for the sake of the children.
> In this quandary I convened a council of my friends, all men . . .

There were four of them; I put the situation to them, and invited their response . . . One of them said I was psychotic. He was a child psychiatrist and psychoanalyst. He had a Scottish upbringing, from the same department as me. He thought it was unthinkable to leave five children . . . To leave was neither a sane option, nor the option of any gentleman. If I was not a cad, I must be mad. (Russell, 1992, pp. 176–177)

Apparently Laing chose not to listen to his friends. The break was painful for all concerned, but much more so for Anne and the children, who in September 1965 returned to a life of hardship and struggle in Glasgow. In the ensuing years, Laing was punctual with support payments, but barring intermittent contact with his favorite daughter, Susie, he had almost no contact with his first family for the next six or seven years. After his return from India in 1972, Laing occasionally attempted to repair the break between him and his first five children—never with complete success, particularly where his daughters were concerned. His second family, with Jutta Werner, would fare somewhat better, though they too would suffer from the corrosive impact of fame on R. D. Laing.

4

IN AND OUT
OF *K*INGSLEY HALL

After two years of informal deliberation and planning, Laing and the Brotherhood—David Cooper, Aaron Esterson, Sidney Briskin, Clancy Sigal, Joan Cunnold, and Raymond Blake—officially founded the Philadelphia Association on April 8, 1965. The P.A., as it is commonly referred to, was initially a charitable foundation devoted the creation of therapeutic communities for people in crisis. Its founders were all firmly committed to the idea that a psychotic breakdown is not a symptom of genetic abnormality or a neurological disorder, but an existential crisis; that it is potentially a breakthrough to a more authentic and integrated way of being; and that professional and patient roles, as understood in mainstream psychiatry, are not conducive to the process of cure. In fact, they tend to undermine any budding sense of solidarity between therapist and patient, and to confirm the mad in their sense of helpless isolation.

To remedy this situation, Laing and his associates set up a series of therapeutic households that would provide those suffering acute distress and disorientation a refuge from the world outside, to facilitate their inner journey in a supportive and nonintrusive environment, free from the stigma of diagnosis and the burdens of involuntary treatment. The first of these houses was run by Sidney Briskin, who opened his own home to four former residents of Villa 21 in October 1964. Briskin's experience, as he later told me, was quite positive and a great morale booster for everyone concerned.

Another house, at a former Laing residence, 23 Granville Road, boarded ten people and was run first by Bill Mason, who had previously worked with Maxwell Jones, and later for a time by Ben Churchill and his wife Lesley (Briskin, 1993; Churchill, 1993).

Encouraged by their results so far, Laing and the Brotherhood began looking for larger premises when, in October 1964, they received a note from a sympathetic student named Philip Cohen, encouraging them to consider Kingsley Hall on Powis Road, Bromley-on-Bow, in London's east end, as a potential cite for a therapeutic community (Mullan, 1995, p. 175). The building was originally a Baptist church known as Zion Chapel. Just before World War I, it came to the attention of Muriel and Dorothy Lester, two adherents of Leo Tolstoy's pacifism, who wished to set up an alcohol-free public house that engaged the local citizenry in harmless diversions like billiards, cards, and chess. Their father, who bought the premises for them, was an admirer of Charles Kingsley, the Cambridge historian who invented the phrase "muscular Christianity," and named his son after him. The Lester sisters renamed the chapel Kingsley Hall, in honor of their brother, who had died recently (Lester, 1937).

Though not all of the local residents shared the Lesters' pacifist and Christian socialist beliefs, during the 1920s Muriel Lester became a widely respected and beloved community figure, serving as an alderman and later as a minister to the local congregation. By the late twenties, Kingsley Hall had become an international center for militant pacifism. In 1931 Mahatma Gandhi, who was in London for a conference on Indian independence, lived there in a little wooden enclosure on the roof of the building. As its activities and resources grew, a nursery, a chapel, a soup kitchen, and a sanctuary room for runaways were added to the building. In short, it was a hub of spiritual and political activity that brought many gifted and renowned people into contact with London's impoverished east end.

In the decade before its occupancy by the P.A., Kingsley Hall had been used mostly by doctors, nurses, and social workers, many of whom lived right on the premises. But by the spring of 1965, when negotiations began, Kingsley Hall had fallen into disuse. In a Seminar at the William Alanson White Institute (January 16, 1967), Laing described Kingsley Hall as collapsed, dismal, and very cold. In view of the limited funds available to the P.A., however, the building's physical state was not a major deterrent, and there followed a series of complex negotiations between Janet Shephard, representing the board of trustees, and Sidney Briskin. Briskin, in turn, got Laing involved. There were two meetings with Muriel Lester. As Laing told it later:

> I went to visit her in her cottage in North London and explained to her what my idea was, which she was quite unfamiliar with but which she picked up very quickly. I explained that I felt that there was a gross violation of primitive human decency in the way we treated people who were mentally out of it as far as other people were concerned. There was just a rampage—lobotomies and electric shocks and comas and incarceration and everything, and that no one cared. Psychoanalysts didn't really address themselves to that wavelength, the nearest people they dealt with were competent businessmen and managers. Basically they had no time for people who couldn't straighten a tie and put on a white shirt and collar or polish their shoes. (Mullan, p. 175)

She liked Laing's pitch. He clinched the deal by promising Lester to "retain the community groups that used the Hall, but that in particular he would do all he could to retain the evangelical black Christian group that met there every Sunday morning, and that he would willingly preach from the pulpit." As Briskin discovered later, to his astonishment, Laing was not at all averse to preaching on occasion and did keep the premises open to local community groups (Briskin, 1994).

When the unexpected breakthrough in negotiations was finally achieved, the Philadelphia Association was offered the use of the building for the symbolic sum of £ 1 a year. And so began a whole new chapter in the social and cultural history of London in the 1960s. Considerable effort was required to get Kingsley Hall into shape. Among those who helped out, as Briskin recalls, were some of the doctors, nurses, and social workers who had recently vacated the premises, who were remarkably generous with their time and support. Though the P.A. took occupancy on June 1, 1965, it was not deemed habitable for another month.

As much as Laing and his associates were united by their antipathy to psychiatry's disregard of human rights, and by their enthusiasm for therapeutic communities, they had different and sometimes discordant visions of what Kingsley Hall should be. At the risk of oversimplifying matters, I will describe these discordant views as Apollonian or Dionysian.

On the face of it, Laing's therapeutic utopia sounded Apollonian enough. It was modeled somewhat on Maxwell Jones's pioneering experiments with therapeutic communities (Jones, 1953) and on the Rumpus Room at Gartnavel Hospital. But there was an important difference. In the earlier communities, the professional distance between doctors, nurses, and their wards, though diminished, was never abolished entirely. Real human bonds were sometimes forged between patients and staff, but there was never any question about who needed help and who should offer it. Though he cited these experiments as embodiments of what they were striving to achieve, in his talks with the Brotherhood Laing emphasized that they were moving into uncharted territory and would have to improvise. He wanted to dispense entirely with professional roles and with preset schedules for communal activity. Laing's preference for spontaneity was later codified into what he called "autorhythmia," the principle of enabling individuals to find their own authentic rhythm, rather than fitting them into a communal pattern. In practice as well as in theory, the results were often anarchic. Basic functions like shopping, cooking, and cleaning up were done poorly, irregularly, and sometimes not at all.

Once things settled down a little, certain communal patterns did emerge. Except for early morning yoga sessions, which were a regular feature in Kingsley Hall, days were relatively unstructured. But at night people converged from the other two P.A. houses for a late evening meal and for intense discussions that lasted late into the morning hours. Laing was usually the featured speaker, discoursing at length on any subject that took his fancy, his style alternating between the ribald and satirical, on one hand, and the scholarly or metaphysical on the other.

Another anarchic influence at Kingsley Hall was David Cooper, who had put his idea of therapeutic utopia into Villa 21. It seems that despite his interest in meditation, mysticism, and so on, Cooper was not on the same wavelength as Laing. During the mid-sixties, Cooper underwent a process of radicalization and began to see himself as an agent for the overthrow of capitalist imperialism, a system of which psychiatry was a part. As Cooper's political commitments were intensifying, Laing's, though left-leaning, remained somewhat diffuse and were scuttled soon after the Dialectics of Liberation Conference in 1967.

Meanwhile, on the Apollonian, organizational side of things were two more important players, Aaron Esterson and Sidney Briskin. Both were convinced of the need for firm policies and ground rules that would give the community some economic and administrative stability. Despite the prevailing mistrust of medicine and psychiatry, Esterson was intent on maintaining clear lines of demarcation between staff and residents and expressed a desire to become the medical director of Kingsley Hall—which contributed to his eventual isolation in the group. Briskin, by contrast, had no investment in perpetuating the old medical roles, but he was a firm believer in sound administration and financial accountability. As Clancy Sigal recalled, he was the one person who kept the place running (Sigal, 1989). He was also a diligent and resourceful fundraiser for the Philadelphia Association, when Laing's scruples did not prevent him from functioning in that capacity—which was most of the time.

Another notable presence at Kingsley Hall was Mary Barnes, a middle-aged Catholic nurse who had been in therapy—first with Laing and then with Esterson—since 1963. Laing told her once that she needed therapy "24 hours out of 24," and shortly after her arrival in July 1965, she promptly demanded just that and regressed to infancy for a period of three years. Others were called on to feed and clean her—an unpleasant task, since she soiled herself, played with her feces, and refused to eat for days at a time. Her behavior provoked a crisis of leadership and considerable envy among the other residents, who resented both her ability to monopolize staff attention and the foul odors emanating from her room.

Eventually the care of Mary Barnes fell principally to Joseph Berke, a twenty-six-year-old American psychiatrist, whom Laing had met in 1963 and who had worked with Maxwell Jones near Edinburgh before joining Laing's circle (Berke, 1990). Facilitating Mary Barnes's recovery was a formidable challenge. Berke gradually coaxed her to stop smearing feces on the wall and on her person and to smear paint on canvas instead. In due course, Barnes improved considerably and, with Burke, wrote a book, *Mary Barnes: Two Accounts of a Journey Through Madness* (1971). A few years later, David Edgar wrote a riveting play about her, which was performed at the

Birmingham Repertory Theatre in 1977 and subsequently moved to the Royal Court, London. This play, and her various art exhibits, brought Barnes into the public eye repeatedly during the seventies.

Needless to say, Mary Barnes generated considerable controversy. For some people, her experience at Kingsley Hall was a clear vindication of Laing's approach to madness as a process of potential self-healing, though Laing himself never spoke of her this way (Mullan, p. 185). At the other extreme, skeptics like Thomas Szasz argued that both her disorder and her recovery were entirely factitious. In an article, "Anti-Psychiatry and the Paradigm of the Plundered Mind," which was first published in the *New Review* in August 1976 and reissued in his *Schizophrenia* (1988), Szasz argues that Mary Barnes followed in the footsteps of Charcot's grand hysterics, who skillfully enacted all the symptoms of hysteria on cue in response to suggestions from the hypnotist. On Szasz's reading, Mary Barnes contrived to become a showpiece for Laingian psychotherapy in collusion with her therapists, who behaved much like con men using a suggestible neophyte to dupe the public and make a name for themselves. According to Szasz, the only real difference between the would-be healers of the Philadelphia Association and actual con artists is that they happened to believe in their own scam, adding self-deception to the list of their many sins.

In *The Female Malady* (1985), however, Elaine Showalter offers a more balanced reading of Mary Barnes's experience. This in itself is somewhat surprising, since her summary of Laing's early life and career is riddled with factual errors and some tendentious comparisons between Laing, John Conolly, and Henry Maudsley—two eminent English psychiatrists of earlier days. Moreover, Laing angrily faulted Showalter for misrepresenting him and events at Kingsley Hall, ranging from his relationship with Barnes to the kinds of festivities that accompanied the evening meals (Mullan, pp. 183–187, 198).

Nevertheless, to her credit, Showalter notes that there was nothing rehearsed about Mary Barnes's breakdown in a Catholic convent, which precipitated a brief hospitalization and a subsequent pilgrimage to Anna Freud, who refused to take her on. Eventually Barnes's pilgrimage took her to a psychiatric social worker at the Tavistock Clinic named James Robertson, who referred her to Laing. As Showalter says, unlike Charcot's prize performers Mary

Barnes "ran her own show" and took no instruction from anyone. Furthermore, unlike the female subjects of earlier case histories, whose voices are filtered through a professional male perspective, Mary Barnes was actively encouraged to speak in her own voice, and she collaborated with her therapist on equal terms in the composition of their book.

Reading Barnes's account of her life, her madness, and her relationship with Joseph Berke, one does get the impression, as Showalter alleges, that many of Berke's psychoanalytic interpretations were crudely Freudian and off the mark, that they failed to reckon with her frustrated ambition and her oppression as a woman in a male-dominated world. But what is even more striking about their book is that no effort was made to minimize their disparate ideas about their curious relationship or to privilege one narrative over the other as what really happened between therapist and patient—surely a first in the clinical literature. Moreover, as Showalter acknowledges, while Berke's interpretations of Barnes's mental state may have been blinkered, parochial, and sexist at times, his ministrations over a three-year period were informed by a spirit of generosity and disinterestedness that few therapists could match. His service is all the more impressive when you consider that Berke, like all the therapists at Kingsley Hall, was unpaid—something Showalter does not mention.

Even without Mary Barnes on the scene, life at Kingsley Hall would have been colorful and anarchic. In a report dated May 1, 1969, the P.A. reported that from June 1, 1965, through November, 31, 1968, six months prior to closing, Kingsley Hall had housed 104 official residents, of whom only 37 were women. Apart from chance encounters between residents—often loud and angry—there were constant informal activities going on, including yoga, painting, singing, and dancing.

Despite the recurrent crises and confrontations that punctuated its communal existence, Kingsley Hall became a refuge for people trying to avoid mental hospitals. As Briskin recalls, people fleeing psychiatric incarceration were often given a night's lodging and advice on where to go for help the next day. There were also regular open houses and Sunday brunches, which generated a little extra income (Briskin, 1993). There was no preordained rhythm or structure to these events, and so, in Laing's words, visitors "took their chances." In addition to offering services and special events, Kingsley Hall hosted lectures by David Mercer, Francis Huxley, David Cooper, and Laing himself—lectures that sometimes drew over two hundred people. And, for a time, Laing and his associates hosted regular monthly seminars on phenomenology and social theory, attended by about fifty psychiatrists and psychotherapists.

In 1965 a frequent visitor to Kingsley Hall from America was Loren Mosher, the chief of schizophrenia studies at the National Institutes of Mental Health from 1968 to 1980, who later founded two therapeutic communities based on the Laingian refuge, but without its chaos and revolutionary pretensions—Soteria House and Emmanon. Like many visitors, Mosher was often uncomfortable during his visits to Kingsley Hall. In retrospect, he reports that what contributed most to his discomfort "was an unspoken rule against carrying on normal social amenities. It was as though introductions, hand shakings and get-acquainted small talk were somehow proscribed." As Mosher experienced it, visitors who indulged in this sort of thing were regarded by residents as sharing in a shabby pretense of friendliness or some slightly sinister conspiracy against the truth and the light.[1]

Since no records were kept, it is impossible to estimate the number of people that visited Kingsley Hall over the years. But the traffic in and out was considerable, and it was not appreciated by the local citizens. In an essay called "Madness and Morals," Morton Schatzman notes:

One Friday night four men whom none of the residents knew, who had been drinking in a nearby pub, broke into the building at Midnight and shouted that we were "loonys," "drug-addicts," and "perverts" who were "stinking" and were "desecrating" a community shrine by our "foul" behavior. A lady in a nearby shop called us "a bunch of nutters and homosexuals." The neighborhood children carried on the eighteenth century French custom of week-end visits to the lunatic asylum to view the inmates: they frequently entered the building on weekends by self-invitation, "just to look around" and giggle. Boys broke the windows facing the street with stones so many times that one winter we decided to freeze rather than spend money to repair them again. Children repeatedly broke empty milk bottles left near the door, smashed the front door with an axe, unscrewed the doorbell, and once put dogs faeces in the ground floor hall. (1969, pp. 308–309)

While vandalism was a serious problem, it would be wrong to suppose that the residents of Kingsley Hall did nothing to provoke their neighbors—though arguably, perhaps, most of their offenses were inadvertent. For example, Schatzman goes on:

Residents alarm people who live outside the building when they behave in ways which are considered strange. A man aged twenty-eight . . . would walk into neighborhood pubs and coffee shops, pick up glasses from tables and counters, drink the contents, and walk out without saying a word. If a door to a house was left open he would enter and sit on a chair in the drawing room until someone of the house would see him. Then he would get up and walk out quietly. He never said anything to threaten anyone and he never touched anyone, but he unnerved people. People would approach him in the street and offer the unsolicited advice that he would "feel better" in a mental hospital. One resident kept people in the house next door awake at night by playing his record player as loudly as he could. He experienced his body as "numb" and found he could give it "life" if he played music loudly. He did not wish to disturb anyone, and when those whom he disturbed, complained, he stopped and apologized. (p. 309)

In view of the problems created by the residents' strange behavior and by the whole nature of the project, which was foreign and frightening to the local citizenry, various efforts were made to reach out for a measure of tolerance and understanding. One form these efforts took was to encourage community groups that had met there before to keep doing so, and for a time, local musical, religious and old people's groups continued to meet in the main hall on a regular basis. In addition, several determined attempts were made to explain to local residents what the nature of the asylum was (Schatzman, 1969; Briskin, 1993). While no doubt sincere, these efforts were not very successful, and the surrounding community continued to view the residents of Kingsley Hall with hostility and distrust.

To complicate matters, not all the visitors to Kingsley Hall were hippies, radicals, or people seeking refuge and advice. For all its revolutionary aspirations, the Philadelphia Association sported an impressive and respectable board of advisers, including Marie Jahoda, a social psychologist from the University of Sussex; Maxwell Jones, chief of the Dingleton Hospital near Edinburgh; Tom Maine, director of Cassell Hospital in Surrey; J. D. Sutherland from the psychiatry department at Edinburgh; Eric Trist, another Tavistock alumnus; Michael Young, director of the Institute for Community Studies in London; and Dame Eileen Younghusband of the National Institute for Social Work Training in London. In the first year of its existence, all of these people visited Kingsley Hall—as did Kenneth Tynan, David Mercer, Timothy Leary, and the young actor, Sean Connery (who dropped by fairly regularly for a time).

Though it was never intended that way, this strange and heterogeneous stream of mad people, hippies, academics, and celebrities was exquisitely calibrated to baffle and antagonize the working-class neighborhood in which Kingsley Hall was nestled. For unlike the celebrities who visited there in days gone by—H. G. Wells, Gandhi, Romain Rolland—this lot was not interested in the local citizenry but was drawn to the increasingly embattled community within a community that Kingsley Hall had become. When the P.A. finally left in 1970, few in the neighborhood were sad to see them go.

Like all groups that reject formal organization, leadership roles at Kingsley Hall were defined informally and inevitably clustered around Laing. His preeminence was not taken for granted at first, but emerged over time. Looking back on Kingsley Hall's second year, Mosher recalls the change in atmosphere. By the fall of 1966,

> topics of discussion and group composition had shifted considerably
> . . . A number of the group's professionals had dropped out or
> attended irregularly . . . No longer were "cases" discussed or advice
> sought. There was usually no formal agenda but often meetings were
> called because a problem had arisen . . . or because of the arrival of a
> visiting dignitary. The meetings changed from being discussions
> among peers about a problem which needed solving to being a forum
> in which Ronnie could put forth his views on various issues. (p. 12)

Having established his position among his collaborators, Laing distanced himself somewhat from Kingsley Hall in December 1966, when he and Jutta Werner moved into a flat at 65a Belsize Park Gardens, where they remained for almost ten years. By his own admission, Laing was tired, and he turned the reins over to three young

American doctors—Joseph Berke, Morton Schatzman, and Leon
Redler. His need to live elsewhere made a certain amount of sense.
Kingsley Hall was a thoroughly exhausting place, and in addition to
running a private practice, Laing was about to launch several new
undertakings that would require clarity and presence of mind.

Nevertheless, Laing's departure was the beginning of the end for
Kingsley Hall. Despite his unpredictable style of leadership, Laing's
charismatic presence had been vital to sustaining the fragile sense of
cohesion that united this motley group of people. Throughout 1965
and 1966, Laing managed to combine his leadership role there with a
busy schedule of lectures and public appearances. Inevitably, perhaps, those who devoted themselves single-mindedly to Kingsley
Hall began to feel that Laing was living a double life—one as a dedicated and charismatic opponent of "the system" and another as a
gifted maverick within it, who observed its conventions sufficiently
to enjoy many of its benefits.

The doubts and dissatisfaction engendered by this growing perception of Laing were compounded by his increasing unavailability
as a therapist. In his own practice, Laing continued to conduct himself more or less responsibly with a varied and interesting clientele,
which included many of England's leading intellectuals and artists.
In addition, he continued to reap monetary benefits. Toward the
end of 1966, however, he did less and less of the hands-on work at
Kingsley Hall and took on a more supervisory role, sending over-
taxed therapists back into the fray with pep talks and leaving others
to cope with the drudgery of maintaining a sprawling, disorganized
household without the benefit of rules and routines.

Finally, for all his intellectual openness and opposition to dogma,
Laing could not long tolerate strong or open differences of opinion
between himself and others, so that if disagreements on policy could
not be settled by friendly persuasion, his temper would flare up,
causing the rifts to deepen. Yet paradoxically, as Clancy Sigal noted
and as John Heaton confirms, those who gave Laing the deference
he demanded also tended to fall in his esteem: his withering contempt for passive or sycophantic people was often turned on those
who worked hardest to win his love and trust on *his* terms.

Though he might have found the comparison odd or contrived,
Laing's leadership style was a little like Freud's. He was privy to his
collaborators' most intimate personal secrets, and the trust and es-

teem they had settled on him through therapy (or otherwise confiding in him) made it impossible for him to relate to them all on equal terms. Moreover, like Freud, he was not above playing favorites, shifting his approval from one person to another as the mood or situation demanded, making the so-called Brotherhood a divided body, torn with sibling rivalries.

This situation could not be sustained indefinitely, and eventually most of the original members left. The first casualty was Clancy Sigal, who had come to Britain in the 1950s to escape the McCarthy blacklist. Like David Cooper, though in a more grounded way, Sigal's sensibilities and commitments were essentially political. In due course he grew disenchanted with Laing's mystical tendencies, which he came to regard as a barely sublimated form of machismo suffused with large doses of megalomania. Sigal detailed his misgivings in a bitter but hilarious satire, *Zone of the Interior* (1976), in which Laing goes by the name of Willie Last, the Philadelphia Association is called the Clare Council, and Kingsley Hall is dubbed Meditation Manor.

Though he claimed never to have read it, Laing was so alarmed by the contents of *Zone of the Interior* that he moved to have it banned in Britain. While many of Laing's friends and followers still treat the book as a vicious caricature, there are some places where the characterizations ring very true. For example:

A romantic, left-wing nationalist, [Willie Last] regarded Scots like himself as "Jews," with the historic mission of filling the shoes of Europe's traditional intellectual-cosmopolitan elite, the Jews Hitler had murdered. He took more or less literally this self-elected Jewishness. England south of Carlisle was a "Diaspora," and Scotland, like pre-Israel Palestine, a marginal land of broken dreams. But one day soon the spark of a primitive kirk-based egalitarianism—the democracy of souls snuffed out by the Culloden massacre and the Act of Union (1707)—would burst into vengeful flame, and Scotland (like Dixie?) would rise again. Then he . . . would hurry back to his native lowlands to raise the consciousness of his awakening countrymen from mere bourgeois nationalism to the heights of psychic revolution.

"But first I'm gointa plunder th' fucken Ainglish like they did us for 250 years!" (pp. 142–143)

Comedy and caricature aside, several disturbing themes emerge from Sigal's narrative. The first is its hero's use of vast amounts of LSD, which was often rationalized as research. Another was the tendency among the men of the place to espouse traditionally dismissive views of women under the guise of being hip—a tendency to type them as "Light Bringers" or "Earth Mothers," according to how they complemented or inspired their male companions (pp. 166–167).

Finally, there was the curious penchant for mixing revolutionary aspirations with religious, mystical, and psychotherapeutic concepts. In fairness to Laing, it may be futile to try to disentangle these spheres of human ideation and endeavor completely. As most anthropologists or historians will readily acknowledge, religion and politics are always intertwined. And as any reflective psychotherapist will admit, spiritual and political issues are frequently addressed (or concealed) in the healing dialogue between two persons.

Moreover, Laing was certainly not alone, since the temptation to fuse and confuse spirituality, psychotherapy, and politics was very much in keeping with the temper of the 1960s. Still, one of the constitutive features of modernity is the attempt to separate religion, politics, and mental healing as far as possible, and the attempt to reverse or defy this tendency—which may be justified in certain contexts—can be taken to absurd and opportunistic extremes. If the florid rhetoric of Willie Last in *Zone of the Interior* is any indication, Laing did just that, seeing himself first as a revolutionary and later as some sort of Christ figure:

His self promotion to a Christ figure coincided with a shift in Clare's attitude toward insanity. Originally, Last had taught me that madness was a comprehensible, but definitely psychotic response to invalidation. By subtler stages it had become something else, a kind of super sanity implicitly superior to the alienation which normals called normality. Indeed, anyone at the Manor who wasn't totally off his chump was treated as a second class citizen. So the competition was to go as crazy as possible the way some kids will try to appear brighter than others for a teacher who gives gold stars for the right kind of answers. Last not only encouraged this worshipful attitude to insanity but also personified it. He had nothing but contempt for social workers and doctors who kept their psychic distance from the mentally ill; such detachment he likened to the voyeurism of the bullfight critic who is afraid to enter the arena. Insisting on the oracular powers of schizophrenics, who were "foreign correspondents back fr' uther wurlds wi' battlefield reports we haven't the wit tae unscramble," he said that the only way to decode such reports was to climb into the schizophrenic's soul—*be* one. (p. 220)

Sigal was not the first or the last person to accuse Laing of glamorizing madness, a charge that Laing steadfastly denied. But if we credit the testimony of many who knew him in those days, it seems clear that he went through a phase between 1966 and 1969 when he did idealize the mad—although in fairness, again, he put that tendency behind him in the seventies.

The next founding member to leave the P.A. was Aaron Esterson. Esterson had studied yoga and Buddhism intensively and was not particularly alarmed by Laing's mysticism. But by the summer of 1966, Esterson was so dismayed at the chaotic state of Kingsley Hall and Laing's intemperate drug use that he began to question Laing's leadership. To buttress his authority, as witnesses recall, Laing quoted Lenin to Esterson—from memory and at length. In response, Esterson took to carrying a biography of Stalin with him at all times.

One night, at Ben Churchill's home, Laing provoked a bitter row by insisting that his friendship with Esterson was doomed unless Esterson, an observant Jew, "would take Jesus Christ into his heart." The implication of this bizarre demand was that Esterson should commit himself unreservedly to Laing's way of seeing and doing things and, more important perhaps, that Esterson should take Laing as he now preferred to be taken, as a spiritual master. Esterson took offense at the remark, and said so. Laing then punched his former friend in the jaw, and a brief but inconclusive scuffle ensued. Esterson resigned from the Philadelphia Association on September 4, 1968, and Churchill, who had joined earlier that year, left without fanfare in early 1969.

Kingsley Hall, now under the stewardship of Joseph Berke and Morton Schatzman, continued to gain publicity and acclaim for a while. But its death knell was sounded in February 1968, when

Muriel Lester passed away. Lester admired Laing and had never wavered in her support. But the remaining trustees thought that the building should revert to its original use. Despite the initial improvements made by the P.A., they noted, the building had deteriorated badly since 1967. In conversation with an American journalist (Goldmann, 1971), Laing himself characterized Kingsley Hall as "an awful shit house," which in light of Mary Barnes (and her many imitators) may have been more than merely a pungent figure of speech. And they were not wanted in the neighborhood. That was crystal clear. So the board of trustees of Kingsley Hall demanded that the P.A. pay them £ 5,000 to restore the gutted building (Redler, Seal, and Yockum, 1970), and gave them a generous period of eighteen months in which to vacate the premises.

Meanwhile, in the spring of 1968, Berke and Schatzman applied for membership in the P.A. and, to their surprise, were refused. There were several reasons for their exclusion. To begin with, Laing, though friendly, was never close to the pair and had scant respect for their background and abilities. Laing later said:

> They were . . . very brashly-declaratively American in the worst sense of the word . . . They were very imbued with this very white mentality—the Yankee, New York number of going to Montgomery on freedom marches on behalf of blacks they had never met and didn't know anything about . . . and of course there was the Cuban missile crisis. This was simply a sensibility I had very little time for.
>
> They were simply unusable for research into the normal families that I was working with . . . I would have had to explain to them how to knock on a door and enter a house and sit down and have cup of tea with a family. (Mullan, p. 197)

Still, Laing conceded, they were students of his, and he allowed them to "hang around" his office. Meanwhile, John Layard, Berke's therapist—who was in therapy with Laing, incidentally—probably shared Laing's antipathy to Americans, since he took Berke on despite the fact that he couldn't stand him. (Evidently Laing did not object to this strange policy.) When Layard finally got fed up with Berke and tried to pressure Laing into severing his connection with him, Laing called a meeting of the Philadelphia Association to discuss the matter. Laing was already annoyed at Berke for coauthoring a book that he was conspicuously prevented from reading and commenting on (Mullan, p. 198). Then he discovered that two new members, John Heaton and Hugh Crawford, did not want Berke and Schatzman aboard because of their lack of grounding in existential phenomenology. Unlike Berke and Schatzman, who were fifteen years younger, Heaton and Crawford were Laing's contemporaries, were well versed in existential phenomenology, and finally, perhaps, were British. That settled it, apparently.

While Berke and Schatzman were excluded, their friend and classmate, Leon Redler, was invited to join the Philadelphia Association, and for many years he was in charge of the Archway communities that sprang up in the wake of Kingsley Hall. Berke and Schatzman went on to found another group devoted to setting up therapeutic communities, the Arbors Association, which is still active and growing. Unlike Clancy Sigal, whose disenchantment with Laing was angrily and eloquently expressed, Berke and Schatzman have been notably diplomatic about their break with Laing. When asked to comment on the P.A.'s refusal of his membership bid, Berke remarked cryptically that it was the biggest favor they could have done him (Berke, 1994).

Was Kingsley Hall a success or a failure? In conversation with Bob Mullan, Laing acknowledged that it "was certainly not a roaring success" but added that it provided valuable lessons for John Weir Perry, the founder of Diabasis House, and for Loren Mosher, among others. Though these experiments were closed down at the end of the seventies, Laing noted that communities modeled on similar lines were emerging here and there. According to him, it was still an open question.

5

THE TURN TO $\mathcal{M}$YSTICISM

Having left Kingsley Hall and moved to Belsize Gardens in December 1966, Laing was poised to launch the next phase of his career, which would catapult him onto the world stage and ignite even wilder controversies. The first big event of 1967 was a series of lectures and seminars delivered at the William Alanson White Institute of Psychiatry, Psychoanalysis and Psychology, in New York City, where Laing was welcomed as a distinguished visiting lecturer by John Schimel, whose home became a frequent refuge for Laing on subsequent visits to New York (Schimel, 1967, 1991).

The White Institute was founded in 1946 by Clara Thompson, Harry Stack Sullivan, Erich Fromm, Frieda Fromm-Reichmann, and David and Janet Rioch. Its founders had run afoul of Freudian orthodoxy or had deliberately disengaged themselves from the administrative and doctrinal constraints of the International Psycho-Analytic Association. Unlike their more conservative counterparts in the Freudian world, the White's faculty shared a broad tolerance for unconventional lifestyles and a skeptical attitude to conventional criteria of sanity.

None of the White's founders was around to hear Laing speak. Sullivan and Fromm-Reichmann were dead, and Fromm was in Switzerland, recuperating from a heart attack. Yet Laing did very well both on and off the podium. The White's faculty was thoroughly impressed with his ideas and his courtesy. And as the progeny of some of the great therapeutic innovators, they were not dismayed by his use of LSD as a therapeutic agent, unlike most of his colleagues in London. The only notable lapse in decorum came at the end of his visit, during a dinner in his honor, when a visibly inebriated Ronald Laing angrily denounced the Vietnam war and challenged his hosts to do likewise. As John Schimel remarked, many of these present experienced Laing's remarks as not merely antiwar but vehemently anti-American.

Though never published, the transcripts of Laing's lectures at the White Institute make fascinating reading. They were not attempts to play it safe or to canvass familiar territory, but to test out ideas that had been brewing in 1965 and 1966. In effect, this series of lectures (and accompanying seminars and workshops) was a dress rehearsal for many themes and variations that would surface subsequently in *Politics of Experience, Politics of the Family, Knots, Do You Love Me?* and *The Facts of Life.* And while he may have aired them earlier on his own turf, so to speak, this particular effort was in front of a new audience on foreign soil; it was not addressed to the familiar, intent, and often adoring adherents who awaited him back home.

Three years before, in *Sanity, Madness and the Family,* Laing urged readers to suspend judgment on whether schizophrenia really exists. In addition to being phenomenological, his approach here was "micro-constructivist" (see Chapter 8), describing how the symptoms of the disorder were identified by family members and psychiatrists in the face of profound mystification and invalidation which, if noted sympathetically, could render the strange beliefs and experiences of the mad intelligible, but which were ignored, as it were, on principle. Now Laing, less cautious, embedded these irrational familial discourses (and subsequent psychiatric invalidation) in a broader social context, arguing that schizophrenia is not a disease entity discovered in the nineteenth century, as psychiatry insisted, but an artifact of capitalist social organization, which both mirrored and reinforced the psychosocial imperatives of the bourgeoisie.

In short, while lecturing at the White Institute, Laing took his theory of schizophrenia to another level of analysis, from *micro* to *macro* if you will, although he repudiated this approach a decade later, saying that the link between capitalism and schizophrenia had been drawn by weaker and more ideological theorists, such as David

Cooper, Felix Guatarri, and Franco Basaglia (Mullan, 1994). Many
of his later reservations may be valid, but the fact remains that the
Marxist ideologues were following in *his* footsteps, a fact he had difficulty admitting, to himself and to others.

Leaving the politics of psychiatry to one side, Laing's lectures at
the White also heralded some new stylistic directions. Among the
handouts that accompanied his lectures were "A Sutra on remembering" (lecture 2), "A Sutra on knots" (lecture 3), and "A Sutra on
going back and going out of one's mind" (lecture 4). These unpublished offerings consisted of anecdotes, poems, observations, and
exhortations that were meant to illustrate the ideas he would offer in
the lectures.

Laing might have called these productions "Thoughts on Remembering," "A Discourse on Knots," or "Reflections on Madness and
Regression," but that would not suit his purpose. He wanted to be
seen as a writer of sutras, religious or philosophical works in the
Hindu and Buddhist traditions. Up to this time, references to eastern philosophy and western mysticism were relatively sparse in
Laing's work. In *The Divided Self*, Laing had made a brief comparison between the schizoid attitude toward the body and the Gnostic
project of achieving disincarnate spirituality. Four years later, in
Sanity, Madness and the Family, he and Esterson made a passing reference to "the veil of Maya" as a way of describing the false consciousness that envelops a family in collusion and denial.
Interpersonal Perception, published in 1966, opened with an allusion
to the Hindu myth of the jeweled net of Indra, which describes the
observable cosmos as a plethora of multifaceted jewels reflecting
one another's reflections, and reflections of reflections, generating
an infinity of images and perspectives. Similarly, "The human race is
a myriad of refractive surfaces staining the white radiance of eter-
nity. Each surface refracts the refraction of refractions of refractions.
Each self refracts the refractions of other's refractions of self's refractions of other's refractions" (Laing, Phillipson, and Lee, 1966,
p. 3).

So far, Laing's allusions to religion and philosophy were service-
able and appropriate to context. For those who did not automatically dismiss mystical modes of experience and thought, they were
illuminating, evidence of both openness and erudition—the kind of
thing one looks for in a thinker of Laing's dimensions. After this

time, however, Laing's stylizings became portentous, often making it hard to discriminate between his genuine thought and superficial mantras mouthed for the sake of being trendy.

It may be that the new style was part of a self-marketing strategy by which Laing hoped to capitalize on the emerging counterculture. Although it perplexed and antagonized his left-wing critics (such as Mitchell, 1975; Collier, 1976; Sedgwick, 1982), in the short run it was a brilliant success, although the effort to promote himself as a guru probably left Laing feeling cut off, and a little disgusted with himself. In the long run, however, Laing's new style was a disaster, since it gave critics all kinds of pretexts to dismiss him, and left him high and dry when the popular tide rolled out.

Despite his stylistic idiosyncrasies, Laing's critique of the concept of adaptation and the psychology of normality, which was another important element in these talks, was much like that of Erich Fromm, as Fromm himself acknowledged (1970, 1991). Long before Laing, Fromm expressed grave skepticism about the use of social adaptation as a criterion of mental health (1955). In fact, for the decades from 1941 to 1980, Fromm wrote about the widespread atrophy of the ability to think critically and to feel deeply in the face of pervasive "filters" acquired in the process of socialization—a problem he termed a "socially patterned defect," as opposed to a neurotic disturbance (Burston, 1991, 1996). Unlike Freudian censorship, which alienates people from the experience of their own desire, but is construed as an intrapsychic agency or process, Fromm's social filters were conceived of as logical and linguistic categories embedded in the culture as a whole. Fromm's goal was to transform psychoanalysis into a humanistic discipline that enables people to recover the wholeness of being human by dissolving the conventional filters, to recover and reintegrate some of the raw, primordial, and transcendental dimensions of experience that society had proscribed for the "normal" human being. Laing's approach to existential psychotherapy was very similar.

The next major event on Laing's calendar for 1967 was the publication (in February) of *The Politics of Experience*. Though it was greeted with less fanfare than the Dialectics of Liberation Conference later that July, its impact on the general public, particularly in

the United States, was far greater. Reiterating some of the ideas he
had tried out at the White Institute, Laing argued that mad people
have lost the conventional social filters and regressed to a level of experience that precedes the acquisition of distinctions between inner
and outer, past and present, real and imaginary, good and bad; but
their anguish and confusion may herald an inner voyage—
metanoia—which in optimal circumstances can result in a recovery
(or rediscovery) of the self. In the meantime their alienation from
the world stands in stark contrast to the forms of self-alienation that
are usually deemed sane. But what are usually described as normal
experiences or ways of being, Laing maintained, are only so many
forms of pseudo-sanity, a product of radical estrangement from the
inner world and the mysterious ground of Being. Those who lose
their way in this world of shadows, who get a dim inkling of deeper
realities that the rest of us routinely repress, who get shattered in the
process—these unfortunates are put away, ostensibly for their benefit. In a troubling, insistent way, Laing urges us to question whether
it is really *their* interests we are defending by labeling and treating
them as schizophrenic:

"Schizophrenia" is a diagnosis, a label applied by some people to
others. This does not prove that the labeled person is subject to an essentially pathological process, of unknown nature and origin, going on
in his or her body. It does not mean that the process is, primarily or
secondarily, a *psycho*pathological one, that is going on *in* the *psyche* of
the person. But it does establish as a social fact that the person labeled
is one of Them . . .
    There is no such "condition" as "schizophrenia," but the label is a
social fact and the social fact a *political event.* This political event,
occurring in the civic order of society, imposes definitions and consequences on the labeled person. It is a social prescription that rational-
izes a set of social actions whereby the labeled person is annexed by
others, who are legally sanctioned, medically empowered and morally
obliged, to become responsible for the person labeled. The person
labeled is inaugurated not only into a role, but into a carrer of patient,
by the concerted action of a coalition (a "conspiracy") of family, G.P.,
mental health officer, psychiatrists, nurses, psychiatric social workers
and often fellow patients . . . degraded from full existential and legal
status as human agent and responsible person to someone no longer in

possession of his own definition of himself, unable to retain his own possessions, precluded from the exercise of his discretion as to whom he meets, what he does. His time is no longer his own and the space he occupies is no longer of his choosing . . . More completely, more radically than anywhere else in our society, he is invalidated as a human being. (1967a, pp. 120–122)

Though extremely influential, *The Politics of Experience* is not Laing's best book. Actually it is a compilation of essays published during the early and mid-sixties which he revised for the occasion, adding a new piece, "The Bird of Paradise," a vivid, rambling psychedelic memoir, at the end. The book in its entirety evokes an author who is wrestling with doubt and despair—a prophet in the wilderness, crying out to "a world that will remain as unmoved as it is avid." But there is also some powerful and thought-provoking prose, including a good critique of positivistic psychology, behaviorism, and psychiatry, and some riveting reflections on existential psychotherapy. The problem is that Laing goes overboard, particularly on the subject of the family. His criticism of the family was not unprecedented, of course. Since the mid-nineteenth century, utopian socialists, communists, and anarchists had made the dissolution of the patriarchal family a rallying cry, along with a call for women's economic and sexual emancipation. Laing was certainly familiar with the works of Wilhelm Reich and Herbert Marcuse, who depicted the family as a repressive institution that limits the realization of people's authentic possibilities in the service of an oppressive and duplicitous status quo (Mitchell, 1975).

In view of the furor that followed, it is important to remember that Laing's previous remarks on the family were not as sweeping as those of Reich, Marcuse, or his colleague David Cooper. In *Self and Others,* published in 1961, Laing argued that *all* social groups, including the family, are held together by social fantasy systems. While this argument presents a rather dismal view of the dynamics of social cohesion, it was one that Laing applied across the board to all institutional structures. The family was not singled out for particular scorn and ridicule.

In *Sanity, Madness and the Family,* published in 1964, Laing and Esterson took a slightly different approach. As phenomenologists they took great care to describe clearly the tangled web of mystification, miscommunication, and invalidation peculiar to each family. Having done that, they suggested that one subtext uniting these seemingly disparate discourses was a parental unwillingness to let children pursue their own lives. This infantilizing tendency prompted parents to interpret a child's developmentally appropriate changes in behavior and attitude as alarming and objectionable signs of mental illness, rather than as first steps toward individuation, and to seek the help of psychiatrists in trying to stop them. Though actually quite frightening, this analysis of family dynamics was more optimistic than the preceding one, since it did allow for the existence of families *not* cursed by this pattern.

Finally, in 1967 Laing published a paper entitled "Family and Individual Structure" in *The Predicament of the Family,* an anthology edited by Peter Lomas (1967). It was a significant intellectual milestone, where Laing outlined his theory of transpersonal defenses (see Chapter 10). Meanwhile, for our purposes, "Family and Individual Structure" is noteworthy because here Laing *explicitly* makes allowance for the existence of families that are not dominated by the fantasy "nexus" (p. 118).

So far, then, Laing had committed himself to two controversial theses regarding the nature of the family. The first posited a model of group cohesion based on fantasy systems, but was devoid of any special animus toward the family per se. The second confined its conclusions to the families under study and others like them, but allowed for the existence of families that were different. Unlike Bateson and his associates, Laing and Esterson did not even claim that the tangled evasions, double binds, and "violence masquerading as love" actually causes madness. They merely said that the peculiar experiences and communications of diagnosed schizophrenics, which otherwise appear so bizarre, become intelligible in light of familial contexts, rendering the diagnostic lexicon of mainstream psychiatry largely irrelevant.

Neither of Laing's positions had elicited universal approval, mostly because he had nothing particularly positive to say about the family. Now, however, in *Politics of Experience,* Laing inserted a note of vehemence into his characterization of the family, which polarized opinion even more. Take the following quote from chapter 3, "The Mystification of Experience." The target of Laing's indignation here was *The Family and Human Adaptation,* by the Harvard psychiatrist Theodor Lidz (1964). According to Laing, Lidz was one of many mental health ideologues who make specious claims to value neutrality, because they assign an essentially positive value to adaptation and to features of the family that drive many people to madness or to mindless, one-dimensional conformity. In contrast to Lidz, Laing insisted:

> The family's function is to repress Eros; to induce a false consciousness of security; to deny death by avoiding life; to cut off transcendence; to believe in God, not to experience the Void; to create, in short, one-dimensional man; to promote respect, conformity, obedience; to con children out of play; to induce a fear of failure; to promote a respect for work; to promote respect for "respectability." (p. 65)

And again:

> The family is, in the first place, the usual instrument for what is called socialization, that is, getting each new recruit of the human race to behave and experience in substantially the same way as those who have already got here. We are fallen Sons of Prophecy, who have learned to die in the Spirit and be reborn in the Flesh.
>
> This is also known as selling one's birthright for a mess of pottage (p. 68).

Quite apart from its oracular tone, this shrill denunciation of the family is new in Laing's work. Perhaps it came in part from Laing's bitter separation from his first wife and family, and his feelings about his family of origin. No doubt he was also affected by his experience as a clinician, where he saw familial violence—both overt and covert—laying waste to his patients' minds.

Another factor, I suspect, was a desire to boost his popularity among segments of the left and the counterculture, who welcomed this kind of intemperate rhetoric. But regardless of whether Laing was after catharsis, revenge, or popularity—indeed all three—the fact is that he suffered subsequently. Book sales rocketed for a time, but his family in Glasgow, after reading the book, was deeply shocked. As much as he wanted to, perhaps Laing could never completely heal the wounds he inflicted then. And though he coped with the growing estrangement of his first family in some ways, his inability to remedy the situation intensified his own malaise (A. Laing, 1994, chaps. 13–14).[1]

In addition, as if this were not bad enough, Laing's anti-family rhetoric in *Politics of Experience* created another problem—which dogged him throughout the seventies and probably beyond. Though still unmarried in 1967, Laing and Jutta Werner started to have children and would have three in all: Adam, Natasha, and Max. Moreover, by the late sixties, Laing let it be known that though he supported alternative lifestyles and experiments in communal living, he was personally committed to monogamous relationships and thought that binding one-to-one commitments provided the best framework for working out unresolved psychological issues (Irwin, personal communication, 1993).

So a curious situation emerged. On the one hand, Laing stubbornly stood by *Politics of Experience* and refused to gratify his critics by reformulating any of his ideas. On the other hand, Laing was clearly embarked on creating a family of his own and formalized the arrangement by marrying Jutta Werner on St. Valentine's Day in 1974. Henceforth, any pro-family critic with a grain of common sense could point to Laing's waywardness and refuse to take him seriously. The anti-family group had a harder time of it. Many had championed Laing as their spokesman and now found themselves reproaching him, publicly or privately, for inconsistency or hypocrisy—David Cooper among them.

Either way, the damage was done. No matter what side of the debate you were on, the sincerity of Laing's position on the family was open to doubt. Laing himself rationalized the apparent contradiction between *Politics of Experience* and his subsequent marriage by saying that his critics failed to get his deeper message, took his statements out of context, and so on. Looking back at the sixties, in an interview with Richard Simon in 1983, Laing said:

> I was writing then mainly about unhappy families. I was trying to describe the family "mangle," the way families manufacture pain for their members. You might say that my writings have been biased in terms of addressing myself to the misery and unhappiness that can occur in families, but I never thought that was the whole story. (p. 26)

In fairness to Laing, his belated attempts at self-justification are plausible in terms of *Self and Others, Sanity, Madness and the Family,* or "Family and Individual Structure." Very few critics have sufficient objectivity to grant him that much. But more casual readers, who know him from *Politics of Experience* alone, may be forgiven some skepticism and incredulity on this score. The tone of his remarks there is too harsh and categorical to warrant any other response.

In view of what followed, one cannot escape the impression that Laing was an unwitting accomplice in his own downfall. In *Politics of Experience,* as Adrian Laing observes (p. 131), R. D. Laing was bent on becoming a preceptor to humanity, like Freud and Jung before him, and for a brief time he was. But he was also setting himself up for a massive crisis of credibility—one that would stymie his faltering career when the collective euphoria of the 1960s wore off and the hangover set in. In retrospect, it seems, he never realized what happened or grasped his own role in these fateful proceedings.

All that said, however, there is some justification in Laing's complaint about being taken out of context. *The Politics of Experience* was an angry, articulate, and *personal* attempt to bring a whole generation to its senses. Whatever your response to the book—outrage, enthusiasm, ambivalence—Laing's message and style ruled out the possibility of a complacent or indifferent response to his ideas. Moreover, his scathing appraisal of the family was part of an all-out attack on alienation and conformity in modern society. And as his references to such contemporaries as Marcuse, Goffman, and Jules Henry indicate, he was not alone.

Unlike Goffman and Henry, however, who targeted specific sectors of society (mental hospitals, schools), Laing spared no one, attacking the family, the educational system, the churches, the military, the political and scientific establishments, and the mental health professions all at once. Anyone who had an ax to grind with one of these institutions could find some solace and instruction in his words. Conversely, those with a stake in one of them might find cause for umbrage.

The problem with Laing's social criticism is that he attempted to cover too much territory. *The Politics of Experience* was too loud, intense, and scattered. Furthermore, it was taken by many of its readers not merely as an impassioned analysis but as an actual call to arms, which only intensified the proverbial generation gap. According to Laing, from earliest infancy young people are forced by a barrage of social pressures to embrace a limited existence, full of pseudo-identities and pseudo-relationships and devoid of genuine

feeling. By the time they reach fifteen, most children are hopelessly
conformist, irrevocably cut off from the wellsprings of their own
creative and spiritual being. And behind this pervasive "violence
masquerading as love" are the schools, the family, the elders.

Laing was certainly not the first to depict relations between the
generations in adversarial terms. In the twilight of Victorianism, the
struggle of the young against the hypocrisy of their elders became a
preoccupation in western thought and letters. Samuel Butler's novel,
The Way of All Flesh, for example, presented this issue with lucidity
and compassion, as did many of the plays of Ibsen and Shaw. These
remarks were written in much the same spirit:

> for many generations we have bowed our necks to the conviction of
> sin. We have swallowed all manner of poisonous certainties fed us by
> our parents, our Sunday and day school teachers, our politicians, our
> priests, our newspapers and others with a vested interest in controlling
> us . . . Misguided by authoritarian dogma, bound by exclusive faith,
> stunted by inculcated loyalty, torn by frantic heresy, drugged by ecsta-
> tic experience, confused by conflicting certainty, bewildered by
> invented mystery, and loaded down by the weight of guilt and fear
> engendered by its own original promises, the unfortunate human race,
> deprived by these incubi of its only defenses and its only reasons for
> striving, its reasoning power and its natural capacity to enjoy the satis-
> faction of its natural urges, struggles along under its ghastly self-
> imposed burden . . . [The] freedom to think freely, present in all
> children and known as innocence, has been destroyed or crippled by
> local certainties, by gods of local moralities, of local loyalty, of
> personal salvation, of prejudice and hate and intolerance—frequently
> masquerading as love gods . . . [that] would destroy freedom to
> observe and to think, and would keep each generation under the
> control of the old people, the elders, the shamans and priests. (Parkin,
> 1987, pp. 61–62)

This is the kind of rhetoric that infuriated Laing's critics. But the
author of this diatribe is not R. D. Laing but Major-General Brock
Chisholm, director-general of medical services for the Canadian
Army, who delivered it during the William Alanson White Memorial Lectures in 1945. Chisholm, a psychiatrist from Oakville, Ontario, was forty-nine years old when he spoke these flaming words,
provoking a barrage of angry denunciations that spanned the length

and breadth of Canada and almost resulted in his dismissal. Chisholm survived, though, and went on to become head of the World Health Organization in 1948—a post he held until his retirement in 1953.

Despite the similarities to Laing, Chisholm's attack explicitly targeted five groups: parents, politicians, the media, educators, and the clergy. The military, medical, and mental health professions were exempt, which is not surprising. After all, the military had just concluded a bloody world war, and the general population was proud of its men, living and dead. Moreover, a man of Chisholm's generation might be excused for believing that psychoanalysis and psychiatry are aligned with the forces of enlightenment, committed to combatting the old order and the enemy within.

Laing had no such faith. For the most part, he despaired of achieving anything worthwhile within the system when he left the Tavistock milieu, and he made no secret of it. If history is any indication, professionals can be dismissive and even vicious with heretics who point an accusing finger at their own fraternity, even (or especially) if the accusations are well founded.

In any case, though Laing deplored this reading of his work, many readers on both sides of the generational divide felt that *Politics of Experience* depicted the young as the victims of the sinister (if unconscious) designs of their elders, whose humanity had been irrevocably compromised by *their* parents and by the mere fact that they functioned passably well in an increasingly dehumanized environment. To others, Laing even appeared to imply that chronic, incapacitating anger, distrust, and despair are the only possible responses left to decent human beings—that anything less is evidence of inauthenticity and evasion. This message played well with followers of Marcuse and with intellectuals and artists who felt misunderstood and who were seeking a good justification for their unconventional lives. Predictably it played less well with more optimistic political activists, who sensed a retreat into passivity and nihilism.

Though Laing disclaimed any intention of casting parents and children in adversarial roles (Evans, 1976, p. xlvi), he seemed almost to absolve the young of responsibility for spiritual malaise. As a pupil of Sartre, for whom the fear of freedom and responsibility for one's own fate is the central issue at any age and at any time in human history, this was an odd way to carry on. At the same time, it must be said that, with all its polemical excesses, *The Politics of Experience* is a remarkable document. Despite its abrasiveness, it elicited a sympathetic response among many parents, educators, clinicians, philosophers, and clergy. These people were not marginal or disaffected, not just hippies, artists, and activists or one kind or another, but responsible members of the establishment, who felt the force and justice of Laing's critique. The fact that their adult lives were enmeshed in the institutions he lambasted did not deter them from recognizing the merit of his arguments, and for using them to illustrate the necessity for reform and renewal, if not for revolution.

This fact underscores the richly ambiguous nature of Laing's legacy, and the attitudes and aspirations that fueled his writing. As anyone who knew him will attest, in writing *Politics of Experience,* Laing was not merely motivated by humane skepticism, by moral outrage and stubborn courage. He had these qualities, to be sure, but he was also driven by his own inner demons and desires. Had Laing been less ambitious, less flamboyant, less categorical, and less despairing; had he been more cautious, comforting, hopeful, and inclusive in tone, he might have been a happier person. By the same token, given the temper of the times, he could not have spread his message as effectively as he did. The tragic upshot of all this was that as times changed, and as his creativity and credibility both declined, he became yesterday's icon, a worn-out, wounded rebel, who jeopardized his chances of getting lasting recognition and continuing scrutiny.

The next major event of 1967 was a conference on "The Dialectics of Liberation," which convened from July 15 to July 30 in the Roundhouse, "a large, circular, barren building originally designed as a railway terminal in Victorian times" in Chalk Farm, north London (Berke, ed., 1969, p. 410). Though nominally sponsored by the Institute of Phenomenological Studies (Laing, Cooper, Berke, and Redler), the idea for this event initially occurred to Joseph Berke who, with Redler and others, gathered some of the best left-wing intellectuals of the day to discuss the emerging global crisis on all fronts. The all-male lineup included Gregory Bateson, John Gerassi, Lucien Goldmann, Herbert Marcuse, Paul Sweezy, Ernest Mandel,

Erving Goffman, Jules Henry, Paul Goodman, Mircea Eliade, Allen Ginsberg, Allen Krebs, and Jacov Lind.

Despite an impressive list of speakers, this was no ordinary academic meeting. Public lectures were given in the morning, followed by seminars and discussion groups in the afternoon, and movies, poetry, and whatnot in the evening. Looking back two years later, Berke wryly described it as an "anti-congress," with hordes of participants occupying the Roundhouse continuously for sixteen days: "meeting, talking, fucking, fighting, flipping, eating and doing nothing, but all trying to find some way to 'make it' with each other and together seek ways out of what they saw to be a common predicament—the horrors of contemporary existence."

During the conference, the poet Allen Ginsberg, Emmett Grogan, and other like-minded people orchestrated various happenings, which made normal scheduling awkward or irrelevant. Furthermore, the assembled experts were not a homogeneous group, intellectually or politically, and personal differences sometimes broke out during the proceedings. Although he was a conference convener, Laing's behavior was not very gracious. He took a particular dislike to Stokely Carmichael, the spokesman for black power, which he indulged at every opportunity with open displays of sarcasm and disdain. Laing argued that Carmichael's philosophy was no more than reverse racism, an inverted mirror image of the ugliness he wished to eliminate. As the conference progressed, Laing's conduct toward Carmichael became so provocative that, in his closing remarks, David Cooper came to Carmichael's defense. Cooper's carefully worded remarks were mild, conciliatory, and generous to everyone concerned (Cooper, 1967b). But privately he was outraged and remained so for many months to come.

In September 1967, Ronald and Jutta welcomed their first child, Adam, into the world. One month later, on October 7, Laing celebrated his fortieth birthday. Though he had authored a body of work that would do credit to a man twice his age, and had never been more prosperous or celebrated than he was now, it was not a particularly joyous occasion. As he confessed to Anthony Clare some twenty years later, at this stage of his life he was becoming increasingly apprehensive about falling into melancholia, as his father and grandfather had at about the same age (Clare, 1985).

Though quiet and prosperous by comparison with the preceding years, 1968 was be challenging as well. Laing's private practice was flourishing, and he was inundated with requests for interviews on television, radio, and various print media. He worked and partied hard as usual but, for the most part, avoided controversy. Yet as he retreated to the relative peace of domestic life and private practice, the world around him was in turmoil. Race riots were ravaging America; there was guerrilla war in Latin America and massive student unrest in Paris, London, and around the world. The antinuclear movement and the feminist movement were gaining ground, and the war in Vietnam was beginning to turn in the communists' favor. For many people concerned with justice, equality, and social change, it was a time of struggle and fear, hope and sacrifice.

In view of circumstances and of his past performance, many people on the left expected Laing to assume some sort of leadership role or, failing that, lend vocal support to many of the causes making headlines around the world. After all, at Glasgow University, he had studied Marxism and befriended the poet Hugh MacDiarmid, a staunch Stalinist. In the early sixties, Laing published in prestigious left-wing journals. Finally, a year earlier, Laing had appeared on the podium with most of the leading leftist theorists in the west and been treated, rightly or wrongly, as first among equals.

To the naive outsider, it might have seemed as if Laing were positioning himself to assume a leadership role of some kind. Rather than join the fray, however, Laing withdrew altogether from politics. As he later told Douglas Kirsner (1980), his mind was elsewhere, preoccupied with symbolic logic and set theory, interests that were reflected in *The Politics of the Family* (1969) and *Knots* (1970).

But, in 1968, the curious mystique of the Dialectics of Liberation Conference continued to grow, fueled by a Penguin paperback based on the proceedings, edited by David Cooper (1967b). It was an instant success. Unfortunately, in the second paragraph of his introduction to *The Dialectics of Liberation,* Cooper claimed that Laing, Redler, and Berke embraced an approach he termed "antipsychiatry"—a label he had coined to describe his own orientation. Now it was Laing's turn to be furious with Cooper, and this put another strain on their friendship.

In the meantime, encouraged by the success of the Dialectics of Liberation Conference, Berke enticed Laing and Cooper to help found a colorful countercultural institution know as the Anti-

University of London, whose brief and turbulent history is related by Roberta Elzey (1969). Shortly after the conference concluded, an ad hoc committee was formed, and with an interest-free loan of £350 from the Institute of Phenomenological Studies, premises were rented, catalogues printed, and secretarial help enlisted for the cause.

The Anti-University of London opened its doors in Shoreditch on February 12, 1969, offering a wide range of noncredit courses, including Experimental Music (Cornelius Cardew), Demystifying Media (Roberta Elzey), Psychology and Politics (David Cooper), Black Power (Obi Egbuna), Politics of Small Groups (Leon Redler), Anti-Institutions Research Project (Joseph Berke), Family as a Counter-Revolutionary Force (Morton Schatzman), The Connection (Yoko Ono), Dragons (Francis Huxley), and Psychology and Religion (R. D. Laing).

Laing's course was billed as an "exposition of some descriptions of 'inner space' in Greek, Christian and Egyptian mythologies." In fact, as Morton Schatzman recalls, he lectured on mythology and cosmogeny as metaphors for the history of consciousness, borrowing frequently from Robert Graves and Mircea Eliade. And though he didn't list Plato in the catalogue description, Laing discussed the *Republic* and *Laws* at length, arguing that the authoritarian political prescriptions of these dialogues were meant ironically, tongue in cheek—an interpretation that is usually championed by conservatives (such as Leo Strauss).

For the remainder of 1968, Schatzman adds, Laing was fairly obsessed with the Gnostic notions of "Pleroma" and "Creatura"—a concurrent preoccupation of Gregory Bateson's and before him, of course, of Carl Jung's. And as Laing confided to Peter Mezan a year later, he was deeply absorbed in the study of Dionysius the Areopagite, whom he quoted at length in his *Sonnets* (1979).

Judging from his own reports and his activities at the time, then, Laing's dominant mood in 1968 was geared toward contemplation, not action. This is not to say that mysticism, particularly western mysticism, always means withdrawal from the world. As Ernst Bloch demonstrated in *Atheism in Christianity* (1972), if we survey the history of western thought we find that messianic and apocalyptic mysticism frequently engenders radical criticism of the social order, coupled with demands for sweeping changes in property laws, class relations, and sexual practices. Moreover, it is interesting to note that there is an impressive body of scholarship linking Neoplatonism and medieval theology (Dionysius the Areopagite, Duns Scotus, Meister Ekhart) to the philosophical roots of Marxist humanism (Fromm, 1961; Bloch, 1972; Kolakowski, 1981). If Laing was aware of this work, which I doubt, he studiously avoided making any connection between Christian mysticism and social activism.

Though documentary evidence on this point is scarce, Clancy Sigal's 1976 satire suggests that elements of the this-worldly mysticism celebrated by Bloch suffused Laing's thought and private utterances until sometime after the liberation conference, when a brief but alarming immersion in spiritualism and magic heralded a turn away from the hope of earthly transformation to the cultivation of gnosis and an increasingly disembodied spirituality. This impression is reinforced by an interview Laing had in 1969, in which he boasted that, through diligent meditation, he had finally relinquished the misguided identification of a man with his body (Mezan, 1972).

In any case, if actions alone are any indication, the kind of mysticism that is historically conjoined with social activism did not appeal to Laing. By the early seventies, he was distinctly apolitical (Kirsner, 1976). In the meantime the impression created by Laing's earlier pronouncements were creating confusion and controversy. Many people on the left treated this apparent about-face as an interlude, a momentary aberration. Yet by the end of the decade it was clear Laing was becoming less and less interested in exploring the political ramifications of his earlier work. In the interview with Mezan, just before his departure for Ceylon and India, Laing put his cards on the table:

> I was never *political* in an activist sense . . . I suppose when people
> think of me as political they're thinking mainly of the Dialectics of
> Liberation Congress . . . I guess I identified myself with the Left by
> being there, but even at the time I made it clear that I really had no
> idea what would come of such an extraordinary conglomeration of
> people. Politically, I think I am neutral, really. (1972, p. 165)

Though he was rapidly loosing interest in global politics, Laing continued to write and reflect on micropolitical events and processes within the family and the mental health system. Thus in May 1968, he delivered a lecture on "Interventions in Social Situations" to the

Association of Family Caseworkers at the National Institute for Social Work. This talk was subsequently issued by the Philadelphia Association and again, in abbreviated form, in *New Society* (September 1969). Phyllis Webb, who was working for the Canadian Broadcasting System, invited Laing to deliver the annual Massey Lectures over Canadian national radio in November and December 1968. These talks were entitled "The Politics of the Family," and were first published by the CBC in Toronto. With minor alterations, the talks were incorporated into a 1971 edition of the same name from Pantheon Books in New York, along with "Interventions in Social Situations" and several other items. Although Laing's characterization of family life here was still disquieting, the book was to the point and not as bombastic as *Politics of Experience.*

Sometime late in 1968 David Laing was hospitalized for senile dementia in Leverndale Hospital, where he remained until his death a decade later. Watching his father's gradual deterioration was a source of recurrent heartache for Laing, who visited the bedside rather infrequently—much to Amelia's anger and disappointment.

As it happens, his father's hospitalization coincided with a visit from Erich Fromm in early December 1968. Though Laing never spoke about their meeting, to my knowledge, Fromm was deeply impressed with Laing and wrote two glosses on his early work. One of these, appeared in "The Crisis of Psychoanalysis" (1970) and the other, written at the same time, was published posthumously in *The Revision of Psychoanalysis* (1992). Curiously, though, the correspondence between Laing and Fromm, which Laing initiated in 1967 just after his return from America, came to an abrupt halt on December 20, 1968, and there is no evidence of further contact between them.

The year 1968 was also important for the P.A, which went through a series of important changes. This was when Laing and his associates started their gradual but thorough process of de-politicizing their work and ideas, and when Laing and Cooper started drifting in different directions. Others left for other reasons. Despite their involvement with Kingsley Hall, Morton Schatzman and Joseph Berke were denied membership in the P.A. and decided to go their own way. Some new members also came on board that year, among them Francis Huxley, Julian's son and a noted anthropologist in his own right.

Another newcomer to the association was Hugh Crawford, a psychiatrist from Glasgow in his mid-forties. During a twenty-year sojourn in the United States, Crawford developed a strong interest in existential phenomenology, Maurice Merleau-Ponty and Bachelard in particular. Unlike Laing, who was a visionary kind of intellectual, Crawford was a sturdier, more reliable, and more nurturing presence in the therapeutic households that soon came under his care; though passionate about his work, as Laing was, he was not concerned with books or publicity. More to the point, in the following decade Laing and Crawford became good friends. During the mid-to-late seventies, Crawford was someone Laing respected, even when he was strongly disinclined to hear out anyone else in the P.A.

The next year, 1969, witnessed the inauguration of a formal training program for the Philadelphia Association and the publication of another bestseller for Laing, *Knots*. Up to this point, the P.A. had been a charitable organization dedicated to promoting therapeutic communities. Now, in response to public demands and various internal pressures, it began to constitute itself as a training program for psychotherapists. The core curriculum was modeled somewhat on courses at the Anti-University and included extensive readings in Freud, phenomenology, and existentialism, as well as Buddhist meditation and Hatha Yoga.

The P.A.'s move toward an accredited training program displeased David Cooper. After all, the introduction of a formal curriculum, of fee-paying students and a regularly repeated program of lectures issued in the kind of social authority he was intent on overthrowing. So in 1969 Cooper devoted more and more time to a commune of young sexual revolutionaries. Though he did not submit his formal resignation from the P.A. until 1971, in June 1969, at the Conference on Madness at Innis College, University of Toronto, Cooper announced to a large crowd that he and Laing were parting ways—that Laing was on a "spiritual trip" while he was on a political trip, in fact about to leave for Latin America to join the struggle against imperialism.

In April, after months of writing and rewriting, Laing finally finished *Knots,* which appeared in early 1970. His slenderest offering to date, *Knots* was an immediate success. Adrian Laing regards it as a popularization of ideas put forward in *Interpersonal Perception,* published in 1966 (p. 147). And so it is, up to a point. In *Interpersonal Perception* Laing used an algebraic notation for "mapping" the interpersonal experience he had unveiled in *Self and Others,* and applied it to the study of marital conflict. Though dry and difficult even for professionals, *Interpersonal Perception* contained some astute reflections on the difference between genuine and pseudo-conflict, and the problems of detecting and resolving real difficulties or drawing out a deeper consensus in couples (hidden because of blocked communications). Despite the daunting length and complexity of the protocols for his interpersonal perception method—IPM, for short—Laing was basically hopeful about fostering understanding and respect among couples, even in highly conflicted relationships, provided that both partners were honest with themselves and one another.

Interpersonal Perception never got the sustained attention it deserved, even from his Tavistock colleagues. When I spoke with him shortly before his death, in June 1990, John Bowlby assured me that though it was developed and published with the Tavistock's personnel and resources, no one at the institute used it after Laing's departure (around 1967). In any case, it appears that Laing resolved to recast his approach as a form of high-brow literary entertainment; it was mercifully free of the algebraic schemata, but replete with a hyperreflexive, paradoxical, and recursive abstractness that defies ready comprehension or application—a kind of intellectual strip-tease. Here is a page:

> There must be something the matter with him
> > because he would not be acting as he does
> > > unless there was
> > therefore he is acting as he is
> > because there is something the matter with him

> He does not think there is anything the matter with him because
> > one of the things that is
> > the matter with him
> > is that he does not think that there is anything
> > the matter with him
> therefore
> > we have to help him realize that,
> > the fact that he does not think there is anything
> > the matter with him
> > is one of the things that is
> > the matter with him (1970, p. 5)

For someone entering into them in the right frame of mind, the schematic disjunctions of consciousness that Laing provides in *Knots* do possess a certain fascination, even some charm and pathos. But coming as they do from a phenomenologist, they raise the troubling question of how close they are to the texture of lived experience, even though in a prefatory note Laing hopes "they are not so schematized that one may not refer back to the very specific experiences from which they derive." Yet reading *Knots* we do want to know how these maddening patterns were derived. We can never be sure because Laing is more interested in their "final formal elegance" and never puts them into a recognizable context. We may conclude that they are stylized versions of Laing's experience of *other* people's experience of themselves and of significant others, and the connection between the two *as interpreted by Laing*, but without the rich case material found in *Sanity, Madness and the Family*.

Whatever else it was, *Knots* was not a cogent theoretical statement. Nor did it have any practical or potential clinical application. Unlike *Interpersonal Perception*, the new book indicated no way out of all these blind alleys and confusion of tongues, so that even when an underlying pattern does emerge, it is never clear what its elucidation is supposed to do. It is as if Laing the therapist were admitting defeat and retreating to a position of detached bemusement or platonic contemplation of "forms." Unlike his efforts in 1967 and 1968, which bristled with criticism of the social order, this work had no social or political relevance—further evidence of his deepening disengagement.

Still, Laing was proud of *Knots*. It was a new departure and won glowing endorsements from eminent philosophers, mathematicians, and composers, who claimed to know what Laing was going on about. He regarded it as a kind of disembodied music and, in retrospect, as the first installment of his poetic oeuvre. Perhaps this is the best way to view it, as a series of etudes whose message is embedded in the structure of the compositions.

By the end of the sixties, Laing's intellectual output, though quite rich, diverse, and provocative, conveyed the impression that he was coming to an impasse. His first book had emphasized the complicity of the mad in the creation and perpetuation of their own inner demons, but it held out the possibility of authentic relatedness to others as a viable alternative to madness. Though articulated in existential-phenomenological language, *The Divided Self* had an obvious kinship with the views of object-relation theorists, such as Fairbairn and Guntrip, who also adopted the therapeutic project of dismantling schizoid defenses and restoring the person's capacity to relate to others.

Self and Others, while recognizing the complicity of everyone, sane or mad, in their self-estrangement, no longer conceived of madness in intrapsychic or developmental terms and tended to construe the mad as the victims of the largely unconscious machinations of others. Gone was any talk of schizoid personality or process or of restoring relatedness. Despite its many virtues, *Sanity, Madness and the Family* continued in this vein, construing schizophrenics almost entirely as victims of sustained communicational deviance and the contradictory demands and attributions of other family members.

Barring some memorable passages here and there, *The Politics of Experience* lacks the subtlety and lucidity of the earlier work. In defiance of the numbing structures and strictures of normality, Laing seemed to be preaching a weird, unlikely mixture of Heidegger, Sartrean Marxism, and eastern mysticism. But if it did seem to indicate a general direction for change, there was little method in his prescriptions and more important, as Douglas Kirsner noted (1977), few grounds for hope.

Knots, composed at the end of the decade, contained nothing about the family, no social criticism, no prescriptions. It conveys the impression that Laing's anger and hopelessness have been transformed into detachment and resignation. And though it has roots in Laing's earlier work and is clearly a work of great ingenuity, it does not appear to lead anywhere. The question now was, where on earth would Laing go next?

6

BIRTH AND *BEFORE*

Although Laing said little and published nothing save *Knots* in 1970, events from the past began to catch up with him. In 1970 Aaron Esterson published *The Leaves of Spring: Schizophrenia, Family and Sacrifice,* a detailed study of the Danzigs, a family from *Sanity, Madness and the Family.* Esterson's ability as a researcher was never in doubt, but the second part of his book, with his reflections on Marxism, psychoanalysis, and Jewish culture, established him as a theorist in his own right and won him a small but loyal following.

Then Morton Schatzman and Joseph Berke, who had apprenticed at Kingsley Hall, founded the Arbors Association, which embraced the practical-therapeutic side of Laing's project but was (and is) less concerned with exploring the larger theoretical and philosophical questions that preoccupied him. As the decade progressed, Berke and Schatzman published books that were widely read—*Mary Barnes* (1971) and *Soul Murder* (1973). Laing was furious at them for leaving and alleged that Schatzman's ideas were cribbed from some seminars on Freud that Laing had given at Kingsley Hall (Mullan, 1995, p. 199).

Schatzman has written to me recently (1995) about these biweekly seminars. They were held at his flat in 1969 and were attended by Laing, Leon Redler, Hugh Crawford, and Jerome Liss. Included was one discussion session on Daniel Paul Schreber's *Memoirs of My Nervous Illness* and one on Freud's treatment of the case (1911), where Schatzman reported on William Niederland's evidence that the persecutory behavior of Schreber's father had contributed to the son's psychosis. Schatzman writes: "When the seminars ended in December, Laing said to us that the one thing he had learnt from them was Niederland's studies, which he had never heard of before." Over the next few years Schatzman developed a theory about Schreber's paranoia that incorporated the father's harsh childrearing practices and, in 1973, published it in *Soul Murder*. In the book Schatzman did not say that he had first presented the material in the seminars, though he did mention discussions with Laing in the preface. "It never ocurred to me to cite those seminars because none of the ideas in my book had come from them, except for my own presentation of Niederland's work." Redler, also present at the seminars, concurs in this explanation, noting that Schatzman first outlined his new ideas in *The Network Newsletter* in 1970, when Laing was off in Ceylon. Sometimes Laing's memory could be distorted by anger, among other things.

In any event, the die was cast. There was competition afoot, and Laing no longer had a monopoly on the kind of theory or practice associated with his name. Right at this professionally troubled time, Natasha, his second child with Jutta, was born in April.

Then, on May 31, 1970, the controversial experiment at Kingsley Hall came to an end. Mourned by some and cheered by others, the departure from Kingsley Hall was a blessing in disguise for the Philadelphia Association. Over the years, in the public mind the P.A. became nearly synonymous with Kingsley Hall, while Kingsley Hall was identified with the story of a single occupant, Mary Barnes. Her celebrity status fostered envy and competition among the other residents, creating all kinds of crises and interpersonal conflicts that clamored for attention and resolution.

In the quieter, more self-contained therapeutic communities that emerged during the seventies, led by Leon Redler, Paul Zeal, Michael Yockum, and Hugh Crawford, there was no public fanfare accompanying breakdowns, and no premium was placed on the regressed behavior that had beguiled the voyeuristic public earlier on (R. Cooper, et al., 1989). Although Laing himself was only peripherally involved in most of these households, more real healing and recovery took place there than in Kingsley Hall, where public

spectacle and private anguish were so injudiciously mixed. Had
these communities not emerged, the Philadelphia Association would
have crumbled altogether for lack of credibility and self-confidence.[1]

Though it survived the closing of Kingsley Hall and the departure
of Sigal, Cooper, Esterson, and Briskin, the P.A. was now polarized
into two factions, each of which attempted to shape the new psychotherapy training curriculum in its image. The first emphasized
the students' need to encounter specifically western intellectual traditions, especially psychoanalysis and existential phenomenology.
Mysticism and meditation were by no means proscribed, but they
were not encouraged either. This faction was led by John Heaton
and Hugh Crawford.

The other group, led by Francis Huxley and Arthur Balaskas, another of Laing's close friends, was more oriented to yoga, meditation, and shamanism, and in due course to spontaneous group
encounters. Here intellectual discipline was considered secondary to
the pursuit of altered states of consciousness. Laing had a hand in
creating and sustaining both groups. Though he might have objected to the analogy, it may be that the two groups personified different sides of Laing's own character, which also came into conflict
as the seventies wore on.

As the sixties drew to a close, Laing was worn-out and becoming
fed up with always being in the public eye. He decided to take himself and his family for an extended sojourn in India and Ceylon, (Sri
Lanka). Toward the end of 1970 he quietly closed his private practice and spent the first months of 1971 making all the legal, medical,
and financial arrangements necessary for taking a year abroad. The
trip was intended both as a retreat and as a pilgrimage of sorts. Since
the mid-sixties, Laing had been a practitioner of yoga and meditation, and he wanted to explore that path more fully. On March 30,
1971, Laing, Jutta, Adam, and Natasha left London and landed in
Columbo, the capital, where they stayed through late September.

As fate would have it, the conflict between the Hindu Tamils and
the island's Buddhist majority, which would later ravage the country, was just beginning, and the Laings were sometimes within
earshot of the shooting and the general commotion that accompanied this unexpected civil war. When violence broke out nearby, the
Laings moved, but this cautious policy didn't please everyone in the

family. In *Conversations with Adam and Natasha* Laing records a fascinating exchange between himself and three-year-old Adam, dated April 1971:

> *Adam:* I want to go to Kandy and kill people and cut them up and eat them for breakfast with a big steel gun and a stiff trigger.
> *Daddy:* Why?
> *Adam:* Because I want to shoot a lot of people and kill them so they'll be dead. Like I did last time . . .
> *Daddy:* How do you mean, last time?
> *Adam:* Last time I was here.
> *Daddy:* Here?
> *Adam:* Last time I was alive.
> *Daddy:* How do you know?
> *Adam:* I remember. I was a soldier. I killed a lot of people.
> *Daddy:* Really.
> *Adam:* Did you kill a lot of people last time, Daddy?
> *Daddy:* No.
> *Adam:* But did you kill a lot of people a long, long time ago?
> *Daddy:* I may have but I can't remember.
> *Adam:* You can't remember? *(incredulously)*
> *Daddy:* No.
> *Adam:* Oh. (Laing, 1977, p. 4)

Throughout his stay in Ceylon, Laing followed a rigorous routine, eating and sleeping little, studying Sanskrit, and meditating for most of the day. After a period of self-guided meditation, he entered the Kanduboda Meditation Center, near Delgoda, for about eight weeks, meditating for seventeen hours a day under the guidance of an elderly Sinhalese monk, the Venerable Sumatipalo Thera. During brief breaks from meditation practice, he would sometimes converse with Nyanaponika Mahathera, who was a friend and teacher to E. G. Howe, Thomas Merton, and Erich Fromm.

Toward the end of September, Laing and the family left Ceylon for Madras and thence to New Delhi, where he stationed his family at the Asoka Hotel while visiting the Buddhist monastery at Bodgaya. From there, in November, they journeyed to Almora, in Uttar Pradesh. After a brief rest at a local hotel, they traveled a few miles northeast to a place called Crank's Ridge. Their modest cottage, nestled in the midst of breathtaking surroundings, was one of

four on the property, two others being occupied by Wayne and Inge
Whymark, a Canadian couple, and a young American couple, all of
whom were intent on avoiding the usual tourist paths. Though
Wayne Whymark chauffeured Laing around the district and Inge
Whymark played for hours with Adam and Natasha, Laing avoided
the other people there.

Laing and his family stayed at Crank's Ridge for seven months,
the longest stop on their tour. Laing studied intensively with Gangotri Baba, a bearded, loin-clothed ascetic who lived in a wooded
crevice one mile from nearby Nanital. He was not the usual Indian
holy man, however. Though his parents were Indian, Gangotri Baba
was reared as a Roman Catholic and spoke English, French, and
German fluently, with a smattering of Japanese as well as several
Hindu dialects. Before adopting a hermit's life, he had trained in
medicine and played the organ, piano, and bagpipes proficiently
(Evans, 1976, pp. 73–75).

Though well versed in western ways, Gangotri Baba was now an
ardent Hindu who had no patience with Christianity or Buddhism,
which was another reason Laing studied with him. As a Shivite
priest of Kali, the Indian goddess of birth and death, he had access
to pre-Buddhist traditions of yoga and meditation that Laing wished
to experience first hand. To that end, Laing spent three weeks alone
with the guru during the early winter months, at an elevation of
9,000 feet. It was congenial company, though Gangotri Baba was
quite misanthropic, as a rule, and though he spent much of his time
in silence, gathering wood or drawing water from a nearby stream
(Mullan, 1995, pp. 242–245). Like Sumatipalo Thera, the instructor in
Buddhist meditation, Gangotri Baba thought Laing quite gifted, although in a somewhat different direction. Buddhist mediation aims
at the achievement of awareness, detachment, compassion, and ultimately Nirvana. At the end of his session, Sumatipalo Thera cred-
ited Laing with having achieved *sotopanna,* which is a form of
consciousness well along the path to Nirvana. The aim of Shivite
yoga, by contrast, is the acquisition of *siddhis,* or occult powers,
which Gangotri Baba claimed to possess; Laing, he said, would be
capable of cultivating them too, if he wished.

After an interval with his family, Laing returned to the guru's
grotto on January 15, 1972, and Gangotri Baba formally initiated him
into the cult of Kali. The initiation was preceded by a communal

meal in which a cake, symbolizing Laing's body, was burned and eaten, followed by the customary bhongs of hashish and a silent vigil from late evening till sunrise to meditate on the rising and setting of the moon in the Himalayan sky (Whymark, 1992). After a few more nighttime vigils, Laing returned to Crank's Ridge for a month or so to study Sanskrit with a local teacher and to converse with a Tibetan lama who lived nearby.

In late March or early April, Laing and his family went to Banaras, where he met with adepts of various kinds (Irwin, 1989). Then they left for home. Looking back on this period, Laing would speculate that his long absences in meditation and study put an enormous strain on his relationship with Jutta, who was terrified that he would abandon her and the children. Though he didn't, as it happens, he was encouraged to do so by his Buddhist friends and by Gangotri Baba who, like religious recluses everywhere, regarded the world as insane and family ties as fetters on the cultivation of the spirit. Moreover, by his own admission, Laing sometimes felt like pursuing this path, even without any prompting from his Asian mentors.

On April 20, 1972, Laing returned to London, relaxed, refreshed, and in splendid health. As his friends and associates recall, he had never looked better. Jutta and the children were not so happy or healthy, but they were relieved to be home. Unfortunately, Laing's vibrant physical and mental health was short-lived. A mere six months after his return, he had resumed all his old haunts and habits. According to John Heaton, this is because in Asia Laing was a virtual unknown, whereas in London he was a celebrity, whose reputation had, if anything, grown even more during his trip. In other words, Laing's metaidentity—his perception of other people's perception of him, which altered considerably abroad—became a renewed source of pleasure, fascination, and torment, fomenting all kinds of lurid theatrics he would have been better off without.

One of the first indications that Laing was falling back into the old ways was his callous treatment of Sidney Briskin, one of the few founding members of the P.A. who had managed to persevere with Laing into the new decade. During Laing's Asian trip, Briskin organized a highly successful fundraiser for the Philadelphia Association. The event lured hordes of celebrities, generating all kinds of publicity, and raised £3,000, which was later used as a down payment on the Grove, the first Archway community. Laing, who was

incommunicado at the time, was not present to veto, control, or revel in these proceedings and, despite the improved cash flow that resulted, was quite nasty about the entire episode. As John Heaton recalls, Laing urged Hugh Crawford and others to echo his deprecations of Briskin, and the situation became unbearable. Briskin left in 1973. It was a terrible way to repay an old friend, and Heaton resigned in protest, only to be coaxed back into the fold some days later (Heaton, 1990, 1994).

Some might argue that in view of his character and his previous conduct, Laing would have to resume his old ways eventually. Perhaps, but in all fairness, as Adrian Laing points out, the immediate cause of his return to the spotlight was financial. After coming back from India, Laing spoke with André Schiffrin, his American publisher, and discovered that he had made some serious financial blunders, spending money he didn't actually have. Though not yet in serious trouble, he was treading dangerously close to an abyss of debt and would have to act quickly to meet his financial obligations or drastically curtail his affluent lifestyle (pp. 164–165). This he could or would not do. The impending disaster prompted the hasty planning of an American speaking tour from November 5 to December 8, 1972, which Laing made in the company of Danny Halpern, a former heroin addict who acted as a surprisingly effective road manager. The odyssey involved public appearances to packed audiences all across the United States.

The journalist Peter Mezan accompanied Laing and Halpern during much of the trip and wrote a fascinating first-hand account of Laing's talk at Hunter College, his appearance (with Rollo May and Nathan Kline) on the *Dick Cavett Show,* another television appearance with Norman Mailer, and filmed encounters with Oscar Ichazo (a mystic), Steve Roday (a political activist), and Elizabeth Fehr (a midwife/therapist). Judging from Mezan's report, Laing was quite candid about his motives for making the tour and confessed to a beleaguered publicist from Pantheon Books that he regarded his public appearances as pure show business (Evans, 1976).

One amusing part of Mezan's article concerns Laing's reunion with his former hosts at the White Institute, who asked Laing about his Asian experience. This prompted a long, rambling discourse on his spiritual development from the age of fourteen up. As the institute's director, Earl Witenberg, told me later, in the interval between his first and second appearances there, most of the analysts at the White had become more skeptical of Laing and his work, and nothing Laing said or did now changed this attitude.

Still this did not deter his steadfast admirer, John Schimel, from giving Laing and his entourage the use of his home in Gramercy Park. In an interview in 1991, Schimel and his wife Phyllis vividly described the chaotic Laing party, which included publicists, agents, admirers, and a remarkably composed and professional film crew led by the filmmaker Peter Robinson. As the Schimels recalled, Laing conducted discussions with people from all across the country, who flew in at odd hours very late at night or early in the morning. He had nothing resembling a regular pattern of sleep, though when he had an hour or so to himself, he retired to his room and played Bach or Scarlatti on a clavichord.

After several weeks of hectic travel, Laing collapsed under the strain. None of the specialists consulted could figure out what was wrong. It is hard to imagine a more dramatic contrast in lifestyles for Laing in 1972. From January to April of that year, he was a disciplined and private person, never far from his family and staying put for two or three weeks at a time. After India he became a major celebrity again, who traveled great distances quickly, slept and ate at irregular intervals, and punctuated his public appearances with intoxicating revelries of staggering proportions.

Another noteworthy feature of the American tour was a new note of conservatism, which Mezan duly noted. Addressing one political activist, for example, Laing said:

> I don't see any way whereby one can take power without overpowering the people who have it with more power. So by the same token that one judges their power to be evil, ours would be a greater evil. And I don't think it's a matter of opinion. Its a mathematical certainty. All power corrupts, and absolute power corrupts absolutely. One would necessarily become more corrupt than they. (Evans, p. lxvi)

Along the same lines, he continued:

> . . . Marx was an enormously alienated man. One of his children died of pneumonia and starvation because he wouldn't deign to spend a few hours a week writing articles. One's got to take that into consideration before one considers him an example to emulate. Having seen

that, I'd expect any present day revolutionary not to fuck up his own
family in the course of pursuing his revolutionary interests. And I
wouldn't entirely trust the large scale vision of a man who had such an
area of blindness. Any Marxism I subscribed to would have to include
among its essential, primary aims the setting of one's own family
aright, and not doing one at the expense of the other. Again and again
I see the lives and families of revolutionaries are as screwed up as any I
can imagine. If they're going to be serious, they're going to have to
stop that. (p. lxviii)

Laing's new attitude toward the family caused a great deal of confusion. Why would someone who had attacked the family as the
"enemy of Eros" seek to rescue it from the neglect and hostility of
misguided revolutionaries? Some saw this apparent change of heart
as a cynical attempt to please a changing mass market. There is
something in this, but it is not the whole truth. Laing's remarks on
the family now were just as heartfelt and genuine as his earlier dia-
tribes. Perhaps more so, in fact. In any event, because of statements
like this, and others like it, Laing came in for some serious scrutiny
on the left and, by the end of the seventies, was the subject of articulate critiques by Peter Sedgwick (1971), Juliet Mitchell (1975), and
Andrew Collier (1976).

Laing returned from his American adventure with the requisite
cash in hand. But he was exhausted, and no doubt toxic from all the
alcohol and drugs he had consumed abroad. Despite his vibrant
state of health only a few months before, he was ensnared in the
pleasures and pains of drink and drugs once more. His weaknesses
were intensified by the discovery, in the spring of 1973, that Jutta was
having an affair, possibly in retaliation for Laing's many absences. It
was a dreadful irony. Having rejected the embrace of the militant
left and the brotherhood of otherworldly ascetics, having returned
at last to the family fold, Laing found himself a cuckold. As Adrian
Laing recalls, the shock nearly killed him (p. 176). Despite their marriage on February 14, 1974, and the birth of Max, their third child,
on June 24, 1975, their relationship continued to go downhill.

Although the debt crisis of 1972 was averted, Laing's financial
troubles grew over the next decade, as book sales declined, particularly in the United States. Another reason was that, as the seventies
progressed, Laing did not pursue his private practice with the same

energy or dedication. But the next major squeeze did not materialize until 1980 or so. Despite falling book sales, he was still considered bankable and received large advances on several books in progress.

Now, in the hope of averting future difficulties, Laing launched a protracted campaign to transform his public image, from psychotherapist/philosopher to poet/philosopher. As Thompson and Heaton recall, he was strongly encouraged by Jutta Laing and Francis Huxley, who disparaged the more staid, clinically minded members of the P.A. So, by the mid-seventies, Laing had distanced himself from many of his colleagues, while continuing to branch out in a theatrical direction. In 1973, he produced a film about natural childbirth and, somewhat later, an engaging television tour of Glasgow. These interesting (but commercially unsuccessful) efforts were followed by a series of disappointing flops, including a musical show based on his *Do You Love Me?,* a tedious record album based on his book of *Sonnets* (1979), called *Life Before Death,* and numerous musical recitals and poetry readings of uncertain quality (A. Laing, chap. 18). To ease his cash-flow problem, he even wrote a personal advice column for the British edition of *Cosmopolitan* magazine and hired an agent, Barry Seale (Thompson, 1994, personal communication).

Despite Laing's best efforts, these projects failed to generate the requisite response: the public didn't welcome Laing's metamorphosis and continued to think of him as the "old" Laing, or else not at all. In retrospect, Laing's declining fortunes were partly the result of mismanagement and profligacy, overexposure, and the decline of the sixties' counterculture. And in dramatic contrast to the preceding decade, his writing no longer came easily. By 1973 Laing was openly complaining of writer's block and of an increasing inability even to sit down at the typewriter (for instance, Laing, 1976, p. 53).

Reports on Laing's state of mind during the latter half of this decade are strikingly diverse. Emmy van Deurzen Smith, who lived and worked in one of the P.A. houses, found Laing reticent and withdrawn, "engaged in battles with deep inner confusion" (1991). Others who sought him out as a teacher or supervisor report similar experiences. According to one close companion, in unguarded moments Laing sometimes confessed to an overwhelming sense of world-weariness, of having seen and understood too much and changed the world too little—a desire, in fact, to die and be done with it.

The latter seventies were marked by another shattering heartbreak. Toward the end of 1975, Laing's favorite daughter Susan, who was twenty-one and engaged to be married, was diagnosed with monoblastic leukemia. She died in 1976, and Laing's handling of the situation sparked off another round of bitter recriminations between Laing and his first wife, Anne, which soon involved the whole family and no doubt brought back many of the old unresolved conflicts (A. Laing, pp. 180–181). Perhaps the death of his daughter, and of his father two years later, contributed to Laing's deepening religiosity in this period of his life. Roger Brooke, professor of psychology at Duquesne University, was in London in 1979, visiting one of Hugh Crawford's houses, and attended a sermon Laing gave in a church near his home on Eton Road. Laing lashed out at those who had come only to hear him speak and were thereby desecrating a house of worship with idolatry.

Judging from these reports, one might infer that, after Susan's death, Laing was in desperate shape, possibly on the verge of collapse. In actual fact, though Laing had his share of rage and anguish, he also enjoyed some interludes of relative peace, when he seemed quietly optimistic, with none of the vehement despair of *Politics of Experience*. Michael Thompson, who was secretary of the P.A. from 1973 to 1980, reports that during most of this time Laing appeared to enjoy life considerably, claiming to have reached a level of contentment that had always eluded him.

After his return from the United States in 1972, Laing started developing a new angle on psychotherapy, one he took to group settings. But, in actuality, the new angle was not at all new. As Laing himself said, he derived the inspiration for this phase of his work from a variety of sources, including Freud, Otto Rank, Francis Mott, E. G. Howe, Arthur Janov, and last but not least Elizabeth Fehr, the American midwife who introduced him to the practice of rebirthing. Rather than blazing a new path into unknown territory, Laing was now following in *their* footsteps. Perhaps he hoped that, by putting an original spin on their work, he could capitalize on the craze for birth-oriented therapies that followed upon Janov's bestselling *The Primal Scream* (1968). Or perhaps he hoped that he could use the new approach on himself, to gain some leverage against his own inner demons. Some evidence for this assertion comes from William Swartley, who headed a network of primal-therapy practitioners in

Canada and United States (the Center for the Whole Person). Swartley toured Europe in fall of 1975 and, in a newsletter to his colleagues and patients, informed them that in London,

> I spent an afternoon with Ronnie Laing . . . Ronnie showed me the galley proof of his next book [*The Facts of Life*], which will assure him a role in the history of psychotherapy as the discoverer of the "implantation primal" (my term, not his), similar to the status of Otto Rank with the birth trauma. Reviewers opinions will vary from concluding that he has finally gone completely mad to speculating that the whole book is some type of mystic message. In any case, Ronnie had a lot of trouble attaching himself to the wall of his mother's uterus eight days after his conception . . . All that was clear is that Ronnie had such a will to be born . . . that he overcame her strong reluctance to the idea. (Swartley, 1975, p. 1)[2]

It may be that *The Facts of Life* was an attempt to provide a rationale for Laing's evolving conjectures about his own history. This heightens one's feeling that many of the clinical vignettes he presents here refer to himself, not to patients. In view of Laing's early development, this fantasy—qua fantasy—makes a certain amount of sense. Much of Amelia's behavior after he was born *was* thoroughly invalidating and might have been annihilating had it not been for the boy's will to survive.

Still, how Laing (or anyone else) could know what transpired in Amelia Laing's uterus shortly after his conception is beyond comprehension. What is most troubling about this theory is its literalism. During the sixties, Laing emphasized the hidden truth of fantasy, once its fidelity to the contours of lived experience is made plain. Seen in context, a neurotic's fantasies or a psychotic's delusions may be intelligible as symbolic representations of actual states of affairs. Now, though, Laing was not treating fantasy as a meaningful codification of a postnatal experience, but as an historical event or process he remembered. This *was* a new departure. In *The Divided Self* Laing had said:

> Biological birth is a definitive act whereby the infant organism is precipitated into the world. There it is, a new baby, a new biological entity, real and alive, from our point of view. But what of the baby's point of view? Under usual circumstances, the physical birth of a new

living organism . . . inaugurates rapidly ongoing processes whereby
within an amazingly short time the infant *feels* real and alive and has a
sense of being an entity, with continuity in time and a location in
space. In short, physical birth and biological aliveness are followed by
the baby becoming existentially born as real and alive. (1960, p. 41)

Existential birth, or the emergence of the self, is something that fol-
lows birth. But the later Laing went on to endow zygotes with memory and, by implication, a certain psychological subjectivity: birth is
not a definitive act but merely "implantation in reverse" (1976,
p. 46). Considering the vast difference in neurophysiological complexity between a fertilized ovum and an infant in utero ready for
delivery, one can only wonder at the oddity of this notion.

In support of his peculiar conjectures, Laing argued that memory
is not situated entirely in the brain and central nervous system, but
in each individual cell of the body. This kind of cellular memory—
for which there is, indeed, some evidence—would presumably account for the organism's ability to store and retrieve impressions
from intrauterine life. But as Laing himself admitted on occasion,
his memory of relatively recent events, even important ones, was
often fickle. So why credit this particular memory?

At the risk of overstating the case, there are at least three more
problems with Laing's theories about prenatal experience. Despite
Freud's awareness of birth dreams, which Laing discussed in detail
(1982, chap. 5), Freud thought that personality formation begins
after birth and that the most decisive traumas for subsequent development occur at the age of three or four. Melanie Klein, by contrast,
argued that the decisive events occur at six to eighteen months. Otto
Rank speculated that the decisive trauma occurs during the birth
process itself. Considered in this light, Laing's "implantation primal," as Swartley termed it, is the logical extension of a collective
tendency among analytic theorists to push the decisive trauma back
to its earliest beginning.

But this tendency to push things back plays into the questionable
clinical ideology which holds that earlier traumas are necessarily
more profound or more decisive than recent ones, or that later conflicts—whether inner or interpersonal—are simply symbolic reen-
actments of earlier ones. This is sometimes, but not always, the case,
and in many instances the single-minded search to uncover earlier

traumas to explain symptoms only provides therapists with a chance to show off their virtuosity. This in turn furnishes patients with handy rationalizations for continuing to evade current *existential* problems.

Another objection to Laing's theory is that an inhospitable intrauterine environment is by no means indicative of a mother's ambivalence or hostility toward her potential offspring. There is no denying that prenatal stresses have an impact on newborns. But to suggest that prenatal stresses almost always stem from conscious or unconscious conflict in the mother, rather than from chance physiological disorders, is both unwarranted and an insult to the many women who suffer from infertility or problems in carrying their babies to term. So even if a person could "remember" an implantation trauma, there is no reason to presume that adverse circumstances occurring within the womb were the product of some antipathy on the mother's part.

In view of Laing's state of mind during the 1970s, and his earlier theories about physical and existential birth, it strikes me that his extravagant conjectures about his own intrauterine experience were a product of displacement, projecting feelings from the postnatal environment backward to the first weeks of conception, implantation, and so on. It also became a potent metaphor for his current stasis and all the adult problems of living in the world. The decade was one of extremes for Laing. One of his poems in the plaintive *Do You Love Me?* (1976) opens with "I die forlorn/I was not born," and ends "I'm past mending/I'm a happy ending."

None of this means that all of Laing's work during the seventies should be dismissed. Though he was preoccupied with rebirthing, Laing continued to embellish older ideas and to scatter fresh insights along the way. Still it is clear that his creativity was dwindling, as his books became increasingly self-referential. For devoted followers, this posed no problem. But Laing's new theoretical and stylistic departures didn't attract new readers, and many of the old ones dropped away.

To complicate matters, some of Laing's associates in the Philadelphia Association viewed his rebirthing phase with suspicion and, in due course, with outright hostility. Many saw it as a lamentable departure from the philosophical groundwork Laing had laid in the previous decade. Not all of them felt this way, however. Francis

Huxley said that the departure represented a deepening of Laing's
shamanistic consciousness. Arthur Balaskas and the body-oriented
therapy faction in the Philadelphia Association embraced the new
ideas enthusiastically and incorporated them into an eclectic repertoire of yoga, meditation, and primal screaming sessions.³

Throughout the late seventies, Laing, Arthur Balaskas, and Janet
Balaskas ran numerous workshops and seminars, involving vigorous
hands-on individual and group activities. Though never codified or
formalized, these rebirthing sessions acquired some of the characteristics of a tribal ritual, in a curious combination of intimacy,
anonymity, catharsis, and exultation. Because of the inevitable
weeping, tremors, convulsions, and trances that accompanied the
sessions, Laing saw to it that these features were balanced by out-
pourings of song, dance, and rhythmic drumming. Although the
therapeutic aims of these gatherings may have been inflated, there is
no doubt that they furnished engrossing experiences for the participants, who had a collective sense of belonging to a groundbreaking
avant-garde. They also helped to keep Laing's waning optimism
alive and compensated somewhat for the dwindling attention of the
general public. As a result, unless you were already part of his inner
circle, the only way to get close to Laing during the late seventies
was to join him in this chaotic song and dance.

Whatever its rationale, Laing's enthusiasm for rebirthing soon lost
all semblance of balance. On August 17, 1978, with the help of
Michael Thompson, Laing organized a program billed as "An Encounter with Carl Rogers and R. D. Laing," which he hoped would
be a major moneymaking event. After some difficult negotiations between Laing, Rogers, and their respective coworkers, the workshop
finally convened in the Grand Ballroom of the London Hilton Hotel
in Mayfair. The turnout was disappointing. Rogers spoke for a
while, and then Laing spent over an hour ridiculing Rogers for denying the existence of evil and for the banality of his other ideas.
Rogers was so taken aback by Laing's attack that he couldn't muster
a cogent defense. Even if he had, he probably wouldn't have had
time to deliver it, because Laing got up and offered to demonstrate
his most recent therapeutic techniques. Those who wanted to could
join in; those who did not could watch.

With the aid of several assistants, Laing then proceeded to "rebirth" two hundred people, many of whom had come just for that

purpose. This bizarre spectacle turned a modest flop into a total disgrace. Many observers saw the proceedings as nothing more than an exercise in mass hypnosis and a mercenary way to make some money. The idea of doing psychotherapy en masse disturbed many members of the P.A., who felt that their name had been used to betray everything they stood for—and what Laing, in better days, had stood for as well.

As the 1970s unfolded, then, Laing encountered a number of converging crises: a credibility crisis, a crisis of creativity and self-confidence, a financial crisis, and a marital crisis in 1980. Since these difficulties compounded one another in so many ways, it is impossible to deal with them singly or sequentially. But in reviewing the decade as a whole, it is important to realize that they did not always intrude on his daily life and that Laing did enjoy periods of relative calm and satisfaction, when life was sweet and his old demons seemed at rest.

In terms of the crises, though, the roots of Laing's loss of credibility went back to the late sixties. His utterances on the family, psychiatry, politics, and mysticism created a public image that became difficult to sustain. One reason was that Laing preached an essentially Buddhist ethos of gentle austerity, nonviolence, and reflection. But as the seventies wore on, his public appearances—often sloppy, provocative, or tedious—were motivated by his increasingly desperate need for cash. Laing was seen as an impulsive, disorganized, and generally intemperate man, who couldn't care less about what others thought of him as long as he collected his fee.

Another factor is that, as Adrian Laing points out, many former associates—Cooper, Esterson, Berke, Schatzman—were now writing books and setting up therapeutic communities of their own, shattering Laing's monopoly on the kind of discourse that he, more than anyone, had started. In addition, Laing alienated a large part of his former constituency by veering away from political issues and turning around his position on the family, blasting it in *The Politics of Experience,* and embracing it a few years later. Laing could never live that down.

Finally, by the late seventies, Laing's retreat from private practice and his increasing involvement with flamboyant group marathons

split the P.A. in two. Many former friends and collaborators felt that
Laing was living out too many personal contradictions and could no
longer be taken seriously. If Laing were to change these views, he
would have to recant some of the things he had said, provide the
public with some new and cogent reflections on the issues that had
made him famous, and heal the rifts in the organization he had created. But none of this could he do.

It seems plausible to suppose that, after his return from Asia,
Laing's renewed reliance on drink and drugs was fueled by his waning creativity and his declining popularity. For though he detested
much of the publicity he received, and claimed to have seen through
the illusion of fame (Evans, pp. lxxi), he still depended on public attention both for his livelihood and for his sense of worth. Though he
may have been reluctant to admit it, the public's flagging attention
troubled him deeply. As he put it in a 1978 poem (*Sonnets*, p. 22),
"I'm nothing now I've lost my funky charm."

7

𝓕ADE TO BLACK

The eighties were a decade of growing obscurity for R. D. Laing, marked by more financial troubles, another bitter divorce, and the dissolution of many old friendships. The first year was punctuated by three events, all of them with dire consequences: the closing of the Archway communities, the death of Hugh Crawford, and a three-week conference on psychotherapy in Saragossa, Spain.

In 1970 the Archway communities had emerged from the ruins of Kingsley Hall under the guidance of Leon Redler, Paul Zeal, and Michael Yokum, and at one point there were as many as nine houses. Though Laing's involvement was peripheral, the Archway network's effectiveness did much to shore up the Philadelphia Association.[1] By the late seventies, however, Yokum and Zeal were gone. Organization and enthusiasm lagged, and there were financial crises. When long-suffering Leon Redler, exhausted from years of overwork, finally withdrew, the Archway project fell apart, leaving only one residence behind, the Grove. Though this did not affect Laing too much personally, it had a dramatic effect on the Philadelphia Association as a whole and exacerbated the friction between Laing and the others.

The threat to morale posed by Archway's demise was compounded by the death of Hugh Crawford, which led to the closing of another cluster of communities in Portland Road. In addition to being a gifted therapist, Crawford had played a large role in ameliorating tensions between Laing and other P.A. members, and he had also counseled Ronald and Jutta over many a bottle of scotch. As John Heaton recalls, Crawford was one of the few people left in Laing's circle who could tell him when he had gone too far. Though some were upset by Laing's apparent lack of sympathy for Crawford during his final days, other P.A. members remember Crawford's death as an event that triggered serious bouts of drinking and abuse.

Despite a shaky beginning to the final decade of his life, in September 1980 Laing had composed himself sufficiently to turn in a creditable performance at the International Conference in Humanistic Psychology at the Monasterio de Piedro, in Saragossa. During the conference Laing was formulating many of the arguments found later in *The Voice of Experience* (1982). Throughout 1981 Laing worked on the book, which he hoped would ensure his comeback as a respectable intellectual. On one level, his effort paid off. Although there is some incredibly bizarre material in the book, it is balanced by considerable insight, sagacity, and cogent argument. Chapters 1 to 4 return to themes from his earlier work, including the chasm between the dehumanizing clinical standpoint and the subjective-experiential approach. In chapters 5 through 12 (and the coda), Laing turned to his more recent preoccupation with prenatal experience and birth, but without the crude literalism that plagued *The Facts of Life*. Anthony Clare, the well-known psychiatrist, called the book "remarkable," which itself is a remarkable statement in view of what Laing said about psychiatry there.

In July 1981, as he was working on *Voice of Experience,* Laing received a call from Roberta Russell, whom he had met at Saragossa. Russell had heard from a mutual friend that Laing was beset by financial and marital problems and thought that he might benefit financially from writing about some of the ideas contained in her recent book, *Report on Effective Psychotherapy: Legislative Testimony,* based on a report she made for the National Accreditation Association and the American Examining Board of Psychoanalysis (Russell, 1981). After conducting an extensive search of the literature and many interviews with patients and therapists, Russell concluded that the key to effective psychotherapy is not the theoretical orientation of the therapist or his years of training and experience. What facilitates change and recovery is the degree of congruence between the values and attitudes of therapist and patient and, above all, the therapist's willingness to engage fully with the patient as a human being. It is the alliance between the patient and the therapist (as perceived by the patient) that is the best predictor of a successful outcome.

Laing sympathized with this point of view. Five years earlier he had cited an American study conducted under the auspices of the National Institute of Mental Health, which appeared to show that sympathetic housewives with a little coaching could perform psychotherapy as effectively as seasoned professionals. Using this study as a point of departure, Laing went on to speculate that many of the best virtues are actually "cultured out" in novice therapists in the process of training (Evans, 1976, part 4).

Instead of writing a book on this theme, as Russell urged, Laing thought they might collaborate. She proposed a book on therapeutic alliances in a non-professional setting, using their own relationship as a model of how to go about it. But when Russell arrived in London on November 2, Laing was in the midst of another domestic crisis. It seemed that Jutta's affections had again strayed elsewhere (Russell, 1992, p. 161). A day or two prior to Russell's arrival, Laing accidentally discovered that Jutta had a clandestine affair while they were at the Saragossa conference, and he was shattered by the revelation (see, for instance, A. Laing, p. 208).

This was not Jutta's first infidelity, nor is it certain that Laing was altogether faithful to her. But the fact remains that certain aspects of Jutta's conduct in this affair came as a shock to Laing. As he later told Michael Thompson, it altered his perception of Jutta irreversibly and left him wondering if he had really known her at all or if he had simply been blinded by love during all the years they lived together. This must have been an enormous blow to Laing's confidence in his powers of judgment. In the past he had often remarked that love is a lucid awareness of the other person in her essential suchness, free of the illusions generated by hatred, fear, and greed or the desire to turn her into something she is not. And unlike indifference—which frequently masquerades as objectivity and sanctions all kinds of violence—love discloses depths in the loved one that are invisible to others. But if that were so, how could Laing make sense of his relationship to Jutta before his disillusionment?

Those thoughts came later, however. In the meantime Laing was still reacting to the new discovery and trying to figure out how to respond. In short, from the standpoint of intellectual work, Roberta Russell could not have arrived at a worse time. Reading the transcripts of their initial conversations, one gets the impression that it was a difficult encounter. Though Russell had been clear about her intentions, and her aim of engaging Laing in co-counseling, Laing flatly declared that he didn't want to change and that the desire to change—rather than to accept—oneself is symptomatic of a deeper existential problem, a lack of genuine self-knowledge.

No doubt Laing's response was attributable to the anger and confusion occasioned by his marital problems. Sensing this, Russell—who was by now in love with Laing—persisted and used the very problems in their relationship as an opportunity for deeper self-exploration. Despite her feelings for him, Russell did not idolize Laing. She found him mercenary and querulous at times, and full of bitter disappointment and an aching addiction to fame.

Though they got off to a terrible start, in time Laing dropped his defensive posture, and as his marriage unraveled, a sustaining friendship ensued and Laing became eager to see their conversations published. *R. D. Laing and Me: Lessons in Love* (1992) is the only collaboration Laing ever undertook with a woman and the only one in which he does not appear as first author. In view of the books that precede it, it is an unusual collaboration, with Russell doing most of the work, blending the self-help and confessional genres in a curious but thoughtful and engaging way. It is also a loving and candid look at Ronald Laing *in extremis,* at his most abrasive and his most vulnerable.

In the summer of 1981, Laing also met Sue Sunkel, a psychotherapist in training at the Institute of Psychotherapy and Social Studies, where Laing was doing some summer teaching. Despite an immediate attraction, Sunkel remembers feeling overwhelmed by Laing's intense anguish over his disintegrating marriage. Though nominally separated, Laing and Jutta continued to share the house at 2 Eton Road. Laing and Sunkel never lived together, but they were a couple for about a year and had a child, Benjamin, born on September 15, 1984. They separated amicably some six months or so after Benjamin's birth, and Laing stayed in regular contact over the years with both mother and son.

Despite the new loves in his life, by 1982 Laing was in very bad shape. John Heaton reports that he was so drunk on two occasions that he assaulted some residents in the P.A.'s few remaining houses (personal communication, 1990). This prompted Heaton (and Chris and Haya Oakley) to lobby for Laing's resignation. Their efforts resulted in a collective refusal to endorse Laing as chairman at the Philadelphia Association's annual meeting in December 1982. Though an honorary consultantship was offered, Laing would not stay on in that capacity and after a year of inconclusive bickering, left in anger.

In response to this uproar, Arthur Balaskas, Francis Huxley, and many other people in the Philadelphia Association's extended network scolded and pleaded for Laing, but to no avail. When their efforts proved fruitless, they left or drifted away, taking the whole birthing and yoga contingent with them and leaving the remaining members to reconstitute themselves as an institute for analytically oriented therapeutic training.[2] Only Leon Redler avoided this collective polarization, remaining on speaking terms with both factions, albeit at the cost of great personal anguish.

As the organization Laing founded was being torn in two, Jutta was publicly consorting with a younger man (Russell, p. 234). Since Ronald and Jutta both refused to leave Eton Road, they decided to have the house partitioned, an effort that disfigured a once elegant home. Division and discord were the order of the day, and participants in the groups run by Laing that year vividly remember the wild pain and rage he often expressed. And it got worse. On November 14, 1983, Laing was scheduled to give a talk to the Oxford Psycho-Analytical Forum, on "Theoretical Influences, from Klein to Bion." To guarantee his presence, Brett Kahr and a colleague drove from Oxford to London to escort Laing in person. To the consternation of his hosts, during the ride back Laing smoked a large hashish cigarette and swigged from a bottle of Calvados. Once at the podium in Oxford, he was greeted with thunderous applause and proceeded to pace up and down the stage for several minutes in an apparent effort to gather his thoughts. He said something disparaging and inconsequential about Klein, stopped abruptly, and started to fiddle with his teeth. He continued jiggling and tugging at one particular tooth until he finally dislodged it, declaring the lecture at an end. Then he embarked on a massive pub crawl that ended in Ascott Farmhouse, a home for former psychiatric patients sponsored by the P.A. (Kahr, 1994).

Like its predecessor, 1984 was a very bad year, despite the relationships with Roberta Russell and Sue Sunkel. On September 18, 1984, he was arrested not far from Eton Road around midnight. He was walking home from a party and impulsively hurled a wine bottle through the window of a local Bhagwan Shree Rajneesh ashram, then sat down on the sidewalk until the police came and arrested him. At the station the police emptied Laing's pockets and discovered a small quantity of hashish (A. Laing, p. 215).

Laing's son Adrian, now a barrister, was called in to help and, despite Laing's monumental stubbornness and his drunken outbursts against the authorities, finally managed to persuade his father to plead guilty. With the aid of independent counsel, Peter Morrish, Laing negotiated a twelve-month conditional discharge on November 27. Though it was not apparent at the time, this episode proved to be the first in a series of events that resulted in Laing's expulsion from the medical profession. We can only wonder what compelled him to throw caution to the winds in such a disastrous way.

Despite their bitter separation, and the newly built walls between them, Laing still shared 2 Eton Road with Jutta. In view of the ashram's proximity to their divided home, this provocation may have been a misguided attempt to bring matters with Jutta to a head. The episode could also be interpreted as a measure of the disturbance caused by Laing's rift with the Philadelphia Association and the disappointing sales of *Voice of Experience,* which he had hoped would revive his career.

Ricki Hornstein, a neighbor and friend of the Laing family, remembers that for two weeks before the bottle-throwing incident, Laing had stalked around her apartment on at least three occasions, denouncing Rajneesh and angrily demanding to know what this man had done to deserve the adoration of so many thousands of followers. Laing was obviously envious of Rajneesh. So perhaps when his envy reached unmanageable proportions, he hurled the bottle (Hornstein, personal communication, 1992). If that was the primary reason, it is another sorry illustration of Laing's craving for fame and recognition.

Laing's provocations did not stop here. One month later, in October 1984, Dr. Stephen Ticktin invited Laing to join him and a well-known person in the mental health field at a local wine bar for a musical evening. Laing arrived with Leon Redler and two female companions, and they proceeded to have a reasonably friendly get-together. To top off the evening, Ticktin's friend suggested a nightcap in his flat. Laing was drinking very heavily and soon got into a heated verbal exchange with his host about the origins of World War II. Being fifteen years Laing's senior and a former communist at Cambridge, Ticktin's friend was not about to be lectured to, not even by the great R. D. Laing. Things looked ominous until Ticktin diffused the situation by pulling out his guitar and playing a few songs that Laing liked particularly well.

At one in the morning, their host announced that he was going to bed and asked his guests to leave. Laing insisted on staying and rudely told the others to do as they liked. Scarcely had he finished saying these words when Laing's host turned on him and knocked out another tooth. Redler and Ticktin bundled Laing out of the flat; when he came to the next day, he blamed Ticktin and his friend for the whole affair.

Sometime in December 1984, Laing finally left Eton Road, and moved to a flat in Maida Vale with his secretary, Marguerite Romayne-Kendon. A native of New Zealand, Marguerite had lived in England since November 1979. Before her job with Laing, she spent several years in Tehran, teaching yoga in Switzerland and Yugoslavia, and assisting a Tibetan lama with the translation of esoteric texts. Though they were never formally married, Marguerite was Laing's constant companion for the remainder of his life, and the mother of his tenth child, Charles, born on January 6, 1988. By all accounts, Laing was very much devoted to his last child.

Laing and Marguerite shared many interests, and one project they embarked on together was variously named Sanctuary, Oran's Trust, or St. Oran's Trust, after a myth-enshrouded Pict warrior (or druid) who converted to Christianity and created a sanctuary for criminals on the island of Orsonay in Scotland. One of their closest associates in this venture was a former monk and a friend of Marguerite's, Kevin O'Sullivan, who became close to Laing. Others involved in the undertaking were Bernard Spalding, Stephen Ticktin, Mina Semyon, and Elena Zanger.

A pamphlet published in 1984 stated that the aim of the trust was to create residential accommodations for people whose lives had become a source of distress to themselves and to others. It went on to describe plans to establish permanent sanctuaries in major cities and in the countryside; to create a central secretariat, library, student center, and resource network. It was an ambitious enterprise, along the lines of the Philadelphia Association.

One of the first people Laing approached to get Oran's Trust off the ground was Sidney Briskin, who well remembers the charm and enthusiasm of Laing's effort to bring him around. Briskin declined to get involved. Despite the shabby treatment he had doled out to this former patient, friend, and fundraiser, Laing was genuinely surprised and hurt at the refusal. His astonishing naiveté points to a strange combination of innocence, aggression, and forgetfulness that could only be sustained by a great deal of denial. Lacking competent fundraising and organizational skills, the Oran's Trust project eventually collapsed.

Up to this point, the eighties had been little more than a dreary series of disappointments. So Laing took special pleasure when on February 25, 1985, his portrait, painted by Victoria Crowe, was unveiled at the National Portrait Gallery in Edinburgh. Despite his raucous conduct in recent years, he was gracious, engaging, and sober throughout the whole event and the accompanying reception (A. Laing, p. 219).

Laing's last book, *Wisdom, Madness and Folly: The Making of a Psychiatrist,* also appeared in 1985 and purported to be an account of his life from birth (and before) to the age of twenty-seven. It was intended as the first of two volumes, but it sold poorly and he never began the second one. In his biography Adrian Laing notes that *Wisdom, Madness and Folly* contains some egregious factual errors and some contradictory assertions regarding David and Amelia Laing, and he infers from this that the book was designed to paint its author as a victim of childhood cruelty and to misrepresent the circumstances of his upbringing (pp. 220–221). While there are indeed errors, contradictions, and omissions in the book—including resounding silences on his romance with Marcelle Vincent, his courtship of Anne Hearne, his friendships with Hutchison, Duffy, Davidson, and others—it cannot be dismissed so easily. With all its defects, *Wisdom, Madness and Folly* gives us an illuminating glimpse into the thoughts and feelings of the brilliant young author of *The Divided Self,* who was wrestling with ethical and epistemological questions that are as relevant today as they were in the fifties. Written in 1984, it also indicates that despite his many heartaches and angry actions, Laing did have some relatively calm intervals that year, which enabled him to work productively.

Another person who was deeply impressed with *Wisdom, Madness and Folly* was Anthony Clare, who invited Laing to do a radio interview on his series *In the Psychiatrist's Chair.* To Clare's surprise, Laing agreed, and their remarkable dialogue was broadcast on July 14, 1985. Clare began the program by giving a brief account of Laing's career and his critique of psychiatry, and asked why Laing agreed to do the interview. Curiously enough, Laing responded that he found the theme of the series quite congenial and potentially useful to people "in our line of business." When pressed, Laing denied that he had ever said that psychiatrists were as deranged as their patients and insisted that he had never been opposed to psychiatric drugs as long as they were not administered involuntarily.

Needless to say, dedicated Laing watchers of old might contest the truth or sincerity of these statements. But accurate or not, they do attest to Laing's desire to be seen as a member of the psychiatric guild rather than as an anti-psychiatrist, which was how he was still portrayed. In response to Clare's probing but sympathetic questions, Laing went on to divulge a great deal about his past life and current state of mind. He admitted that his marriage was in ruins and that he entertained some sad thoughts on problems of faith. But unless you were already deeply hostile toward him, this was not the sort of thing that would put Laing's mental stability in question.

Laing did not stop there, however. He also admitted that he was prone to paralyzing depressive spells and that he sometimes drank to the point where, on waking, he couldn't remember the events of the night before. Though he denied that his drinking impaired his effectiveness as a psychotherapist, he hinted that his occasional blackouts—which he described with a burst of laughter—had prompted him to consider total sobriety as a next step.

Laing's candor was commendable from a personal point of view. But when it came to the attention of the General Medical Council, which regulates the medical profession in Britain, the doctors were not amused. Laing had offended too many of his colleagues far too long for anyone to be reassured by his attempts at collegiality or rapprochement. Very soon they would let him know it.

In December 1985, Laing attended a prestigious gathering of mental health professionals in Phoenix, Arizona, on "The Evolution of

Psychotherapy." Among those attending were Thomas Szasz, Bruno Bettelheim, Rollo May, Judd Marmor, James Bugenthal, Virginia Satir, Jay Haley, Salvador Minuchin, Carl Rogers, Murray Bowen, and Joseph Wolpe. Despite several challenges from participants and the press, as Michael Thompson reports, Laing was courteous and composed throughout.

But on his return to London in January 1986, Laing was confronted with a letter from the General Medical Council. It outlined a complaint lodged by a patient who alleged that he had been intoxicated and unprofessional on two occasions. His fitness to practice medicine was open to doubt. Adrian Laing was notified, and father and son strategized together about how to handle the situation. As usual, Adrian had to cajole and admonish his father not to indulge in gratuitous gestures of defiance, to address the problem with the seriousness it deserved, and finally to seek independent counsel. Although the initial complaint was dropped eventually, the General Medical Council continued its investigation, citing Laing's prior arrest and his public confession of alcohol abuse on the radio (A. Laing, pp. 225–227).

As the council was deliberating, Laing left London for Burch House, a Laing-inspired residential retreat in rural New Hampshire, run by a former student and friend, David Goldblatt. On November 10, 1986, around 10:00 P.M., Laing received a message that his mother was dying in a Glasgow hospital, and he asked Goldblatt to inquire after her because he wasn't up to placing the call himself. Over the telephone an attending nurse informed Goldblatt that Laing's mother had passed away an hour or so before. Laing told Goldblatt to ask if anyone had been there, and the nurse replied that Amelia had died alone.

On hearing of his mother's death, Laing wept briefly and then declared stoutly that his biggest regret in life was that he had not hurt his mother more. After a few moments' silence, he and Goldblatt moved toward the piano in an adjacent room where they sang an old Victorian song Laing was fond of, "A Boy's Best Friend Is His Mother" (Goldblatt, 1994, personal communication). The following morning, Laing made travel arrangements and returned to Glasgow. He wept uncontrollably at the service for Amelia and, despite mounting money problems, spent lavish sums in a riotous reunion with John Duffy, Lennie Davidson, and his first family.

When the wake and the reunion were over, Laing returned to
New Hampshire to work on a new book, *The Lies of Love: A Study
of Sexual Jealousy and Deception.* As Michael Thompson recalls,
Laing embarked on this project at the urging of Rollo May, who felt
that writing a book of this kind might help Laing to purge himself of
the pain that continued to plague him in connection with the separation from Jutta. Whether Laing was helped is open to doubt: *The
Lies of Love,* which remains unpublished, is appallingly trite and dis-
jointed.

On July 26, 1986, David Cooper, who was fifty-five, died of a heart
attack in Paris. By all accounts, he literally drank himself to death,
and Laing did not attend the funeral. Perhaps he lacked the time or
money or was uneasy at the prospect of encountering Cooper's
friends and followers, who might try to elicit a last gesture of solidarity. Perhaps he feared being hounded by some avid journalist
seeking a definitive statement on anti-psychiatry. Perhaps he feared
a similar end, drinking himself to death. In any case, Douglas
Kirsner, a friend of both men, found Laing quite cold when discussing his former associate's death. There was a subdued ferocity
and a barely concealed scorn for Cooper in Laing's tone that was
odd and unnerving.

By March 1987, the General Medical Council had completed its
inquiry and on March 31, Laing—who was at the Naropa Institute in
Boulder, Colorado—was invited to withdraw his name from the register of practicing physicians in Great Britain "voluntarily," with no
penalty or censure. In exchange they offered him the opportunity of
rejoining the profession later, if he could demonstrate his fitness to
practice. Laing promptly withdrew. By April 1987, Laing was a once-
famous man with no profession, no fixed address, and no funds.
Moreover, despite efforts to sober up, his health was failing and he
knew it.

In the summer of 1987 Laing decided to leave London for an envi-
ronment that would be more conducive to giving up alcohol. He
and Marguerite rented a flat in the town of Going, in the Austrian
Tyrol, where he continued to work on *Lies of Love.* A frequent visi-
tor to their flat was a former student of Laing's, Theodor Itten, from
St. Gallen, Switzerland, who talks about a vivid transformation in
Laing before his death. As Clancy Sigal, among others, has noted,
Laing was generally averse to doing any kind of domestic work.

Now, for the first time in his life, Laing busied himself with domestic chores, washing dishes, chopping wood, tending Charles, and he actually seemed to enjoy it. Itten recollects that Laing was warm and optimistic, and deeply sad and thoughtful by turns. He claimed to be sober and planned to stay that way till the day he died. And though he acknowledged the possibility of imminent death, he spoke with great enthusiasm about his latest schemes, as if he had many years ahead of him.

Early in 1988, Laing was approached by Bob Mullan, professor of applied social studies at the University of Wales in Swansea, and a producer at Anglia television, for permission to write an authorized biography. Laing agreed and was interviewed by Mullan for several hundred tape-recorded hours. The edited transcripts of these conversations were published after Laing's death in *Mad To Be Normal: Conversations with R. D. Laing* (1995). Mullan justifiably characterizes this book as a sequel to *Wisdom, Madness and Folly,* or "the memoir he never lived to write."

In response to Mullan's questioning, Laing delved into the relationship between his parents, between his parents and himself, his musical education, his university studies, his training in neurology and psychiatry, his first love, his first marriage, his analytic training, the founding of the Philadelphia Association, Mary Barnes and Kingsley Hall, the dialectics of liberation conference, his relationships with mentors and colleagues, his differences with Leary and Alpert, his attitudes toward critics, and more.

Notably absent, however, are in-depth discussions of the troubling events of the 1980s. The period that goes unchronicled is inconsequential, as far as intellectual output is concerned. In all fairness to Mullan, Laing may have been unwilling to discuss it because of the painful emotions involved. Still, these years are part of the bigger picture and add to a general understanding of his life. Another problem with Mullan's book is that, through no fault of his own, the sole source of information on R. D. Laing is Laing himself. Although Laing speaks with authority and is cogent throughout, sometimes his account of events clashes with those of his teachers, contemporaries, and family, and sometimes he is transparently self-serving.

Nevertheless, *Mad To Be Normal* gives us a wealth of new information and a vivid impression of the breadth of Laing's mind and

the passion, lucidity, and integrity he brought to his work. Though
his memory is sometimes slanted and selective, this is Laing's authentic voice, and we are lucky to hear it.

As he was working with Mullan, Laing was also trying to put the pieces of his life back together. He reached out to his estranged children and renewed contact with some old friends and allies he had abandoned, alienated, or simply lost touch with. One such person was James Templeton, another army psychiatrist who had known Laing in grammar school. While visiting his Aunt Ethel between March 7 and 11, 1989, Laing stayed at Templeton's home in Largs and, as Templeton recalls, was warm, lucid, full of impish humor, and completely sober.

A few months later, vacationing in Europe, Laing met an American psychologist, Robert Firestone. In St. Tropez on August 23, 1989, Laing and Firestone played tennis in the grueling summer heat. Laing competed with his customary ferocity and was leading four games to one when he collapsed on the court with a heart attack. Efforts to revive him failed; he was only sixty-two. A few days later, Laing was buried a short walk from the home of his daughter Karen in Glasgow. There was a funeral service in Glasgow Cathedral and memorial services in London, New York, and other cities around the world.

Despite a few strident dismissals, there was a strong measure of convergence among the many tributes and reminiscences that flooded the British and American press after Laing's death. Despite differences in emphasis, they all praise *The Divided Self,* Laing's first book, and lament the decline in creative power that seemed to follow on his increasing infatuation with fame. One piece, by Clancy Sigal, noted:

> Games . . . were central to Laing's outlook. His notions—that you might actually enjoy a part of your inner torment, and that misery, if handled gently and with humor could yield profoundly therapeutic insights—threw me temporarily off balance. But, true to his word, he pitched himself headlong into all kinds of role reversals that I found both awkward and appealing. During our sessions together, anything went. . . .

Laing died only a day or two after the Black Panther leader Huey Newton was shot to death on a drug-infested street in Oakland, California. They had in common an inner violence that was never satisfactorily purged. They also shared a terrific charm, a potential for greatness and an inability to break out of whatever sacred madness it was that happened in the Sixties. In the heaven he did not believe in, or in the hell he thought he existed in only on this despised earth, I hope he is as wryly amused as I am that he should have passed away while playing tennis in St. Tropez. He always told me normal life was the most dangerous. (*The Independent,* August 30, 1989)

James Hood, who knew Laing in the Glasgow University Moutaineering Club, reached farther back in his recollections:

We were contemporaries at Glasgow University, and afterwards as psychoanalysts in training in London. Our ways did not diverge until the mid Sixties, when Laing was living in Kingsley Hall . . .

I consider that the publication of *The Divided Self* marked a . . . turning-point in British psychiatry . . . largely because Laing was able to collate, digest, synthesize and crystallize ideas that were already current or latent in continental Europe and North America. Laing's originality lay in his power to complete the task and in his capacity to present the ideas which had by then become his, with clinical illustrations, in such a way that a very large number of people were persuaded, and continue to be persuaded, that he was right. (*The Independent,* August 29, 1989)

The psychiatrist Anthony Storr had only a nodding acquaintance with Laing, but he arrived at a similar assessment:

[*The Divided Self*] was a triumphant success, and deserved to be so. Laing had an unrivalled capacity for empathy with the alienated and psychotic . . . He felt that the diagnostic process was itself demeaning. Labelling the patient mad and the psychiatrist sane increased the distance between them, and compounded the sense of being alienated and misunderstood . . .

Unfortunately, the world-wide success of his early books transformed him from a psychiatrist into a prophet. His insistence on treating the discourse of schizophrenics as true led to his losing his own capacity for objectivity. A schizophrenic's statement that his family is persecuting him may validly reflect his own experience; but it does not follow that his family is in fact responsible for his illness. (*The Observer,* August 27, 1989)

Morton Schatzman was a bit more generous in assessing Laing's later work:

> As a political libertarian, Laing thought everyone, even psychotics, must be free to decide where, how and with whom they spend their time. Once, at a formal meeting of Irish psychiatrists, he said that people were put into mental hospitals not because they were suffering, but because they were insufferable. It was not received well . . .
>
> The main thrust of Laing's work was upon our understanding of schizophrenia, and this is one area where his legacy must be judged. The prevailing view today is that whatever schizophrenia is, it is almost certainly a brain disorder, and probably has a genetic component. However, there is much about this disorder upon which the scientific jury is still deliberating. (1990)

The following year, James Gordon, an American psychiatrist, wrote a lengthy article in the *Psychiatric Times* (April 1990). He said that Laing's contribution to the understanding of mental disturbance transcends diagnostic categories—that more than schizophrenia is illuminated by his work. Having read the obituaries in the press, Gordon complained that most of Laing's critics were ungenerous. It makes no sense, he observed,

> to tax any pioneer with not having covered all of truth's bases or anticipated its mutations. Laing's problem was less the incompleteness or inaccuracy of his perspective than it was his difficulty in expanding or growing beyond it.
>
> Laing, I think, allowed himself to be limited not by the refutations and attacks he expected, but by the unexpected adulation he received. The delicate balance between the pessimism and mistrust that were relics of his childhood and the hopefulness that galvanized his work was upset by his extraordinary reception and the demands it put upon him. Like the schizoid patients he had described 30 years before in *The Divided Self,* he was in retreat from those who wanted to define him, to make him their own. But in his retreat, he cut himself off from what had infused his work with life—his capacity for disciplined empathy, his willingness to look at social situations with great intelli-

gence and freshness, and his sustained engagement with troubled and troubling people. (1990)

Finally, some months later, Joseph Berke published an appreciation of Laing in the *British Journal of Psychotherapy:*

Ronnie usually identified with the underdog. He saw his patients as a sort of emotional proletariat, in Fanon's terms, "the wretched of the earth," fighting to survive an unjust and oppressive family or a capitalist or institutional "system." But I think this is an area where he can and should be criticized. He tended to idealize the patient and overlook the damage that this person, as an active agent in an extended family drama, was able to inflict on his parents and siblings. Now the worm has turned the other way, and groups like the National Fellowship for Schizophrenia tend to exonerate the family and blame the diagnosed member for causing all the difficulties. Neither view is correct . . .

A second factor which Ronnie overlooked was the damage that his patients did to him. Over the years he saw many terribly wounded, but also wounding, individuals, and this seems to have contributed to a certain callousness and self-abuse as time went by. He began to respect the pain rather than the person. He neglected the impact that personal notoriety could have on himself and others. These are problems that can afflict the most experienced therapist. They did not pass him by.

Thirdly, I think Ronnie overestimated the healing potential of a psychotic regression. It may be a way that some individuals shed their false selves and achieve a new and vital relationship with themselves and the outside world. This is a phenomenon which Jung, Winnicott and Balint, among others, have observed and described. Yet, more often than not, malicious intentions fuel the breakdown of the self and contribute to a negative outcome. Ironically, it may be that Ronnie's failure to explore the destructive functions of regression has contributed to the present unwillingness on the part of many therapists to appreciate that some types of psychosis are self-limiting and enriching. (1990, p. 176)

There is merit to Berke's claim that Laing's need to identify with the underdog issued in a tendency to idealize madness, and it contributed mightily to the present climate of opinion in psychiatry,

which is hostile to Laingian ideas. One of the tragic ironies of
Laing's life is that his brief but incredible hold on the public imagination galvanized the current reaction against communication-
oriented research or therapy for schizophrenia. The anti-Laingian
reaction is so well organized and so militant that Laingian approaches, which were clearly catching on in the early seventies, have
been rendered marginal in the field today. The deliberate neglect of
Loren Mosher's highly successful therapeutic community, Soteria
House, is a signal case in point.[3]

Then, too, there is merit in Gordon's observations on the deleteri-
ous effects of fame on Laing. Laing's difficulty in handling criticism
was apparent to everyone, but his inability to handle fame—and the
gradual loss of fame—requires a deeper knowledge of the man.
Laing was not only a passive recipient of the public's uncritical adu-
lation. Despite his repeated claims to have transcended the desire
for fame, he actively cultivated this kind of response and was not
above playing to the gallery, even though he scorned the kind of uncritical enthusiasm engendered in the process.

What led Laing to behave like this? The simplest answer is that it
filled his pocketbook and fed his ego. But that isn't the whole truth.
From boyhood on, Laing was skeptical of other people's ideas about
him. He realized that the Ronald Laing whom other people experienced as being or behaving in certain ways was not who he really
was. In the Sartrean terminology the early Laing preferred, his
being-for-himself and his being-for-others were never properly
aligned. Or, as he might have said around 1966, his identity and his
metaidentity were divergent.

Judging from his writings in the seventies, Laing never stopped
feeling that way, except perhaps in brief interludes. One wonders
whether Laing used his fleeting fame and wealth to compensate himself for the trials of his childhood. The problem with this interpretation is that it depicts the adult Laing as the victim of childhood
deprivation, rather than of his own greed and egotism. Both interpretations—Laing as glutton, Laing as victim—are half-truths. It is
simplistic to see his hunger for fame as a substitute for the unconditional love he missed as a child. As an existentialist, Laing was committed to the view that individuals are not merely the creatures of
circumstance or environment, but play an active role in shaping the
kind of the person they become.

If we take all this into account, we are now confronted by the possibility that the split in Laing between his public and private selves was at first a strategy developed to protect his sanity. No one knows what he would have been like in less trying circumstances, when he might not have felt compelled to adapt in this manner. In time, however, the strategy became a character trait, a way of being-in-the-world, which he embraced and was unwilling to part with, even when it wreaked havoc in his life. But let us leave that troubled life behind and proceed to a closer study of Laing's thought. Despite some notable problems, there is still much to explore and to celebrate in his work.

8

A TOPOGRAPHY OF $\mathcal{B}$ABEL

Whatever we may think about the vagaries of R. D. Laing's life, his body of work covers an impressive area, including theories of madness, schizophrenia, transpersonal defenses, and more generally the whole interpersonal approach to the human mind. Before looking at his contributions, it may be useful to survey the field and to map the boundaries of the schools or models that exist today. No contribution as extensive as Laing's can avoid touching all of these paths.

In terms of conceptual underpinnings, the mental health field can be divided into six basic models of human nature, with corresponding methods of research and remedial intervention. These models cut across professional and disciplinary boundaries (psychiatry, psychology, social work) and frequently overlap. Yet for heuristic purposes, and for clarity and economy of exposition, it is advisable to treat them separately and to recognize that while hybrids and compromises exist, each model has its loyal and committed adherents.

The models are (1) the neurobiological or medical model, (2) the behaviorist model, (3) the cognitive and information-processing model, (4) the psychoanalytic model, (5) the existential-phenomenological model, and (6) the social-constructivist model. These models can be compared in at least four dimensions: the kinds of causal factors they stress in the shaping of human behavior; whether they situate the sources of disordered thoughts, feelings, or behavior inside or outside the individual; how they define psychological health and disorder; and what degree of active agency or responsiveness they deem characteristic of human beings.

Briefly, the _neurobiological or medical model_ holds that the way we think, feel, and behave is determined primarily by biological events and processes that occur within the body or brain of the individual. Though the environment is understood to play a facilitating or injurious role, when some gross disorder occurs the locus of pathology, or the source of the disturbance, is situated squarely inside the body and the brain, and remedial interventions are tailored accordingly. Health is defined by the absence of morbidity, or a defect or deficiency in the basic structures, tissues, and regulatory systems of the body according to age- and gender-specific norms that are presumed to be universal, with minor local variations. Illness is defined as an organismic dysfunction, which is ascertained diagnostically by degrees of deviance from the aforementioned criteria.

While medicine and neurology have sometimes regarded the organism as passive and reactive—thanks in part to Cartesian mechanism, the ideas of Sherrington, Hughlings-Jackson, and Pavlov—the consensus among neurologists today is that the organism is essentially active in relation to its environment, and that even simple perceptions involve complex (albeit unconscious) processes of searching, tracking, configuring, and such—something that idealist philosophers like Leibniz and Kant realized long ago (Luria, 1973; Burston, 1986; Gardner, 1987).

In dramatic contrast to the medical model, the _behaviorist model_ holds that behavior determines thought and feeling. And how we behave, in turn, is determined by environmental contingencies and the schedules of positive and negative reinforcement that obtain randomly in nature or society or, in the laboratory, by design. In this model, events and processes occurring inside the organism or mind are bracketed as irrelevant or as mere epiphenomena, such as B. F. Skinner's "black box" concept. Moreover, in behaviorism, past events or environmental conditions are deemed insignificant in comparison to current circumstances in the shaping of behavior.

Significantly, by its very nature, the behaviorist model lacks intrinsic criteria by which to differentiate between health and illness. Inasmuch as all recurrent patterns of behavior are the product of conditioning, "behavior is behavior is behavior." That being so, for a thoroughgoing behaviorist the only cogent rationale for develop-

ing interventions are those based on personal or social expediency,
custom and convention, common sense or social control. (Behavior-
ists offer different rationales for treatment, such as the patient's happiness and well being, but these come from other ideas and values.
They are themselves not grounded in their scientific outlook.)

Finally, radical behaviorism regards all organisms as essentially
passive automata that respond reflexively to stimuli from without.
Disregarding the vastly different constraints and capacities inherent
in different animal species, stemming from evolution and cortical
development, they construe more complex and purposeful activities
of the mind and brain, and the many inflections of human personality, as simply more and more complex bundles or aggregations of
conditioned reflexes and, therefore, as differing only in complexity,
not in kind, from the behavior of rats, pigeons, and worms.

The *cognitive model* of human behavior holds that what we think,
and how we think, determines how we feel and behave in the world
around us. In this cognitivist view, human beings are primarily
information-processing entities, and sound cognitive strategies issue
in favorable organismic, social, and environmental outcomes. Conversely, irrational beliefs and expectations lead to specific kinds of
bias, error, and selective inattention, which lead in turn to maladaptive behavior.

Unlike the behaviorist model, with which it is often associated in
North America, the cognitive model tends to situate the source of
disturbance in the individual, albeit not primarily in the body or
brain as such. Its criteria for demarcating health from disorder are
not medical but commonsensical. Is the person happy? Does she
think and behave rationally and adaptively? Its view of the mind as a
problem-solving apparatus means that the mind (and the organism
that sustains it) is goal-directed, oriented to the world in an active
manner, and capable of independent initiative.

Having said that, I should also point out that cognitivism is never
a single, monolithic entity. For heuristic purposes, the cognitive field
can be divided along several different axes, which serve to highlight
differences in the theoretical inflections and backgrounds of its theorists. To begin with, the field can be divided into those who model
human cognition by analogy with computers, information-processing
machines, and those who dislike the machine analogy and subscribe
to a more organismic point of view (such as Jean Piaget, Michael

Polanyi, Howard Gardner). Contemporary cognitivists can also be grouped according to those who promote updated, mostly American versions of pragmatism, rationalism, and individualism (such as Albert Ellis, and Aron Beck) those who synthesize continental traditions such as idealism, empiricism, and dialectical thought (Polanyi, Piaget), and those who regard individual rationality, such as it is, as merely a more local and differentiated expression of a rationality that suffuses the whole natural order (Polanyi, Bateson).

Finally, cognitive theorists can be differentiated according to those who regard the unconscious dimension of information processing as relatively superficial and accessible to introspective awareness, except in pathological instances, and those who regard information processing as "deep" and difficult to access or reconstruct, either in health or in illness.[1]

By contrast with cognitivism, which emphasizes the primacy of thought over feeling, the _psychoanalytic model_ asserts the primacy of affect. For the analytic theorist, how we feel and what we wish for—unconsciously, for the most part—determines what and how we think, and how we are likely to experience the world around us. A further stipulation is that our current feelings, wishes, and experiences are largely determined by past experiences, and that the cause of personal idiosyncrasies can be found in the individual's life history. Analytic theory insists that when organic pathology is not present—and often when it is too—the content or pattern of disordered thoughts, feelings, and behavior emanates from a repressed conflict between disparate needs and desires.

In analytic theory, unconscious emotional conflict can give rise to symptoms that mimic those of organic illness (conversion hysteria) or exacerbate and even create illness in their own right (psychosomatic disease). Ideally, therapy consists in bringing unconscious conflicts to consciousness through free association, dream interpretation, and so on. But when the problem is too severe, the best solution is to aid, not undo, the forces of repression and to strengthen the person's defensive and adaptive capabilities.

Unlike the other models, psychoanalytic theories vary considerably in the degree to which they situate the sources of pathology inside or outside the individual. In theory, Freud always emphasized the interaction between constitutional and environmental factors. In practice, however, his early theories have an environmentalist cast,

while his later work veers sharply toward biological determinism.
Since Freud's day, influential theorists such as Melanie Klein have
taken Freud's reliance on endogenous factors to far extremes.

As for the assessment of health and illness, psychoanalysis is noto-
riously vague. Some theorists, following Heinz Hartmann, insist that
psychological health consists in the adaptation of the ego to its surroundings, with the absence of disturbing symptoms (depression,
anxiety, sexual dysfunction. antisocial behavior). This essentially
negative definition of health enjoys wide currency, chiefly for its
pragmatism. Other theorists insist that a well-adapted persona is by
no means a proof of health. In many instances, the absence of manifest pathology may result from a false self superimposed on an impoverished, confused, and undeveloped real self, repressed early on
in the person's development in response to environmental demands.
As such, it conceals a profound personal tragedy, which is no less
real for being disowned or disguised on the level of appearances.

Alternatively, some think that an adapted persona may be indicative not of personal misfortune but of a more widespread phenomenon, determined by faulty or excessive socialization. Conformity, for
example, an incapacity to think critically and question authority,
may constitute evidence of a *socially patterned defect,* to borrow
Fromm's term.

On one point, though, psychoanalysis is not in the least ambiguous. Like the neurobiological model, from which it emerged historically, psychoanalysis sees the organism as always striving. In
Freudian theory, dreams preserve the state of sleep by deflecting
spontaneous impulses (hunger, thirst, lust, fear, anger) that would
otherwise rouse the person to consciousness along (hallucinatory)
sensory pathways. This would not be necessary if the organism were
simply an automaton activated by external pressures. Paradoxically,
even Freud's principle of constancy, the tendency to reduce internal
tensions to the absolute minimum, is a drive, a pattern of dynamic
striving, that can never be shut off or relinquished save at death. As
long as we are alive, we are driven, even if the ultimate goal of our
striving is quiescence or the death of desire (Freud, 1920).

Although intended as a mode of clinical psychopathology from the
outset, analytic theory had a tendency to generalize its conflict model
of dreams, symptoms, and so on, to all types of human conduct. Thus
all human behavior represents the direct or indirect expression of

some instinctual urge to action, a conflict between two instincts or groups of instincts, and so on. Freud's tendency to generalize indiscriminately from neurotic symptomatology gave analytic theory a determinist orientation, which was congruent with nineteenth-century materialism but out of step today. This tendency was first expressed in Freud's principle of psychic determinism, which states that all psychic events and processes are shaped by the confluence of and conflict between unconscious needs and desires, or by specific instinctual motives that are not immediately present to consciousness.[2]

A more balanced expression of this same determinism was Freud's later insistence that the executive side of the personality, the ego, is simply a more differentiated portion of the instinctual id. This formulation leaves some scope for autonomous choice or volition on the ego's part, but it is still limited. For the most part, the ego does not pose its own problems and objectives, so to speak, but must solve the problems posed for it by the insistent demands of the id and superego. The ego's domain of choice consists of where and how it will placate, deflect, or negate the id and superego in compliance with the demands of reality. It cannot freely elect to have the desires or fears that prompt it to action. And while it can somewhat modify the environment to comply with its own needs, it can only do so only if it has wrested enough energy from the id. In short, in classical theory the autonomy of the ego is a precarious and essentially relative affair.

Though it is seldom construed in this light, least of all by Laing, ego psychology is an attempt to escape the deterministic and increasingly fatalistic features of classical Freudianism by granting the ego greater scope for autonomous action. This results in a more positive definition of psychological health, since the absence of manifest pathology was now predicated on the presence of a strong enough ego. Whether this idea of a conflict-free sphere of ego operation is a logical extension of classical Freudianism, as Hartmann alleged, is debatable (Fromm, 1970). Even so, ego psychology won widespread acceptance in North America because of its more optimistic and voluntaristic outlook. A similar tendency can be found in the so-called interpersonal schools of Fromm, Karen Horney, and Sullivan, which did not hide their differences with Freud and therefore won their way into the analytic mainstream gradually and against considerable resistance.

Of all the various approaches, the *existential-phenomenological model* is the most difficult to summarize. Arguably, it is not a model so much as a broad spectrum of approaches to psychology and psychiatry that arose in response to Freudian determinism and to any approach that can be called behaviorist. This creates confusion for laypeople, who hear or read of thinkers (or therapists) labeled variously as "existential," "phenomenological," "existential-phenomenological," or even "existential humanists."

It might help to note that mental health professionals who espouse such definitions tend to draw heavily on continental philosophy, chiefly from the works of Kierkegaard, Nietzsche, Husserl, Heidegger, Buber, Marcel, Sartre, Merleau-Ponty, and Levinas. Despite their individual differences, what unites these philosophers is an emphasis on the primacy of lived experience and on one or more of the following themes:

1. Certain human needs and experiences, such as the search for meaning, authenticity, or transcendence, are universal; and they are not an outgrowth of biological needs but are rooted in the "human condition."
2. The primary determinants of human behavior do not lie in the person's past or in biological processes, but in the way the person relates to their *Mitwelt,* their interpersonal environments and contexts, and their ability to envisage a viable future.
3. The direction of any human life is shaped as much by the person's choices and intentions as it is by heredity or environment.
4. Many of Freud's core constructs, such as the id-ego-superego triumvirate and the unconscious, are useful heuristic fictions at best and, at worst, reified abstractions that distort the interpersonal nexus, the primary datum of all psychology.
5. There is a marked or exclusive preference for qualitative over quantitative research methods, based on the conviction that our way of being-in-the-world, which includes choice, self-consciousness, and the awareness of death, precludes the heavy-handed application of methods derived from the natural sciences, i.e. that the human or behavioral sciences require their own distinct methodology.

Humanistic psychologists subscribe to some of these principles as well, but they are less philosophically inclined and characteristically emphasize that all human beings strive to realize their latent emotional, intellectual, and spiritual potential, and that human happiness is contingent on this process of self-actualization. The existential outlook emphasizes the inevitability of suffering and values authenticity as the chief human virtue. By contrast, humanistic theorists believe that the seemingly pervasive role of suffering, and of inner and interpersonal conflict, can be transcended by a robust sense of well-being conferred through becoming self-actualized. Whereas the existentialist glamorizes anxiety and despair, the humanist's tendency to predicate personal happiness on self-actualization can also be profoundly misleading. Many people are quite happy without beginning to realize their manifold potentialities, and many who are committed to self-actualization can also be profoundly unhappy.

Many ideas that germinated in the existential-phenomenological and humanist camps are now featured in the writings of well-known psychoanalysts. Fromm, for one, placed equal emphasis on authenticity and self-actualization, and tried to harmonize these commitments with a continuing fidelity to Freud (Burston, 1991). Indeed, psychoanalysis and existential phenomenology have been engaged in a deepening and fruitful dialogue ever since the late 1920s. Accordingly, in summarizing the differences between these models and psychoanalysis, I am deliberately overlooking the more recent inflections of existentialism, phenomenology, and humanism to be found in the analytic corpus, particularly in self-psychology; I use classical Freudianism as the basis for comparison.[3]

According to the existential-phenomenological outlook, the basic determinants of human behavior reside not in the past but in the present, in the kinds of choices people make to shape their future. In addition to environmental contingencies and instincts—both of which are genuine springs to action in their own right—people are motivated by specifically human needs, whose denial is likely to be pathogenic. Characteristically, the existential-phenomenological approach locates disturbance neither inside the individual nor outside, but in the area between: the interpersonal field. Health and illness are defined not by the level of adaptation but by the quality of relatedness between self and others, by the capacity to assume responsibility for one's actions and choices and by the preponderance of honesty and authenticity over self-deception.

Obviously, in a world like ours, the hierarchy of needs, interests, and principles created by such criteria of psychological health put a premium on integrity and sincerity at the expense of adaptation, and when acutely felt and acted on, they are not necessarily a recipe for happiness. Still most existentialists would insist that real happiness is impossible without authenticity, regardless of the satisfactions afforded by the environment.

Finally, we come to the *social-constructivist model.* Though it is rapidly gaining ground in America, it too has roots in continental philosophy but with a greater emphasis on the social sciences, especially the later Marx, Wundt, Durkheim, G. H. Mead, Lev Vygotsky, the later Heidegger, Lévi-Strauss, Goffman, Bateson, Lacan, Jules Henry, Foucault, Thomas Szasz, and more.

This school is divided into two camps, which overlap somewhat in practice but should be kept distinct for our purposes. One camp, the "micro-constructivists," has been influenced by anthropology, sociology, cybernetics, and systems theory. It has an essentially interactive approach to individual problems in living. Many of the problems and processes that are characteristically ascribed to individual psychopathology in the medical and analytic models are not so much the products of organic illness or of distorted psychodynamic functions, but of pathological communications or structural defects within the person's family and social network; the so-called identified patient becomes the scapegoat or lightning rod for collective psychopathology.

Of course, none of these theorists would deny that being a scapegoat has tragically debilitating effects on a person's well-being, which can then be assessed medically or analytically. The point is, however, that they regard these as the symptoms and not the causes of the real disorder that permeates every aspect of the person's familial or social network.

Another group, which can be called the "macro-constructivists," has been influenced more by such disciplines as political economy and cross-cultural studies. These theorists believe that the causes of individual disturbances are primarily (or exclusively) social, economic, and political in character, reflecting structural inequalities in the distribution of power. So the various nosological schemes used to describe the varieties of mental anguish and deviance are not neutral scientific describers of underlying disease entities, but social constructs that serve specific functions such as role definition or the allocation of resources, control and oppression of disenfranchised groups, including racial and sexual minorities. Hence the social roles and remedial interventions mandated by institutions designed to segregate and treat the mentally disturbed tend to perpetuate or indeed manufacture the very symptoms of what they are supposed to heal.

So far, the macro-constructivists and micro-constructivists sound pretty much alike. Theoretically, the two approaches can be reconciled simply by supposing that the structural problems that afflict individuals in their immediate setting (say, the family) reflect broader sociopolitical tensions. In practice, however, many people subscribing to variants of micro-constructivist theory prefer to regard the family as more or less a closed system.

Furthermore, these ideas are all loosely compatible with the perspectives of some theorists committed to an existential or humanist approach. Yet a fundamental incompatibility emerges when we examine the axiomatic assumptions of a second, more extreme group of macro-constructivists. This small but increasingly influential subgroup is greatly influenced by structuralism and poststructuralism, deconstructionism, postmodernism, and Lacanian theory. Radical macro-constructivists hold that the self, so called, is a social artifact, if not a complete (but convenient) fiction. The very idea of a universal human nature, a transhistorical, cross-cultural "essence" shared by all, is a corollary delusion. So any attempt to frame a normative conception of psychological health and disturbance is repressive, naive, enthnocentric, and ultimately futile.

In short, social constructivism of the extreme variety posits no binding or universal criteria for psychological health and illness, nor does it allow for the existence of a generic substrate to human experience. The self is a chimera, a creature of social pressures and conventions. (Note the resemblance to behaviorism.) Since it does not recognize the existence of mental illness as such, or as something that exists independently of the social order, it tends to attribute the cause of all human suffering and confusion to social evils like scarcity, domination, racism, sexism, and so on, leaving individual agency out of the picture.

Consciously or otherwise, radical constructivists have broken with the existential-phenomenological position, although some of them continue to regard phenomenology as a useful propaedeutic to their own work. Their American counterparts, in psychology especially, pay comparatively little attention to European antecedents and contemporaries, stressing certain currents of indigenous thought (Richard Rorty, Kenneth Gergen, Edward Sampson).

Note that I have labeled the six approaches "models of human nature," not of "mental illness," because they purport to explain more than the deviant or pathological manifestations of human nature. Furthermore, to call them models of mental illness would be tendentious and inexact, inasmuch as some of the approaches, including Laing's, acknowledge the reality of mental anguish and confusion, of disturbed and disturbing states of mind, but do not regard disordered conduct as the necessary result of an underlying individual "illness," to the manifest neglect of the social surroundings.

In designating these approaches as models, I question the wisdom of those who prefer to describe them, after Thomas Kuhn, as paradigms (Ingelby, 1980; Reznek, 1991). In my view, it is self-defeating to apply a concept from the history of the natural sciences to the human sciences when the basic intent is to show that methods of study appropriate to one field have no place in the study of social and interpersonal processes. Besides, the use of "paradigm" is inappropriate when we consider what Kuhn's notion actually entails. According to Kuhn (1970), when scientific communities share a single theoretical frame of reference, they go through periods of relatively stable and unspectacular development, elaborating on what went before. Eventually anomalies emerge that do not make sense within the prevailing paradigm, and they ultimately exceed the existing paradigm's ability to accommodate or dismiss them. Thus cosmological coherence breaks down and a new, more persuasive paradigm will emerge from the rubble of the old, creating periods of spectacular growth that irrevocably alter our concept of the universe.

While undoubtedly useful in the history of the natural sciences, Kuhn's concept of paradigms is irrelevant to the history of the human sciences, where the clash of different models is continuous and unceasing. In the mental health field as well, competition among many models is the norm, not the exception, despite the fact that the medical model continues to be dominant. More to the point perhaps, old paradigms are not exploded or discarded as new ones appear, but are revised to fit the contours of new facts and experiences, often quite unreasonably.

Finally, in considering the history, contours, and contemporary impact of these models, we must make a clear distinction between the idea of models and the idea of a scientific *theory*. The two are far from identical. In the human sciences, one and the same model can encompass many contradictory theories. For example, the medical model of schizophrenia encompasses the theories of Kraepelin, Bleuler, Meyer, Kretchmer, Rumke, and many more recent theorists, which are by no means compatible. Similarly, the psychoanalytic model encompasses several different theories of gender, which mandate different modes of intervention. Behaviorism encompasses the ideas of Pavlov, Watson, Skinner, and countless neo-behaviorists, while cognitivism subsumes a wide range of theories derived from old-fashioned rationalism, those built on computer or machine analogies, and others allied to biology and neurology.

Let me call attention to these facts again to emphasize that one model can encompass many different theories of human behavior—rational and irrational, sane and disordered—and that the reason for grouping them in one conceptual category is not because of any consensus that prevails. On the contrary, *within any given model, the normal state of affairs is controversy and competition between divergent theories or between different schools.* Paradigms, in Kuhn's sense, are nowhere to be found.

Still, if one probes the welter of conflicting theories, one will eventually find that there are certain family resemblances between contending theories that reflect a metatheoretical consensus about human behavior which puts them all in the same universe of discourse. This is not to say that the researchers and practitioners who subscribe to these models are necessarily aware of the axioms that govern their research. Far from it. More often than not, these axioms function as a kind of unconscious metaphysic underneath the whole theoretical edifice. For lack of a better word, those who share in the *metatheoretical* assumptions that govern their own group's activities belong to the same epistemic community.

Finally, it is important to note that while specific theories can be tested by appeals to logic, experience, and experiment, history demonstrates that models of human nature and mental disorder have a life of their own. Any one model—more accurately, any epistemic community—will generate numerous theories about the causes or meanings of human behavior. Any one theory may also be tested and found wanting (for one reason or another). But in practice the axioms that define a model's boundaries are not susceptible to straightforward refutation and function more like unspoken (and often unconscious) articles of faith.

History demonstrates that the currency enjoyed by these models is not determined solely by the plausibility or correctness of the theories they generate. A variety of social, political, and economic factors also contribute to their popularity or decline. In *Madness and Civilization* Foucault characterizes the history of psychiatry not as a dialogue with madness, but as "a monologue by reason about madness." This influential metaphor, while doubtless well intended, and quite consistent with Laing up to a point, is misleading if taken too seriously. The discourse of psychiatry and the mental health professions is not always rational, and it is never a monologue: it is a thundering cacophony, a veritable tower of Babel, where many discordant and mutually incomprehensible voices battle for our attention.

Furthermore, many of these voices, which purport to speak on behalf of reason, do nothing of the kind. They actually replace calm, lucid skepticism with different varieties of rhetoric and unselfconscious scientism. Two examples from the history of the field will illustrate this point.

My first example concerns the rise and fall of phrenology. In the early 1800s, psychiatry was dominated by the ideas of Franz Josef Gall on the determination of mental capacity by the shape and size of the skull and brain. In view of the paucity of evidence at the time, the amazing popularity of phrenology among alienists and asylum keepers was clearly not a function of rationality. When men give credence to unsubstantiated assertions—no matter what their social standing or educational background, and no matter how plausible the assertions appear on first inspection—they are behaving irrationally. Although there was little evidence to demonstrate the truth of phrenology, it had a marked influence on physical anthropologists into our own time, leading to, for example, pernicious theories about brain size and racial superiority.

Nonetheless, in some respects phrenology proved to be a productive fallacy, which generated much useful research. Had it not been for efforts to prove or disprove various phrenological theses, advances in the modern neurosciences might have taken much longer to accomplish.

My second example of collective irrationality is insulin-coma therapy, introduced by Manfred Joshua Sakel (1900–1957) in Vienna. In 1930 Sakel stumbled on the idea after accidentally giving an insulin overdose to a patient who was diabetic and a drug addict. When she regained consciousness, her craving for morphine subsided, and so Sakel proceeded to experiment with other addicts, claiming great effectiveness for his new technique. By 1933 Sakel was trying this approach on psychotic patients, and in 1936 his treatment was introduced to England and the United States, where it won widespread acceptance.

Arguably, insulin-coma therapy did work in rare instances, although it had nothing to do with Sakel's reasons, which were pure science fiction. Most patients getting the treatment knew that they could die as a result. In ordinary circumstances, these same patients were often starved for attention and care. When the artificially induced life-or-death crisis intervened, followed by the patient ministrations of a team of doctors trying anxiously to avert the patient's death and to ensure recovery, the massive psychological repercussions of this collective ritual might have been sufficient to turn a handful of cases around, just as ritual exorcism sometimes works.

But there were three striking things about this craze. One was that Sakel had no plausible theory of therapy, no reasonable way of explaining how his technique actually worked. Another was that he claimed a success rate of 88 percent, which could not be replicated even by his most ardent followers, some of whom were leading psychiatrists of the time such as Joseph Wortis, Willi Mayer-Gross, and Ewan Cameron, (Valenstein, 1984, chap. 3). The third astonishing thing about insulin-coma therapy was that it lasted so long. Perhaps the only explanation is that uncritical enthusiasts with reputations at stake prefer to institutionalize their errors rather than admit them openly, even (or especially) when patients have suffered or died as a result.

Today it is commonly conceded that Sakel's astronomical rate of cure was the product of delusion, fraud, or both. At the time, however, he was heralded as "the Pasteur of psychiatry" and enjoyed a sterling reputation well into the 1960s, when insulin-coma treatment was finally discontinued. One notable skeptic was Oscar Diethelm, who warned Sakel and his associates—Joseph Ladislas von Meduna, inventor of metrazol coma therapy, and Ugo Cerletti, inventor of electroshock therapy—that their heroic new methods, which were untested and based on pure conjecture, were "an expression of therapeutic hopelessness in a naively hopeful physician" and of "too strong an enthusiastic drive to help where others have failed, or to find an answer to what had been an unsolved riddle" (Diethelm, 1938). Unfortunately, almost no one was listening.

Looking back at phrenology and insulin-coma therapy, how do we account for their uncritical acceptance by hundreds of learned men and women? This is obviously a complex question, beyond the scope of this book. Suffice it to say that the mental health professions came into existence when society was beginning to shift its allegiance away from organized religion and to acknowledge the competence of psychiatry to deal with mental disturbances. Unlike the priest, who could provide solace, support, and occasionally some genuine instruction, psychiatrists treated mental disorders as physical diseases and promised to provide cures.

As a result, for the last two hundred years society has expected psychiatrists and psychologists to produce remedies for all kinds of problems, and to afford some leverage against the baffling complexities of mental disorder. Having promised to deliver a substantial bill of goods, researchers and clinicians alike are engaged in a collective game of "catch up," trying to make good on the claims of their predecessors and to prove the scoffers wrong. Rather than admit their limitations, specialists in the treatment of human misery often grasp at straws, huddling round the idols of their tribes for mutual solace and reassurance that they have something useful to offer.

In such instances, however, we lose sight of Socrates' maxim— that wisdom begins with an appreciation of your own ignorance, of knowing that you do not know—and the overpowering need for certainty clouds the mind with all kinds of pseudo-knowledge and misinformation that masquerade as the genuine article. The victims of this charade are invariably the patients, who become guinea pigs in ill-conceived experiments to vindicate the claims of psychiatry.

Though he was not a historian of psychiatry or psychology, Laing was far more aware than most professionals of the irrationality in the mental health field. One of his illuminating observations was that a man who calls himself an automaton is regarded as schizophrenic, whereas a scientist who claims that all human beings are automatons is regarded as a clear-sighted observer (1960, p. 23). Indeed, this scientist's theories may have an appreciable impact on how schizophrenics are actually treated.

Even today, this grim irony is lost on most mental health professionals, who dismiss it is a clever but essentially irrelevant observation. But surely it is a telling commentary on the frightening culture of irrationality that suffuses psychiatry. The point is that there is often a tacit double standard in the allocation of diagnostic labels, and if mental health professionals rigorously applied their own criteria to themselves, they would have to question their own fitness to practice and the firm line of demarcation that divides "us" (the professionals) from "them" (the patients). Indeed, as Laing observed in his seminars at the White Institute, "they" provide "us" with our raison d'etre, so that many of us are strongly invested in *not* seeing that we construct others in our own image and in dismissing those who call attention to this collective denial.

These considerations bear mostly on the issue of the diagnosis or classification of mental disorders. What about other aspects of the medical model—treatment and research? Though this is seldom acknowledged by Laing's critics, the fact remains that Laing respected medical methodologies, as long as they were applied to phenomena that were within its legitimate domain and as long as the methods employed were scientific, not mere contrivances for promoting an ideological agenda. Take the subject of genetics and schizophrenia. For decades the psychiatric profession claimed that the genetic basis of schizophrenia was proven by the studies of Franz Josef Kallman and Eliot Slater (Kallman, 1953). In fact, as Laing demonstrated, they were as flawed as Sakel's insulin coma (Evans, 1976b, appendix), and today no self-respecting geneticist endorses them.

In short, despite his "far-out" reputation, Laing had a discerning eye for methodological flaws within the medical model, and he called attention to them in no uncertain terms. More recent methodological critiques of Kallman (such as Lewontin, Rose, and Kamin, 1984; Breggin, 1991) have not improved on Laing's critique in any substantial way.

Regarding the treatment of mental disorder, it is often forgotten

that Laing did not categorically rule out the possibility that some varieties of psychosis may be cured by medication (Evans, p. 16). But
at the level of etiology he cautioned that the mere fact that chemical
interventions may produce salutory effects does not prove causality.
As Laing insisted, our neurophysiological systems are profoundly affected by our emotional states and by social and environmental
processes. Radical changes in the social or environmental fields can
cause physical changes just as surely as the latter produce behavioral
anomalies.

Accordingly, unless they are the result of lesions or abnormalities
of the brain that are clearly *not* the result of medical interventions—
such as iatrogenic effects of neuroleptic medication or ECT, which
account for many of the brain abnormalities observed in schizophrenics—we should not automatically assume a priori that a psychotic disorder originates in a person's brain. Existential, spiritual,
and social crises may all be in play, and their resolution may be more
crucial to the recuperation of patients than what is going on inside
their skulls.

Moving on to the next model, Laing had nothing but contempt
for behaviorism (1967, pp. 44–45). Science won a decisive victory
over animism when it persuaded us that the inanimate world is not
populated by sentient beings with good or malevolent intentions,
except in our imaginations. But when science deprives *human* beings of agency and experience, it oversteps its bounds and degener-
ates into scientism. The behavior of inanimate objects may indeed
be governed by impersonal laws of physics and chemistry, but objects do not experience the forces that act upon them and, unlike
people, do not endow them with intelligence of any kind. Studying
human behavior in isolation from its experiential roots robs it of its
meaning and becomes a straightforward exercise in reification.

Whereas Laing scorned behaviorism, his view of cognitivism was
more complex. He loathed the machine analogy for the human psyche and had no patience with the computer-oriented enthusiasts.
And unlike the American promoters of cognitive therapy, Ellis and
Beck, Laing was not an old-fashioned rationalist but a dialectical rationalist, whose methodology was more influenced by Mead, Sartre,
and Goffman than it was by mainstream approaches (Esterson,
1992).

Still, Laing never assumed that a patient's conscious thoughts are a mere palimpsest of unconscious conflicts, and he accorded far more causal efficacy to conscious cognition than most analysts do. But he also maintained that the cognitions that affect us viscerally always occur in a social context. In other words, it is not merely what I think that shapes my moods and behavior, but also what I think *you* think. Furthermore, if I am bluffing or positioning myself in a complex negotiation, what I think you think I think will have considerable impact on what I say or do next, regardless of what I actually think. In matters of collective strategy—in business, politics, or military affairs—what we think *they* think also matters enormously, whether they are enemies or allies. And what we think they think we think is also germane to our conduct, particularly if we happen to be wrong.

In recent years, cognitivism has begun to take social and interpersonal contexts into account. So far, though, nothing like a systematic theory has emerged, and most research is still focused on the individual. Despite impressive work with dyads in *Interpersonal Perception* (1966), Laing had no systematic theory either. But he made intriguing suggestions and observations, and the various "positions" of consciousness he describes, in which people's cognitions are shaped by their place in the prevailing scheme of social relations, bear closer scrutiny.

Laing's complex relationship to social constructivism is best approached through his scattered reflections on personality. He never outlined a theory of personality as such. Even so, there are two distinct phases discernible in his various writings on the subject. In *The Divided Self,* chapter 11, Laing posited the existence of hereditary predispositions in children that shape mother-infant dynamics for good or ill. In this way he felt he could account for the striking difference between his patient Julie, who was passive, dependent, and guiltily hated her mother, and her older sister, who was openly rebellious but relatively intact. Similarly, in chapter 9 of *Self and Others,* he speculated that when mother and child double-bind one another incessantly, there may be a fundamental mismatch between them. Though he didn't attribute this misalliance to temperamental differences, he didn't rule them out either.

Laing's later, more constructivist phase began around 1964 and is characterized by an absence of any conjectures about endogenous traits or dispositions, with repeated reminders that there is no such thing as a basic personality apart from specific social contexts. Because of the paucity of evidence on this point, it is unclear whether Laing ever recognized the apparent contradiction between his interpersonal theses and his later attempt to introduce an intrauterine phase of psychosexual development.

As the case of Nan illustrates (see Chapter 2), Laing never abandoned his belief in personal agency altogether. As much as her posttraumatic personality changed, and as much as her second self was shaped by the meanings thrust on her by others, Nan was not a puppet of environmental contingencies. As Laing saw it, Nan actively took up these imposed elements of identity and shaped them into a meaningful personal gestalt. In short, the creation of personality, or identity, is a dialectical process in which the person actively participates.

Another area where constructivist sympathies are in evidence, of course, is in Laing's ideas about madness. His deepest affinities here were probably with Bateson, Goffman, and Foucault. In the late fifties and early sixties, those men looked at the existing medical model of schizophrenia and demonstrated that there are alternative ways of construing madness which have commendable rigor and explanatory power. The family, the mental hospital, and society at large have a role—indeed, a vested interest—in the creation of madness, although this is not readily apparent if one approaches the problem from the standpoint of neo-Kraepelinian psychiatry, which finds the source of individual problems within the body or brain.

Laing's appreciation for Goffman and Bateson is well known. But though it seldom registers in his published work, he set Foucault even higher. As he said to Theodor Itten, he regarded Foucault as one of a handful of stellar intellectuals—including Sartre, R. D. Laing of course, Emmanuel Levinas, and Paul Feyerabend—who led the way in the latter half of the twentieth century.

Whatever else they were, Bateson and Goffman were not Marxists. Nor was Foucault, for that matter. But by the mid-1960s, Laing's ideas had attracted the interest of many Marxist intellectuals, not least because of his admiration for Sartre and because terms like mystification, alienation, and nexus, which he used repeatedly, were derived from Marxist sources. Moreover, the work of his colleague David Cooper, explicitly Marxist and anti-imperialist, was frequently read as an extension of Laing's. Yet, after the Dialectics of Liberation Conference, Laing lost no opportunity to emphasize his indebtedness to Kierkegaard, Nietzsche, and Freud, distancing himself from Marxist politics. At that point, as noted earlier, he started to cultivate an image of himself (and of the Philadelphia Association) as politically neutral and disengaged. On a biographical level, it is interesting to note that in the early 1980s, Laing remarked to Michael Thompson that politically he was well to the right of Mrs. Thatcher and Ronald Reagan. Apparently he meant it, since he made the remark with some feeling.

Laing's remark was probably an exaggeration. By the same token, though, we cannot dismiss the possibility that Laing went through a gradual shift from left to right, as some of his left-wing critics insist (Kovel, 1980; Sedgwick, 1982). The problem with this interpretation is that, while we can't dismiss it, we can't prove it either. Laing's nature often prompted him to adopt a position exactly opposite to the one attributed to him: he wanted to remain an enigma, and he was loathe to retract anything he had said or to acknowledge inconsistencies between his past and present views.

As Peter Sedgwick states, Laing's shift to the right may have been an attempt to regain a measure of credibility in the academic and cultural mainstream. Then again, it is also possible that Laing's earlier left-wing affinities were the self-promoting ones, and his shift toward the right could have been more indicative of his true feelings. In any case, Laing's apparent move to the right raises the question of his relationship to another noteworthy figure in the social-constructivist camp, Thomas Szasz. He is a self-proclaimed right-wing radical (Szasz, 1990) who, like Sedgwick on the left, attacked Laing in 1976 for equivocating and backtracking on certain important issues. Drawing on chapter 3 of *Politics of Experience,* where Laing alludes to Marx, Orwell, and Fanon, Szasz characterized Laing and his associates as socialists and communists. While the attribution may have had some credibility prior to 1967, it was not true after 1968. Szasz also charged Laing and the Philadelphia Association with making the ordinary British citizen pay for the maintenance of their therapeutic households—a charge that was patently false (Kirsner, 1977).

Though Laing did not reply to Szasz directly, he was distressed by the virulence of the attack, and often wondered why Szasz didn't have it out with him in person before resorting to such harsh polemics in print. Without delving into all the specifics, there were some notable differences between the two men that probably contributed to Szasz's rude criticism. Though he frequently denied their existence—in public, at least—Laing saw his contradictions as a source of creativity and potential strength, and no reason for self-reproach. Throughout his adult life, Laing labored under a veritable compulsion to say something fresh and unheard, never to dwell too long on anything he had said before. This may help to account for the thematic inconsistencies and unfinished projects he left behind, not to mention his crisis of confidence when he ran finally ran out of new things to say.

By contrast, Szasz's most notable characteristic is his relentless consistency in returning to old themes. It is only natural that a man of consistent temperament would criticize Laing. But it is true that most creative theorists often express different and sometimes contradictory positions in the course of their careers. Though it is our right to point out contradictions, there was an ad hominem quality to Szasz's critique that was uncharitable. Had he approached Laing in a more humane spirit, he might have allowed that at least some of the contradictions in Laing's utterances and ideas were not the result of insincerity and hypocrisy, but of an ongoing struggle to sort out the bafflements of mental disorder and the ethical issues surrounding it. And he might have refrained from embellishing his critique with factual errors—or at least apologized for them later.

Since my next chapters explore Laing's relationship to existential phenomenology and psychoanalysis in some detail, I will canvass the rest of the territory at hand with a brief survey of Laing's relation to humanistic psychology. During the seventies and eighties, when most psychiatrists, analysts, and radicals were loosing interest in him, many of Laing's loyal readers in the United States were psychologists or psychotherapists who described themselves as humanists. Paradoxically, Laing had no patience for mainstream humanistic psychology, arguing that the fame once enjoyed by Carl Rogers and Abraham Maslow was a dreadful reflection on American culture. He reproached Maslow for acquiring guru status by "selling" a derivative version of Nietzsche's ideas (Mullan, 1994). His objections to Rogers were more complex. In an interview with Richard Simon, Laing recalled that he once asked Rogers:

> "What's your personal experience of evil?" He said, "I have no experience of evil in my whole life. I know nothing about evil. I've never had an evil thought, an evil imagination. I've never done anything evil in my whole life." So I said, "How do you connect with your clients?" And he said, "I sit and listen to them and learn about evil from them."
>
> He told me about a meeting he had with Martin Buber in the late 40's in which he told Buber that schizophrenics were the most evil people in the world. Buber was very much in agreement with that and told him schizophrenics were incapable of an I–Thou relationship.
>
> Some time later Rogers did expose himself to a therapeutic relationship with a schizophrenic lady that drove him over the edge. He went completely crazy himself, but had the social prudence to get out. One day he got in his car and disappeared from his family and his practice and drove up to Canada. It was three months before he found his balance again. When he came back, he decided to never, ever, listen to a schizophrenic again. (Simon, 1983)

Assuming this information is correct, there were three things about Rogers that alienated Laing: his characterization of schizophrenics as evil, his refusal to listen to them, and his holier-than-thou self-appraisal, which to a skeptic like Laing could only suggest someone who is very repressed, very dull, or very dishonest. Laing also implied that Rogers lacked the inner strength to listen to someone who was disturbed without "loosing it" himself. There is another element to Laing's contempt for Rogers that doesn't surface here but is apparent in the interviews with Bob Mullan: his Eurocentrism. Like Fromm, Laing felt that mainstream psychology in America was a flimsy affair, intellectually speaking, and he attributed the weight of his own ideas and convictions, right or wrong, to his immersion in continental philosophy, and literature.

That said, however, the preceding quote attests to more than Laing's dislike of Rogers. Again like Fromm, Laing was often reproached by critics as a naive environmentalist, who explained the many varieties of mental suffering as so many instances of social injustice, victimization by others, and so on. In fairness to the critics, there is some basis for this complaint. Laing believed that our inclination to self-destructive acts is radically intensified by the treatment we receive at the hands of others. But Laing, who admired Augustine and Kierkegaard, had an equally keen appreciation for the inherent evil in all of us. Violence and deception, done by us or to us, are not mere products of alienation, mystification, invalidation, or competing interests. Evil often springs from sources deep within us that we prefer to disavow.

9

PHILOSOPHICAL
ANTHROPOLOGY

In this chapter I examine the axioms underlying Laing's view of the human condition and the human passions. Laing had some forceful things to say about our basic needs. But his notions of the embodied and disembodied self, though intriguing, are equivocal, and his views on solidarity and social groups are also open to question. Still, since existential phenomenology and psychoanalysis inform his work throughout, we should first take a look at these discourses.

The psychoanalytic and phenomenological traditions emerged independently but simultaneously around 1900, in the work of Sigmund Freud and Edmund Husserl, two students of the philosopher Franz Brentano. But Brentano rejected the idea of unconscious mental processes, and so Freud developed his model of the mind primarily along lines suggested by J. F. Herbart, Arthur Schopenhauer, Friedrich Nietzsche, Eduard von Hartmann, and Theodor Lipps, who spawned voluminous theories about the unconscious, sexuality, aggression, and self-deception, which Freud seldom cited but often took to heart. True to his medical training, however, Freud tried to fit his evolving ideas within the framework of the mechanistic materialism of Hermann Helmholtz, Ernst Brooke, and his own esteemed teacher, Theodor Meynert. Arguably, this was an impossible project, but in any event Freud came to regard the psyche as a self-enclosed system of reciprocally inhibiting and facilitating energic impulses and structures, governed by necessity and

Fechner's principle of constancy. Moreover, Freud's theory of human nature is predicated on the unbroken continuity between men and beasts in the animal kingdom. As Freud remarked to Ludwig Binswanger, people are far more animal (or bestial) than they care to imagine.

For his part, Husserl drew extensively on Brentano, who anticipated many of his formulations on intentionality in human perception, awareness, and thought. Husserl shared Brentano's distaste for the notion of unconscious mental processes and, in dramatic contrast to Freud, attempted to construe psychology as a branch of *Geisteswissenschaften,* the human sciences, or sciences of mind and spirit. To that end, Husserl drew on the philosophical work of Wilhelm Dilthey. Dilthey noted that applying the methods of natural science to the study of human behavior is misleading, because behavior is intelligible only in light of a person's experience and intentions. Furthermore, following Vico, Dilthey argued that human experience and action are always embedded in culturally and historically constituted situations, and are never simply determined by immutable natural laws. The fact that people make their own history, that they create meaning, culture, and language, makes human existence qualitatively different from those of other animal species.

In view of their disparate origins and orientations, psychoanalysis and phenomenology developed more or less independently until the 1920s, when Husserl's friend and colleague, Max Scheler, began to incorporate psychoanalytic ideas into his work. A year before Scheler's death in 1928, Martin Heidegger, Husserl's pupil, published *Being and Time.* Heidegger's answer to Husserl's phenomenology engendered the existential-phenomenological tradition that influenced Laing. During the 1930s, Binswanger attempted to integrate Freud's ideas with those of Husserl and Heidegger in a system known as *Daseinanalysis.* As much as he respected Freud, though, Binswanger insisted that human experience and motivation cannot be explained solely in terms of physiological drives or biological determinism. Other needs and experiences, distinctively human, are also in play and may be even more decisive in understanding the nature of mental disorder (Binswanger, 1936).

Binswanger's critique of Freud's biological reductionism has been endorsed ever since by most existential phenomenologists. Furthermore, in the clinical offshoots of this tradition, the critique of

Freud's biologism is linked to a more or less explicit philosophical anthropology, or a model of basic human needs and experiences that Binswanger called phenomenological anthropology.

In the last few decades, however, theorists influenced by the later Heidegger have argued that the whole notion of philosophical anthropology is outdated and repressive. Among the first critics was Michel Foucault, whose groundbreaking *Mental Illness and Psychology* (1954) laid the foundation for recent debate along these lines. Theorists who follow Foucault lean toward poststructuralism, social constructivism, deconstructionism, and postmodernism, and tend to dismiss the existential dimension of madness, arguing that cultural and social forces alone create, define, and stigmatize "mental illness." Characteristically, they also insist that any notion of a basic or universal human nature simply reifies one particular cultural-historical way of being-in-the-world and thereby obscures the specifically social process that creates and defines madness.[1]

It is interesting to note, again, that Laing had great respect for Foucault. Indeed, Foucault's bestselling *Madness and Civilization* first appeared in English (1961) in a series Laing edited, Studies in Existentialism and Phenomenology, with an introduction by David Cooper. Nevertheless, rightly or wrongly, Laing never repudiated philosophical anthropology, as Foucault did, and so remained closer to the traditional existential approach.

As his work progressed, Laing never outlined an explicit philosophical anthropology. On the contrary, most of his ideas on the subject have to be inferred from his texts. Commenting on the vagaries of clinical practice, for example, Laing said:

> no matter how circumscribed or diffuse the initial complaint may be, one knows that the patient is bringing into the treatment situation, whether intentionally or unintentionally, his existence, his whole being-in-his-world. One knows that every aspect of his being is related in some way to every other aspect, thought the manner in which these aspects are articulated may be by no means clear. It is the task of existential phenomenology to articulate what the other's "world" is and his way of being in it. (1960a, p. 25)

While acknowledging that every person is unique, however, in *The Politics of Experience* (1967) Laing alluded to a distinctively human way of being that transcends any individual's particular way of being. He declared that "a critical theory must be able to place all theories of practices within the scope of a total vision of the ontological structure of being human" (p. 41). Or again, that "any theory not founded on the nature of being human is a lie and a betrayal of man" (p. 45).

But Laing never spelled out this "ontological structure of being human," leaving it to us to guess what he meant by that arresting phrase. Fortunately, a careful reading of Laing's work discloses a distinctive form of philosophical anthropology that merits attention.

The first element in Laing's philosophical anthropology concerns the situated and relational aspects of our being-in-the-world. In *The Divided Self* Laing said

> The words of the current technical vocabulary either refer to man in isolation from the other and the world, that is, as an entity not essentially "in relation to" the other and in a world, or they refer to falsely substantialized aspects of this isolated entity. Such words are: mind and body, psyche and soma, psychological and physical, personality, the self, the organism. All these terms are abstracta. Instead of the original bond of *I* and *You*, we take a single man in isolation and conceptualize his various aspects into "the ego," "the superego," and "the id" . . . This difficulty faces not only classical Freudian metapsychology but equally any theory that begins with a man or a part of man abstracted from his relation with the other in his world. (1960, pp. 19–20)

Another important feature of Laing's philosophical anthropology is his dialectical approach to the concepts of selfhood and identity. Laing endorsed the thesis advanced by Hegel, Husserl, Merleau-Ponty, and Buber (among others) that the experience of personhood, of an "I" as a locus of experience of and action on the world, presupposes a "Thou," an other, in terms of whom one's own existence is understood. Whether we exist in a close, distant, complementary, or adversarial relationship, self and other are always reciprocally constituted. So one's sense of identity is never simply a product of unmediated introspection, but a selective synthesis of refracted self-appraisals, elements of the self that are expressed in dialogue (and in conflict) with others. This dialectical perspective is apparent in *Self and Others* and later in *Interpersonal Perception,* where Laing notes:

Self-identity (my view of myself) and meta-identity (my view of your view of me) are theoretical constructs, not concrete realities. *In concreto,* rather than in *abstracto,* self-identity ("I" looking at "me") is constituted not only by our looking at ourselves, but also by our looking at others looking at us and our reconstruction and alteration of these views of the others about us. At this more complex, more concrete level, self-identity is a synthesis of my looking at me with my view of others views of me. These views by others of me need not be passively accepted, but they cannot be ignored in my development of my sense of who I am. (1966, p. 5)

However, while one's sense of self, one's being-for-myself, is always constituted through others, there is another realm of human experience that is not dialogical but deeply private. Indeed, Laing speculated, the loss of this sense of unqualified privacy is a hallmark of madness. Accordingly, while one may communicate with other human beings, another person's experience "is never available to me as a primary datum of my experience." To paraphrase Laing, I cannot experience another's experience. I can only experience another *experiencing* the world in certain ways, and all my ideas about another person's experience are built up through inferences from my own. Hence Laing's emphasis on "the inexorable separateness between man and man, that no love, nor the most complete experience of union, can annul" (1961, p. 130).

Another feature of Laing's philosophical anthropology is his notion of authenticity. He noted that everyday speech abounds in expressions that describe the self's relations to its own actions and the resulting states of mind.

One says that a person "puts himself into" his acts, or that he is *not* "in" what he says or does . . . He may seem to be "full of himself" or "beside himself" or "to have come to himself" again after "not being himself." These expressions are attributions about the person's relations to his own actions, and are used quite naturally as the language of the "man in the street." In them all the issue is the extent to which the act is seen or felt to *potentiate* the being or existence of the doer, or the extent to which the action makes patent the latent self of the doer . . .

The intensification of the being of the agent through self-disclosure, through making patent the latent self, is the meaning of Nietzsche's "will to power." It is the "weak" man who is not potentiating himself genuinely who may counterfeit his impotence by dominating and controlling others, by idealizing physical strength or sexual potency, in the restricted sense of the capacity to have erections and to ejaculate. (1961, p. 126)

Laing's notion of authentic self-disclosure has an immediate application to clinical problems like guilt, depression, schizophrenia, and the dynamics of sexual deviance. Although his thoughts on deviant sexual desires and practices are confined to a single book, *Self and Others,* they furnish an illuminating point of departure for assessing the relation between philosophical anthropology and clinical practice.

In Freudian theory, deviant sexual practices and fantasies are alleged to be symptomatic of a fixation at or regression to a specific point in an ontogenetic series. In Laingian usage, by contrast, they are enactments or expressions of an existential position or predicament:

> The man who does not reveal himself or is not "seen" by the others when he does, may turn, in partial despair, to false modes of self-disclosure. The exhibitionist who shows off his body, or a part of the body, or some highly prized function or skill, may be despairingly trying to overcome that isolation and loneliness which tends to haunt the man who feels his "real" or "true" self has never been disclosed to and confirmed by others. The man who compulsively exhibits his penis can be in "bad faith." He can be substituting self-disclosure through this "thing" rather than through living . . . He wishes to put his would-be "true" self into his penis. But instead of making patent his latent self and thereby intensifying his being, he holds himself in (inhibits himself) while he holds out (exhibits) his penis. (1961, p. 131–132)

Laing's remarks on exhibitionism are indebted to the work of Medard Boss. But they also show a deep affinity to the thought of someone seldom associated with existentialism: Erich Fromm. Like Fromm, Laing regarded the inevitability of death as a problem with no predetermined solution, one that everyone faces and addresses (in one way or another) in their style of life and relatedness to others (Burston, 1992, chap. 4). Laing's use of the term "authenticity" is

also similar to Fromm's notion of "productivity," or the unalienated
objectification of the latent powers of the self through one's praxis
in the world. From both perspectives, then, inauthentic actions estrange individuals from their core or ground, creating a false self
that produces boredom, depression, and a sense of futility and
anger, no matter how efficacious they may be in terms of results or
external success and recognition. This kind of self-estrangement can
exist quite independently of the vicissitudes of the libido.

Along the same lines, in contrast to Freud, Laing and Fromm regarded the passions and privations that animate deviant sexual practices as largely nonsexual, as disturbances in the soul desperately
enacted in a metaphoric language of the body. Fromm's first discussion of this point appeared in the *Zeitschrift für Sozialforschung,* the
house organ of the Frankfurt School, in 1936 and 1937, where he observed that feelings of profound powerlessness and isolation beget
sadomasochistic tendencies, which may or may not take overtly sexual form. This idea was explored further in *Escape from Freedom*
(1941) and later in *The Art of Loving* (1956).

Another clinical application of Laing's philosophical anthropology concerns the psychology of orgasm, impotence, and frigidity.
The larger context for Laing's discussion was a meditation on the
origins of envy, the sense of helplessness, and destructive fantasies.
Melanie Klein believed that envy and destructiveness are innate, endemic to early infancy (or an adult regression to infantile positions).
But Laing thought that envy, helplessness, and destructive fantasies
are not necessarily the products of persisting infantile trends, but are
perennial possibilities in all human relationships, because of our
need for reciprocity and recognition from others. In relationships
based on mutual affirmation and respect, envy and destructiveness
have little leverage in the long run. In disturbed interpersonal relationships, however, our need to give and to be confirmed in our capacity as givers becomes the occasion for others to frustrate us by
withholding confirmation of our worth or potency (and vice versa).
In his words:

Consider this in relation to sex. Two basic intentions in sexuality are
pleasurable relief from tension, and change in the other. Sex may be
felt to be empty if the other is not dancing as well. The pure self-
gratification of rise and fall of tension can be eminently frustrating.

Any theory of sexuality which makes the "aim" of the sexual "instinct" the achievement of orgasmic potency alone, while the other . . . is a mere object . . . ignores the erotic desire to make a difference to the other. When Blake suggested that what is most required is "the lineaments of gratified desire" *in the other,* he indicated that one of the most frustrating possible experiences is full discharge of one's energy or libido, however pleasurable, without making any difference to the other.

Frigidity in women is often the refusal to allow men the triumph of "giving" satisfaction. Her frigidity is triumph and torment. "You can give your penis, your erection, your orgasm, but it doesn't make any difference to me." Indeed, erection and orgasm are very limited aspects of potency: potency without power to make a difference to the other. The impotent man, analogously to the frigid woman, is often determined not to give the woman the satisfaction of satisfying him. (1961, pp. 84–85).

Clearly, then, the passions that drive one's sexual conduct and fantasies are not simply libidinous. They also involve issues of power, including the power to give and to gratify and the power to frustrate, deprive, or diminish others. Another feature of Laing's philosophical anthropology that merits comparison with Fromm's is his conception of existential needs. The term "existential needs" is Fromm's of course, but it evokes what Laing apparently had in mind. In Fromm's work, existential needs are not directly derived from the exigencies of satisfying drives. But they affect our sanity and well-being as surely and directly as instincts do.

Though scarcely irrelevant in the present context, I will not rehearse Fromm's discussion of existential needs in detail here because I have done so elsewhere and because the nature and number of needs Fromm listed kept changing over the years. But, in fairness to Laing, we ought to see what existential needs figure most prominently in his work.

As far as I can establish, there are six existential needs that Laing acknowledged, some already alluded to, including (1) authentic self-disclosure and (2) the confirmation of one's power to give, or to make a difference to others. These needs logically imply the existence of (3) relatedness to others, without whom self-disclosure and the experience and expression of one's powers of "giving" would not be possible.

Elsewhere Laing discussed needs for (4) <u>ontological security</u> and a corollary sense of agency, autonomy, and self-worth, (5) <u>transcendence</u>, and (6) <u>truth, or freedom from deception</u> (Laing, 1976). Judging from Laing's clinical vignettes, the disappointment of these needs will have adverse psychological consequences, which vary with the quality and intensity of the frustration experienced. For example, in the absence of authentic self-disclosure—whether from lack of opportunity or ability or both—the self becomes impoverished and lapses into boredom and a sense of futility. The frustration of the need to give or "to make a difference," and to be confirmed by others in that capacity, engenders envy and destructiveness. And so on.

For heuristic purposes, the various needs Laing touches on could be discussed separately, as if their fulfillment or frustration depended on independent processes, actions, and events. Clearly, though, this cannot happen. Judging from Laing's own descriptions, these needs are not distinct but intimately intertwined, and constantly operative in every human being. In his discussion of schizoid processes, Laing notes that the ontologically insecure individual fears relatedness as such

> because his uncertainty about the stability of his autonomy lays him open to the dread lest in any relationship he lose his autonomy and identity . . .
>
> The main manoeuvre used to preserve identity under pressure from the dread of engulfment is isolation. Thus, instead of the polarities of separateness and relatedness based on individual autonomy, there is the antithesis between complete loss of being by absorption into the other person (engulfment) and complete aloneness (isolation). There is no safe third possibility of a dialectical relationship between two persons, both sure of their own ground and, on this very basis, able to 'lose themselves' in each other. Such merging of being can only occur in an authentic way when the individuals are sure of themselves. (1960a, p. 44)

To summarize, moments of "authentic merging" between human beings are predicated on their basic separateness and on their having (and maintaining) a sense of autonomy. These thoughts are not original to Laing, of course. They were stated in Buber's "Distance and Relation" (1951). Laing took Buber's reasoning one step further, to point out that the individual's need for relatedness to others cannot be satisfied as long as he or she is terrified of being engulfed by the other. So there is thus the faint but unmistakable suggestion that the satisfaction of some needs, such as ontological security, takes priority over others, or that the failure to satisfy some needs will preclude the satisfaction of others.

Conceptualizing human needs in terms of differential urgencies, or of varying degrees of priority, may seem to imply a hierarchy of needs or a developmental table, like Maslow's hierarchy of needs or Erikson's development theory. But Laing's ideas, though similar up to a point, are not couched in terms of a hierarchy or an epigenetic series or a developmental itinerary. If there is any sequence here, it is an existential and logical one, not a maturational process in which one need comes to the fore as each preceding stage is mastered. And despite moments of satisfaction, there is never a definitive "mastering" of any given need, which supposedly allows the person to move on to the next stage.

So far, we can see a philosophical anthropology predicated on the constitutive paradox of human existence—that, whether we realize it or not, we live profoundly communal and private existences at the same time. Judging from Laing's work, however, the communal dimension of our lives takes precedence, because before you can be self-conscious, you must be "for others," that is, you must experience yourself as the object of another's intentional acts (Laing, 1960, pp. 108, 139). And as his remarks on infant development suggest, these experiences of being-for-others need not be mediated through words alone, but can be accurately expressed in the language of the body and eyes (p. 116).

Though Laing did not say so in quite these words, in *The Divided Self* he suggests that the dualism at the core of human existence has strong repercussions on the way in which sanity and madness are experienced and defined. In the usual course of events, Laing notes, being-for-oneself and being-for-others are conjunctive. The person you take me for is, if not identical, then very similar to the person I think I am. When there is a radical disjuncture between who (or what) I think I am and who (or what) you think I am, or what I in

turn think of you, one of us will probably be deemed mad: say, if I
insist that I am Napoleon or a savior in disguise, while you steadfastly refuse to recognize me as such . . . Or if you maintain that you
are a real psychiatrist, while I insist that you are a posturing phony,
despite your numerous diplomas, and so on.

In such instances, consensus about who each of us is (or is not)
will determine who is labeled mad and who does the labeling. A
general principle of interpersonal phenomenology is that madness,
real or alleged, is a function of a radical experiential disjuncture of
some kind, a rupture between being-for-oneself and being-for-
others. But apart from the specific diagnostic constructions put on
our interpersonal attributions, which vary from one culture or century to another, Laing insists that if you endeavor to construct an
identity entirely detached from consensual validation and other people's experience of you, you are truly, *existentially* mad, not merely a
victim of collective fear, intolerance, or duplicity. The construction
itself is unattainable, however faithfully and diligently pursued.[2]

So far so good. But problems arise when we try to reconcile
Laing's earlier emphasis on our need for a sense of autonomy with
his later discussion of the transcendental impulse, which supposedly
severs us from our "egoic consciousness" and our bodily existence
(1967). There are also disparities in Laing's reflections on the theme
of embodiment. In *The Divided Self* Laing said that he regarded
"any particular man as finite, as one who has had a beginning and
who will have an end. He is born, and he is going to die. In the
meantime, he has a body that roots him to this time and place"
(p. 26). But he went on to qualify his position, in odd but important
ways. He begins by contrasting ontological security and insecurity.
A secure person experiences her self as differentiated and autonomous, continuous in time, having inner consistency and worth,
and being "spatially co-extensive with the body" and thus liable to
extinction at death. By contrast, the individual suffering from ontological insecurity "may feel more unreal than real; in a literal sense,
more dead than alive; precariously differentiated from the rest of the
world, so that his identity and autonomy are always in question. . . .
He may feel more insubstantial than substantial, and unable to assume that the stuff he is made of is genuine, good, valuable. And he
may feel his self as partially divorced from his body" (p. 42).

According to Laing, these two ways of being-in-the-world constitute the greatest difference imaginable, except that "normal" people also dissociate from their bodies when subject to extreme stress or trauma. By contrast, the schizoid individual normally experiences his bodily existence as a perpetual threat to his real, unembodied self and as a result never fully inhabits his body. Contemporary culture takes the embodied self as normal, and the unembodied self as abnormal or pathological. But as Laing was careful to point out,

> it is of considerable practical importance that one should be able to see that the concept and/or experience that a man may have of his being may be very different from one's own . . . In these cases, one has to be able to re-orient oneself as a person in the other's scheme of things . . . One must be able to effect this reorientation without prejudging who is right and wrong. The ability to do this is an absolute and obvious prerequisite to working with psychotics. (1960, p. 26)

Thus any attempt to understand the world of the schizoid or schizophrenic person phenomenologically must preclude value judgments as to whether their experiences, ideas, and aspirations are abnormal. Leaving methodology aside, the inability to do so may prevent genuine participation in their subjective reality, undermining their already impaired capacity for trust and their need to communicate. In short, entertaining value judgments about a patient's project for achieving or defending a disembodied spiritual existence will be profoundly untherapeutic.

Yet the fact remains that what Laing says about the schizoid state gives rise to the impression that the misery experienced by the disembodied person is the product of a disturbed mind. He notes, for example, that ontologically insecure individuals have a shadowy or fragmentary sense of self and lack the ability to sustain satisfying interpersonal relationships. They experience the world as a menacing, hostile place and can only maintain an intermittent sense of personhood in isolation from others, because what the individual deems to be her authentic self "is experienced divorced from all activity that is observable by another" (1960, p. 73).

As a result, "the unembodied self, as onlooker to all the body does, engages in nothing directly. Its functions come to be observation, control and criticism vis a vis what the body is experiencing and doing, and those operations which are usually spoken of as purely mental" (p. 69). To compensate for its unfulfilled existential needs, the self retreats into fantasy. But fantasy "without being either in some measure embodied in reality, or itself enriched by injections of reality, becomes more and more empty and volatized" (p. 85).

As if this did not warrant a suspicion that something is amiss here, Laing himself reminds us that "*the sense of identity requires the existence of another by whom one is known;* and a conjunction of this other person's recognition of one's self with self-recognition. It is not possible to go on living in a sane way if one tries to be a man disconnected from all others and uncoupled even from a large part of one's own being" (p. 139). His formulation of the principle of mutual recognition and the inherently communal character of human life are amplified in the resonant utterance of the patient Peter, who toward the end of his treatment volunteered: "I've been sort of dead in a way. I cut myself off from other people and became shut up in myself. And I can see that you become dead in a way when you do this. You have to live in the world *with* other people. If you don't something dies inside. It sounds silly. I don't really understand it, but something like that seems to happen. It's funny" (p. 133).

Despite pleas for tolerance, then, Laing's own characterization of schizoid states in *The Divided Self* suggests that in rejecting the corporeal and communal aspects of being, schizoid persons are in flight from their basic humanity. Still Laing wrote with equal urgency: "it is possible to suggest that the individual should try to disentangle himself from his body and thereby achieve a desired state of disincarnate spirituality" (p. 66). To buttress this point, Laing quotes an anonymous Gnostic author cited by Rudolph Bultmann in *Primitive Christianity* (1956), who informs us that the body is "the dark prison, the living death, the sense-endowed corpse, the grave thou bearest about with thee, the grave thou carriest around with thee, the thievish companion who hateth thee in loving thee, and envieth thee in hating thee."

With this strange interpolation, Laing probably thought that corroboration from an ancient source would dispel whatever misgivings one may entertain about his argument. And as if this were insufficient—and it is—he insisted, quite rightly, that it is not possible to gauge sanity by the degree of embodiment a person experiences or espouses in daily life.

Let us grant Laing this last point for a moment. The relative degree of embodiment that a person enjoins is not in itself an indication of sanity or madness. Many religious people would agree that the real self (or soul) has to be disentangled from the body, and they are not insane for saying so. Nevertheless, and on the more general point, Laing finally fails to persuade. "It is," he says, "not possible to go on living indefinitely in a sane way if one tries to be a man disconnected from all others and uncoupled even from a large part of one's own being." At the very least, this remark implies that the Gnostic ideal of "divorce of soul (real self) from the body," which resembles the schizoid manner of being-in-the-world, is a flight from (or attack on) one's own humanity.[3]

The question arises: what relevance might Laing's notion of existential needs have to a totally disembodied mind (or subject)? Not much. The notion of needs in Laing's early work is free of crude biological determinism. But his notion of personal being presupposes a conscious, bodily being, whose relation to its own existence is articulated in and through its relations with other embodied selves.

That said, however, it is important not to fetishize Laing's concept of ontological security. Like Freud's pregenital and genital characters, Jung's introverted and extraverted types, and Klein's schizoid and depressive positions, Laing's account of ontological security and insecurity is a first-rate heuristic device, a splendid typological fiction. In our day and age, the defining attribute of the ontologically secure person is probably not the sense of agency, autonomy, and so on, but the realization that our essential relatedness to others and our separateness from them are mutually constitutive or dialectical polarities in human life, not logical or ontological alternatives, and that the one is meaningless without the other.

At the same time, as Alan Tyson observed three decades ago, *The Divided Self* struck a deep chord in millions of readers because schizoid feelings, attitudes, and experiences are so prevalent and intense in our society. As Erich Fromm said in 1955, chronic low-grade schizoid processes are part of what he termed "the pathology of normalcy" and are abundant in contemporary art and letters (Sass, 1992). In present circumstances, perhaps anyone who feels secure on a more or less uninterrupted basis is young or wealthy or stupid: more probably, all three. At the very least, such people would lack negative capability—the capacity for doubt, uncertainty, and mys-

tery—that Laing himself valued so highly. I dwell on this aspect of
Laing's work because it has continuing relevance. It does direct our
attention to his assumptions about the nature of our needs and passions and what it is to be a human being. And though scarcely free
from contradiction, it suggests that philosophy and psychotherapy
can be linked in a rigorous and systematic fashion.

So far, this analysis of Laing's existentialism is confined to the interpersonal field, to me and you, and the ongoing dialectic between
separateness and relatedness that suffuses human existence. Still, it
is also true that a sense of self is rooted in an individual's experiences in the social groups that constitute his or her social and cultural environment. By and large, the sense of "I am" presupposes a
sense of "we are," as well as a sense of "they" or that collective
Other in terms of whom one's corporate identity is experienced and
defined.

In view of the difficulties encountered with the issue of embodiment, it is not surprising that there are also contradictions in Laing's
handling of the communal aspects of human life. We find early evidence of this in an undated letter to Marcelle Vincent, written sometime in 1951, where Laing comments on the debate between Sartre
and Camus. Laing notes that Camus asserted the existence of a
"metaphysical solidarity with our fellow men," a shared essence or
nature: it is only through the emergence of a "we are"—established
through man's revolt—that I can really say "I am." Laing, significantly, sides with Sartre. He finds the very notion of "we" suspect,
arguing that there is no universal essence and that the essential relation between man and man is adversarial, not fraternal.[4] Indeed, like
Sartre, Laing excommunicates Camus, arguing that his ideas on
human solidarity go against the very grain of existentialism.

What, then, is the status of community and solidarity in Laing's
published work? How is it addressed, explained, or criticized? And
can we relate his ideas to his own project of therapeutic communities? Before tackling these questions, we should remember that the
word "solidarity" does not denote a single, homogeneous mode of
relatedness to others. On the contrary, like the word "love" it is a
multifaceted phenomenon expressed in many ways. To begin with,
solidarity may be based on kinship, language, faith, and on the de-

gree to which our sense of self is comprised, invested, or entangled in our vocations or professions and in regional or national identities. The fact that our individual lives are situated in specific social and cultural groups shapes our sense of ourselves: as parents and children; as English, French, or Arabic speakers; as Christians, Muslims, or Jews; as doctors, lawyers, laborers, or artists; as northerners, southerners, or westerners. In fact we can go further and say that *individual identities are syntheses of these social categories of inclusion,* and to that extent they are social constructions. This need not imply that identity is only an artifact—that you have no choice in how to appropriate and interpret these categories, for better or worse. Nor does it preclude conflict with other individuals in your reference groups. But it does mean that ordinarily your sense of rootedness in a social entity outweighs your sense of distance from it.

For many people, solidarity of this kind is the most common thing in the world. It affords a sense of embeddedness in a cultural community, if often at the expense of reason and compassion where nongroup members are concerned. After all, many of the categories of inclusion that the individual internalizes are categories of exclusion as well. Thus the rules of kinship dictate that a child may be a parent, in certain circumstances. But a man is not a woman, a Christian is not a Muslim, an Asian is not an African. So when it comes to defining a group's boundaries and identity—virtually the same thing in many cases—an "us" presupposes a "them." Difference, the Other, is the condition of all identity.

Yet experience also shows that solidarity can be extended to those who ordinarily are not participants in the construction and maintenance of our everyday world: the homeless, the hungry, the oppressed, refugees, foreigners, and the mad. To the extent that we identify with these disenfranchised groups and consider their plights to hinge on the beliefs and practices of the mainstream, rather than on their own weakness, we may even develop an oppositional identity, rooted in a sense of identification with those beyond the pale.

Curiously enough, the only kind of solidarity Laing describes in positive terms is empathy for the mad, which is so beautifully expressed in his own work. Undoubtedly this counts as an instance of solidarity with the outsider, or what Fromm called "love for the stranger" (1956). All other instances of solidarity Laing examines, from *Self and Others* through *Politics of the Family,* are instances of in-group solidarity and, as such, are destructive. They are not based on a real recognition of the other as a fellow human being, but on the interlacing of cognitive activity with collective fantasy systems; Laing called this *co-inherence*. In "Family and Individual Structure" he notes:

> If I think of certain others as together with me, and certain others as not together with me, I have already undertaken two acts of synthesis, resulting in *we* and *them*. The family is a common *we*, in contrast to *them* outside the family. But in addition, there are subgroups within the family, we, me, you, them, *we* parents, *those* children, *we* children, mother-and-child *we*, father as him, and so on. In order that any identity be formed as me as one of us, you have to make a similar synthesis, or in a triad, you and he or she and me, each and all have to become *us*. In such a family we, each of us, recognizes not only his or her own private family synthesis, but that such a synthesis exists in you, him and her also . . .
>
> Thus the family is united by the reciprocal internalization by each . . . of each other's internalization. The unity of the family is in the interior of each synthesis and each synthesis is bound by reciprocal interiority with each other's internalization of each other's internalization. (Lomas, 1967, pp. 110–111)

One interesting thing about Laing's co-inherence is the way in which the experience of "we-ness," of sharing in the same supraindividual identity, is taken to be a product of cognition or fantasy alone, and not of other social, cultural, economic, and historical constraints that shape the pattern of kinship. Laing does not ask if these constructions—or syntheses, as he calls them—might reflect deeper realities in the social fabric that are reflected or distorted in the individual's mental activity. By default if not by design, Laing implies that the family (or any other social entity) is invented simultaneously in the minds of all its participants. In the final analysis, it is nothing more than a thought construction.

Of course Laing did acknowledge in passing that there are other "group modes" or structures, but that they are not particularly relevant to his concerns (p. 118). Yet there is no denying that his discussion of family cohesion centered on its role in fomenting psychological disturbances, not in enhancing growth. A similar pattern prevails when he discusses the dynamics of national, racial, or ideological groups. In *Politics of Experience,* "The Obvious," and other papers, his remarks on group solidarity focus specifically on the fantasy nexus and its role in fomenting the myriad conflicts between "us" and "them." These conflicts run the gamut from the family feud to racism and world war, furnishing endless excuses for aggression, mystification, and mutual misunderstanding (1967a, 1967b, 1969).

In discussing social fantasy systems, Laing relied extensively on psychoanalytic theory. But he also used concepts like dialectics and mystification, derived from Marxism. So it may be helpful to contrast Laing's remarks on group cohesion with the ideas of Marx. In various works and in various ways, Marx suggested that people's beliefs and actions are motivated primarily by class interests based on material conditions, which create forms of social action in the furtherance of economic agendas. While the interests and conditions that unite people are generally real, in the end the preeminent social praxis intended to buttress shared objectives (short of actual violence) is the elaboration of ideology, or a system of belief whose function is to legitimate their political and economic agendas.

In other words, Marx did not deny the role of illusions in promoting social cohesion. On the contrary, he acknowledged that ideology posits fictive entities and relations between them (mystification) to disguise, disown, or distort historical actualities. Still, ideology and collective illusions do not create class (or group) cohesion, though they support it by disguising reality when the truth about social reality is too raw and disturbing to acknowledge. But even as he criticized ideological illusions, Marx also anticipated a postrevolutionary social order that would abolish class interest, and create a kind of solidarity rooted, as he said, in our *species being* (presumably foreshadowed in the aims and activities of the industrial proletariat, which Marx clearly mistook for a "universal class"). A classless society would create a social order purged of ideological illusions and predatory social relations. In such surroundings, our sense of solidarity would embrace the whole human species, and elements that divided us historically—religion, class, nationality—would wither away.

Though he did not explicitly rule it out, Laing never thematized a mode of solidarity based either on objective social realities or one that goes beyond parochial perspectives. On one—admittedly early and unpublished—occasion, Laing flatly denied that species-consciousness was possible, citing Sartre as his authority. Twenty-five years later, in *Reason and Violence,* Laing's concluding remarks allude to the remote possibility that the overcoming of scarcity might lead to the transcendence of predatory relation among individuals in a classless society. Unfortunately, these remarks are obscure, and Laing said nothing about how it might be done (Laing and Cooper, 1964, pp. 172–176). Nor did he indicate whether the scarcity that engenders adversarial relations is a given or an artificial (market-driven) scarcity created by certain groups in order to maintain their hegemony.

Thus Laing's discussion of human solidarity, sociability, and scarcity left many fundamental questions unanswered. The possibility of the attenuation of social antagonisms was an afterthought, not a vital option and a project for emancipatory struggle. Despite the lacunae in his theoretical work, Laing founded an organization, the Philadelphia Association, whose very name bespeaks concern for human solidarity. Is there a contradiction here? If the basic relation of one person to another is adversarial or antagonistic, as Sartre insisted, there is little likelihood that healing would take place in artificial communities like these. Indeed one could go further and ask how a therapeutic community could ever exist. And what rationale would there be for creating such communities, apart from utilitarian ones such as mutual defense or shared aggression?

Significantly, the residents of Kingsley Hall and related households never articulated their goals in terms of recovering the sociability that is distorted and disguised by scarcity and domination. Instead their project was to deconstruct the false identities and dualistic categories internalized in the process of socialization, heralding a kind of existential rebirth. At one point Laing and his followers even appeared to believe that people could disentangle their sense of self from the various forms of corporate identity and collective fantasy that suffuse the individual's mental life.

The attempt to divest oneself of every form of collective identity, while realizable in periods of mystical transport perhaps, is not attainable for any individual all of the time. At the very least, those who achieve the requisite detachment from collective illusions during meditation would tend to group themselves with the rare and heroic souls who have pierced the veil of Maya, with those who are "in the know," members of an elect or epistemic elite. Accordingly, Laing's pursuit of rigorous detachment from collective fantasy invites comparison with other paths to liberation.

In some ways, the fairest comparison would be to Vedanta and to the Neoplatonic Christianity of Dionysius the Areopagite, which were the proximal sources of Laing's vision. But though fair as far as it goes, this is not as illuminating as comparisons to two other intellectual traditions, Stoicism and Gnosticism (particularly in view of Laing's earlier ties with Marxism). The Stoic philosophers of Greece enjoined their followers to renounce all the particularisms of language, nationality, faith, and class, and to see themselves as world citizens, as rational beings living in a universe governed by natural law. If rational people see through the illusions of man-made laws, of class and ethnic divisions, and if they will the emergence of a universal order based on brotherhood and reason, then the will of God comes to eventual realization.

The Stoics' search for rational sociability, infused with secularized but profoundly messianic sensibilities, filtered through the legacy of Kant and Hegel, inspired young Marx's theory of species-consciousness. This philosophical tradition locates the divine within the worldly sphere. And by not excluding anyone from the participation in universal truth and the designs of Providence, it has generally been democratic in character.

Laing's affinities lie elsewhere, however. In contrast to the Stoics, the Gnostics taught that only a handful of human beings—the elect—can pierce the veil of ignorance obscuring our true nature, and the only law of nature in this fallen world is a malignant will to power, embodied in Jehovah and his archons (Jonas, 1961). Rather than obey nature, the elect should seek to transcend and defy it, to root their sense of identity in a cosmic deity—variously known as Abraxas, Pleroma, and so on—whose being is completely outside this world. Some of Laing favorite metaphors and rhetorical tropes—that we are asleep while dreaming we are awake, that we are dead but imagine that we are alive—are derived proximally from Gurdjieff or Sufi masters, to be sure. But ultimately they are Gnostic in derivation, and his frequent reliance on these colorful figures of speech says a great deal about his work. The Gnostic spirit is deeply distrustful of worldly power and authority, exquisitely attuned to the pervasive role of self-deception in human affairs. But it is also profoundly elitist, irreconcilably at odds with the things of this world (the body and its appetites among them).

At the risk of tremendous oversimplification, it could be argued that the history of Christian philosophy is a series of conflicts and compromises between Stoic/Hebraic and Gnostic sensibilities. Augustinian theology leaned toward otherworldly and Gnostic ideas and aspirations, while the scholastic synthesis of Thomas Aquinas reintroduced a more Stoic sensibility into mainstream Christian thought. The same might be said of Protestantism, although it is no accident that Martin Luther began his religious vocation as an Augustinian friar, and Augustine, in turn, began his as a Manichean.

As it happens, the Calvinist creed in which Laing was reared owed more to Augustine than to Aquinas. So it is interesting to note that Laing was much taken with Augustine and that, despite its name, which proclaims a mission of brotherly love, the Philadelphia Association during the Kingsley Hall period devoted far more energy to the task of extricating itself from the pervasive effects of mystification, collusion, and so on, than to restoring any latent sociability (Mezan, 1972). Perhaps they did not see what they were doing as an attempt to join the elect, but that essentially defined their concept of liberation.

The problem with this approach is that it attempts to define a communal project in purely negative terms, in terms of what the community is not and what it wants to avoid or eliminate. This *via negativa* makes no provision for (and no theoretical link with) Laing's tacit conception of existential needs and the overaching problems of scarcity and domination. The question then arises: can people be healed simply by the shedding of their false selves, if the environment they inhabit does not address their existential needs or eliminate the adversarial quality of human relations? These were questions that Laing never answered satisfactorily.

In his defense, it might be argued that Laing was fruitfully inconsistent: that his desire to foster therapeutic communities signaled a greater faith in people than he was willing to entertain in theory, or that his withering critique of social fantasy systems acknowledged the possibility, however remote, that people will see through them and recognize the humanity of their adversaries before mutual annihilation results. That was certainly the hope he expressed in chapter 4 of *Politics of Experience*. From this point of view, Laing's discussion of the role of fantasy systems in creating a sense of solidarity could be construed as a critique of *pseudo-solidarity,* not of the genuine article. But even this defense entails the dubious assumption that solidarity based on delusions is somehow less real or effective than solidarity based on truth and reality. (Were the Nazis any less effective in achieving their goals because of their collective delusions?)

The fact remains that Laing never achieved clarity in this area: the practical and theoretical connections and disjunctions between basic human needs, the structure of the family, conditions of scarcity and domination, the nature and function of therapeutic communities, were never fully explored in his work. As a result, since Laing's day members of the Philadelphia Association have approached the problems of therapeutic communities in Heideggerian or Lacanian idioms, and not by reference to its chief founder—which is a telling statement in itself.

10

THE CRITIQUE OF
$\mathcal{P}$SYCHOANALYSIS

As the preceding pages attest, Laing's relationship to psychoanalysis was fraught with ambivalence. In his clinical practice, Laing expressed a sovereign disregard for the standard protocols of psychoanalytic therapy. As he remarked to Richard Evans (1976), he felt that most of the rules and procedures of the analytic hour were designed for the therapist's benefit, not for the patient's. So Laing's patients were not obliged to use the couch but could sit on a chair or on the floor or pace up and down, whatever they preferred. At his invitation, they generally addressed him as "Ronnie" rather than as "Dr. Laing," and he was utterly indifferent to the conventional regulation of the timing and duration of analytic appointments, usually seeing patients for about an hour and a half once or twice a week, but sometimes seeing people for two or three hours at a time and keeping extended vigils with them in periods of crisis. He was not averse to nonsexual physical contact with patients, and his willingness to turn former patients into friends and colleagues (and vice versa) is well known.

Clinical conduct aside, however, Laing's published work shows that he harnessed his ambivalence productively, in a bold critique of many psychoanalytic concepts—one that presages many recent developments in the field. His early distrust of Freudian theory is shown in an astonishing letter to Marcelle Vincent, written around 1949. Here he viewed Freud's notion of unconscious mental processes with open suspicion, arguing that the idea of unconscious mental processes is not original to Freud but comes from Schopenhauer and von Hartmann. He said he admired Freud for championing such an idea "in the face of its evident absurdity" and went on to characterize him as what André Gide called "an imbecile of genius"—a creative man afflicted with tunnel vision, who is utterly unmoved by the rational objections of others. If we were to judge from this statement alone, we might imagine that Laing's skepticism would preclude a deeper engagement with psychoanalysis. But that was not the case. In *The Facts of Life* Laing recalled how, as a college student, he was drawn to it:

> although I thought I wanted to study embryology, and neurophysiology in particular, I found that I could not keep away from psychoanalysis. From the start, I had grave misgivings as to whether psychoanalysis was a science, since I doubted that it proceeded by a scientific *method*. But my fascination overruled my qualms. (1976, p. 150)

Though Laing's fascination got the better of him, he continued to doubt the scientific underpinnings of psychoanalysis. In *Reason and Violence,* coauthored with David Cooper, Laing even said that psychoanalysis "does not conflict with a Marxist philosophical framework, since it has no theoretical basis but is simply a technique, and an extremely good one, for investigating a vital sector of human reality" (1964, p. 23). Laing would later waver on the merits of psychoanalysis as technique, suggesting that it was developed in the service of ignoble or technocratic ideals. In a conversation with Roberta Russell, for example, he said:

> Basically, Freud is a popularizer of Nietzsche. We only see the emergent spray of what's going on behind our consciousness. We see it with a view to dominating it, controlling it, categorizing it, manipulating it, and one way or another exercising power over it. All our impetus to knowledge through awareness is motivated by power. (Russell and Laing, 1992, p. 189)

To judge from these musings, it appears that as a student in the late 1940s, Laing stressed the derivative nature of Freud's ideas and questioned their validity, if not their "fructifying influence." By the 1960s, now an analyst himself, Laing dismissed Freud's metapsychol-

ogy and questioned his methodology, but he regarded psychoanalysis as a useful technique "for investigating a vital sector of human reality." Two decades later, in 1981, he once again stressed Freud's
debt to earlier thinkers, this time to Nietzsche rather than to
Schopenhauer and von Hartmann. And like Foucault, he now characterized the motive behind the creation of psychoanalysis as a sublimated pursuit of power, or the hegemony of reason.

These brief assessments, culled from different periods in Laing's
life, are instructive because Laing seldom offered global appraisals
of psychoanalysis anywhere in his published work. He preferred to
address or attack specific features. Before surveying Laing's opinions and ideas, it may be useful to note the topics he *neglected* to explore. There is no need to be mean-spirited here. If Laing did not
address certain issues with the depth and seriousness that others
brought to them, this is not grounds for reproach; nor does it vitiate
what he did have to say in his own domain.

Laing's best work concerned the ways in which we become estranged from our own experience—whether through our own unconscious activity and choices or through the agency of others intent
on shaping our reality to conform with their own designs. Yet, by
his own admission, there is very little in Laing on the psychology of
gender and sexual difference—no theory of character, no developmental models or tables, no theory of psychic energy. Indeed, many
traditional topics of psychoanalytic inquiry go begging in Laing's
published work. When Laing did address these issues in passing, he
seldom fails to be illuminating. For example, in *The Divided Self:*

> It seems that the loss of the mother, at a certain stage, threatens the
> individual with the loss of his self. The mother, however, is not simply
> a *thing* that the child can see, but a *person* who sees the child. There-
> fore, we suggest that a necessary component in the development of the
> self is the experience of oneself as a person under the loving eye of the
> mother. (1960, 116)

Laing goes on to suggest that the emergence of the self as an existential subject, a being-for-itself, is conferred on the growing child by
its awareness of being an object for another's intentional activities—
looking, holding, feeding, bathing. As a result, being-for-oneself and
being-for-others are dialectically intertwined, and when the two
break apart, disjunctive, disturbance results. These remarks—

Hegelian in spirit—antedate D. W. Winnicott's germinal essay on the "Mirror Role of Mother and Family in Child Development" (1967) and Heinz Kohut's self-psychology. Even so, the point is that these Hegelian-cum-existential reflections on the emergence of the self is the exception, not the rule, in Laing's first decade of productive work. Though not particularly noteworthy now, perhaps, in its own day the assertion of the mother's pivotal role as "mirror" was quite avant-garde.

Though he anticipated later trends, in 1960 Laing was addressing an audience made up mostly of mainstream psychoanalysts and their patients. Though critical of analysis, he both needed and courted the more open-minded members of the analytic community. So he stopped quoting Gide's characterization of Freud as "an imbecile of genius" and described him instead as a "heroic" thinker. But Laing's ambivalence was not yet erased. It merely hinged on a different issue. According to Laing, Freud's reliance on medical metaphors in his assessment of psychological disturbances involves psychoanalysis in a unwitting process of reification and depersonalization that is endemic to all systems of psychopathology. Furthermore, Laing added, the model of the id, ego, and superego treats the individual as a self-contained monad existing in isolation from others (1960, chap. 1).

Laing's charge that classical Freudianism treats the individual as a self-enclosed monad may say more about the way Freud was taught to Laing as an analytic candidate than it does about Freud himself. In the introduction to *Group Psychology and the Analysis of the Ego* (1921), Freud makes it abundantly clear that it is impossible to understand other human beings without taking into account those whom they love, hate, idealize, identify with, and why. In short, Freud would have scorned the idea that one can deal with the individual in isolation.

On the other hand, there was some merit to Laing's reservations about the whole notion of "psychopathology" that Freud inherited and revised. In the mental health professions, conventional wisdom and prevailing linguistic usage suggest that "pathology" and "normality" are mutually exclusive. Indeed, normality is defined by the absence of pathology or by the degree of consensual validation attached to a particular thought, feeling, or behavior. But consensual validation, by its very nature, is a cultural or statistical artifact, which prescribes specific norms of conduct and belief considered appropriate to a person's age, gender, and social class. Like dress codes, manners, and linguistic usage, these prescriptive norms vary considerably with the person's social and historical milieu.

Medicine, on the other hand, attempts to generate norms of health and illness that are universally valid. Whereas cultural views of conduct and belief vary widely, the judgments of medicine are presumably rooted in the anatomy and physiology that all human beings share, no matter what their social context or moment in history. The problem, as Laing discerned, is that many mental health professionals are systematically trained to make conventional and culturally specific judgments about a patient's conduct, character, and beliefs that have little to do with their organismic well-being— or the lack of it—and then to invest these judgments with a specious universality and value neutrality, calling this "science."

Freud, for all his genius, did not help to clarify this situation. On the contrary, as Laing observed, the very title of his second book, *The Psychopathology of Everyday Life* (1901), suggests that Freud saw all kinds of incipiently pathological phenomena as part and parcel of the normal condition, which adds nothing (Laing, 1990). Arguably, Freud's attempt to situate normal and neurotic behavior on the same explanatory continuum was evidence of his humanism and his desire to foster empathy with those in psychic distress. But, as Laing observed, for most analysts, beginning with Freud, psychotics are generally not included on this continuum; they are beyond the pale because they lack the capacity for transference and, by implication, for relatedness to others. Evidently Martin Buber and Carl Rogers followed Freud in this. Laing heartily disagreed with this conclusion, and so he opted to jettison the medical model rather than tinker with it, since he thought that any modifications introduced *within* that frame of reference were doomed to sterility or self-deception. Instead Laing endorsed a existential-phenomenological approach, which conceptualizes mental disturbances as the expression of an individual's being-in-the-world.

The next installment in Laing's critique of analytic theory came in *Self and Others* (1961). The opening pages of this book are devoted to a trenchant critique of Susan Isaacs' codification of Melanie Klein's theory of unconscious fantasy. Laing noted that in making interpretations, an analyst often claims privileged access to a domain of the patient's experience that patients themselves lack. Analysts may claim, say, that without realizing it, a patient wants to be nursed by the therapist, to seduce or be seduced, or that they hate the therapist, despite vigorous disclaimers on the patient's part.

Laing observed, however, that the inferences analysts make about patients' unconscious experience usually entail a host of subsidiary assumptions about mental structures, processes, and functions, many of which are dubious at best. Laing took on the constitutive dualisms of analytic discourse, such as mental and physical, psychic and physical reality, inner and outer, and concluded that even in the absence of the meanings attached to them in different contexts by different authors—that is, even if usage were consistent, which it is not—these dualisms involve us in intractable theoretical conundrums and undercut most renderings of the term "unconscious."

Also, if the Freudian metapsychology is wrong, then inferences based on it are bound to be faulty. The unstated implication of Laing's view is that if interpretations are correct, it might be by sheer coincidence or simple intuition, not from any special intellectual rigor attributable to the analytic method. As it happens, Laing was not just attacking the epistemic status of analytic concepts, but the whole cult of the expert that pervades the psychoanalytic profession. According to Laing, an analyst's inferences and attributions about a patient's motives and states of mind are just that, inferences and attributions. Like any other set of judgments, they should be subject to the same criteria and evidential processes that apply elsewhere. In the absence of such scrutiny, analytic interpretations may be no more than shots in the dark, which patients must accept if they wish to stay in therapy.

Unfortunately, Laing noted, the logic of interpersonal experience and attribution—of who attributes what to whom, in what circumstances, to what effect, and why—had never been satisfactorily elucidated, though Heider and Buber had made bold beginnings in this direction. The question then arises: what would a science of interpersonal attributions and inferences be like? Laing would soon expound on the methodology for the study of interpersonal attributions in *Sanity, Madness and the Family* (1964) and *Interpersonal Perception* (1966). Meanwhile, in *Self and Others* he devoted more space to showing what the appropriate methodology is *not*.

Echoing Dilthey and Husserl, he noted that the natural science approach to psychology obstructs the rigorous study of interpersonal processes, since the objects of inquiry in the natural sciences are not persons. As a human being, I experience my own actions as motivated by (and intelligible in terms of) my experience of the world and of others in it. When I observe other people, I infer from my own experience that their actions are a function of *their* experience, however concealed it may be.

But since others' experience is not directly accessible to me, all my ideas about their experience—conscious or unconscious—are mediated by empathy and inference, both through dialogue and nonverbal communication. This is not the case in the natural sciences. Atoms, molecules, tides, and stellar nebulae cannot communicate ideas or intentions to their interrogators, nor can investigators ever hope to know what it feels like to be the objects of their study. And apart from the most intelligent animal species, most objects of the natural sciences have no ability or desire to communicate or to conceal their experience from observers—or from themselves, for that matter. They do not experience their experiencers or regard them in a potentially friendly or hostile light.

So Laing concluded, it is impossible to derive the logic of a "science of persons" from the natural sciences. If analysts confined themselves to the attribution (or inference) of agency, motives, intentions, and experiences that the patient disclaims and is unaware of, psychoanalysis might engage meaningfully with existential phenomenology. In the meantime, there is "an extraordinary exfoliation of forces, energies, dynamics, economics, processes and structures to explain the 'unconscious'" (1961, p. 29). These hypothetical processes are used to explain other hypothetical experiences, motives, and meanings of which the patient is supposedly unaware, rendering them "doubly chimerical" in Laing's estimation.

It seems obvious that using one hypothetical process or entity, such as a defense mechanism, to explain the existence of another hypothetical entity, which the patient vigorously disclaims, such as an unconscious wish, fantasy or conflict, is an undertaking filled with risk and uncertainty. We can see the dangers of this in Freud's own writings. In some case histories, Freud makes interpretations to suit his theoretical preconceptions, quietly seething with disappointment when patients fail to find his constructions persuasive and refuse to go along. Yet, as a seasoned clinician, Laing knew well that people really do have thoughts, feelings, wishes, beliefs, and conflicts they are not conscious of, and they must exist if one is to make sense of a person's conscious experience and behavior. Despite his reservations about psychoanalysis, Laing never wavered in this view. From *Reason and Violence,* for example: "There is plenty of room for a phenomenological examination of unconscious phantasy, in so far as the latter is conceived in its reality as experience and not as a series of mechanisms to be imposed on the subject objectified in the psycho-analytic situation" (Laing and Cooper, 1964, p. 25).

Looking back, we are apt to forget that Laing's rejection of the natural science approach to psychoanalysis, which is now quite common, was considered radical in the early 1960s. By formulating his critique of mainstream theory so forcefully, Laing was courting rejection. One anecdote speaks to the reception *The Divided Self* and *Self and Others* received in the analytic establishment. In 1962 Charles Rycroft attended a meeting of the British Psychoanalytic Society, at which James Home read a paper called "The Concept of Mind" (Rycroft, 1994). Home argued that psychoanalysis is essentially a semantic theory, one of the humanities or moral sciences—or one of the *Geisteswissenschaften,* as Dilthey or Husserl might have said.

In response to Home, Rycroft recalls, the faithful rose en masse to denounce this heresy and to affirm their unwavering faith in Freud's notion of psychic determinism and the natural-scientific basis of analytic theory. To appreciate how irrational this collective response was, we should bear in mind that the deterministic belief in immutable laws of natural causation was waning during Freud's own lifetime. In the late nineteenth century, mechanistic materialism was being overturned by a probabilistic and statistical orientation that was more in keeping with modern physics (Hacking, 1991). Thus Freud's belief in psychic determinism, supposedly derived from the scientific world view, was already anachronistic in the 1920s, never mind in 1961 when Laing published *Self and Others.* The model of the natural sciences most analysts espoused when Laing began writing was already obsolete.

Though largely ignored by the psychoanalytic establishment, elements of *The Divided Self* and *Self and Others* anticipated several major developments in the analytic world by a decade or so. Begin-

ning in the mid-1960s, a student of David Rapaport's, George Klein,
became exasperated with the obvious errors and inconsistencies in
Freud's metapsychology and attempted to extract a clinical theory
from the writings that would be faithful to observed phenomena
without making false assumptions on "metapsychological" matters.
George Klein's initiative sparked a round of debate and theorizing
among Rapaport's students that issued, among other things, in Roy
Schafer's "action language," which came closest to Laing's theoretical ideal of fidelity to experience without multiplying hypotheses or
treating the patient's actions and attitudes as attributes of independent "agencies" within the psyche.[1]

Few exponents of humanistic or hermeneutically oriented psychoanalysis have acknowledged Laing's priority or importance in this
area. Two noteworthy exceptions are Erich Fromm and Charles
Rycroft, whose theoretical position since the mid-1960s shifted in a
somewhat Laingian direction under the influence of James Home
and Susanne Langer.

In any case, despite dire warnings about slipshod methodology and
scientism, Laing was not just an insightful critic but an important
theorist in his own right. His most important contributions lay in his
concepts of unconscious fantasy and transpersonal defenses, which
revised the two approaches to analytic theory that were current in
Britain at the time. When Laing arrived on the scene, the study and
elucidation of defense mechanisms was the domain of Anna Freud,
and the concept of unconscious fantasy was pursued most avidly by
Melanie Klein. These concepts were designed to elucidate patients'
experience of themselves (and their analysts), predicated on the assumption that conscious experience is profoundly affected by unconscious conflicts and desires.[2]

For the sake of discussion, let us suppose a patient believes that
he is a prophet sent to save the world from imminent catastrophe.
Taken at face value, this delusion is not an unconscious fantasy, but
a imaginary construction that is consciously experienced and expressed. The problem is that the patient has lost the ability to discriminate between the fantasy and the reality. So the fantasy is not
experienced as a fantasy, but as a compelling and irrevocable fact.
Still it is not repressed. On the contrary, the patient is obsessed by

the fantasy, which psychiatry would classify as delusions of grandeur with messianic overtones.

Unless we happen to believe the patient's claim to savior status, the disjunction between his experience of himself and our experience of him is so vast that it must be explained. To account for the situation, the medical model posits the existence of some disturbance of neurophysiology or some structural-anatomical defects, whereas the psychoanalytic approach would focus on unconscious conflicts. A Kleinian analyst might suggest that the savior idea, and the patient's fear of the end of the world, represents a projected fear and desire from earliest infancy, in which the child hoped to spare its mother the devastating effects of its own destructive rage, which it feared would engulf her, destroying himself and his world in the process. In short, his conscious fantasy is an unconscious transposition of infantile wishes from the preoedipal (and preverbal) period of his life, which had never entered consciousness before.

Another way of interpreting the delusion is as a defense. An analyst might say that the patient's delusions of grandeur are reaction-formations against repressed feelings of worthlessness, inferiority, and powerlessness that originate in unresolved oedipal difficulties. Either way, though, psychoanalytic therapy is predicated on the assumption that the only way to dissolve the distortions of unconscious fantasies and defense mechanisms is to render them available to awareness. And the technical method for transposing fantasies, fears, and desires from the patient's unconscious and into her conscious experience is called "interpretation."

The problem, as Laing noted, is that categorical distinctions between conscious and unconscious experience, between fantasy and defense mechanisms, and so on, all beg the more fundamental question of what experience actually *is* (1967, p. 42). Unless we are clearer on that point, we may simply be chasing our tails. So to begin with, what is experience?

Laing often posed this question, but he never answered it systematically. Instead he offered an array of compelling reflections that are widely dispersed through his books and papers. They demand integration, but that is a daunting task. As Juliet Mitchell has noted, Laing's use of the word "experience" was sometimes narrowly empirical, more or less equivalent to perception or conception, and sometimes studiously vague and mystical. Laing used the word in diverse senses as needed, to suit his shifting polemical purposes and to buttress his mystical-transcendental project with a semblance of common sense (Mitchell, 1975).

But Laing felt that there was no inherent contradiction in using "experience" in several senses. Is there any thread of consistency to lead us through the labyrinth of his texts? I believe there is. But first it is instructive to note what "experience," by Laing's reckoning, is *not*. Experience, like the self, is not something palpable, not an entity that can be touched or seen, not something that exists "out there" in space and time, to be dissected, measured, and observed. This has led some people to imagine that experience is essentially an inner process. And in one sense, of course, it is. At the same time, as Brentano and Husserl stressed, experience is always an experience *of* something, and this has led some to confuse experience with the processes of perception.

As Laing observed, however, you cannot explain experience by studying the anatomy and physiology of sight, smell, touch, hearing, and so forth (Laing, 1976). Experience is *mediated* by the senses, to be sure, but each sensory organ or perceptual modality contributes merely one part of the integrated gestalt of our sensorium, and for those people who lose or regain the use of a sensory modality, its absence or recovery—say of sight or hearing—is itself a process of experience, a transformation of our personal awareness (Sacks, 1993).

Thus one might be tempted to speculate that experience, while not identical to any single sense modality, arises from the integration of all our perceptual processes. That is a closer approximation, but still falls short of the truth. After all, the attempt to explain experience in terms of the cross-modal integration of various sensory modalities focuses on the "contents" of experience and the processes whereby the perception of such objects is possible. It addresses the "how" of experience, not the "what" of experience itself. Meanwhile, everything we know about the process of experiencing (including our knowledge of the brain) is based on inferences derived from experience, which in an important sense remains primary and unaccounted for. While attempts to reduce experience to specific sensory organs and brain processes may be doomed to failure, philosophically speaking, they are illuminating to the extent that they emphasize the *object-centered* quality of experience. Experience may be an inner process, but by the same token it is always an experience *of* something. And as Laing at first defined it, experience presupposes an experiencing subject as well as an object to experience.

At first glance, all of this seems to imply that experience is something that originates inside the experiencer but refers to something outside. Laing rejected this view, arguing that one's experience of the world is not something that occurs in one's head, so to speak, but happens out there as well. Besides, in his study of schizoid self-consciousness, Laing noted that experience has a self-referential aspect, where the person is simultaneously the subject and object of experience. At a basic level, we may experience our own states of bodily arousal (hunger, lust, fear, fatigue) and our emotional states (joy, excitement, perplexity, ennui). At more complex levels, we can *experience ourselves experiencing* an inner or external object, with a view to appreciating, understanding, or distancing ourselves from our ideas, feelings, attitudes, and so on—a process traditionally termed introspection or, more recently, reflexivity.

Though the notion of experience presupposes an experiencing subject and an object of experience—even if that object is oneself, finally—no one, Laing least of all, maintains that experience is a stable, continuous process. Even to a naive observer, the process of experience undergoes innumerable shifts and fluctuations. Two people can experience one object, event, or situation in radically different ways, depending on their mood, their levels of anxiety or fatigue, their cultural and social background, or religious and political affiliations. And as experiments in social psychology have shown, a person may experience objects and events very differently in the presence of others, depending on what role or status those others have, and what degree of consensus regarding what is real or true obtains (Asch, 1950; Milgram, 1967).

Finally, it is important to remember that people may not allow themselves to experience themselves feeling, thinking, remembering, or willing, in which case we usually say that their experience is unconscious or repressed. This does not mean that the ideas, feelings, or fantasies cease to influence behavior. They simply do not register in a person's consciousness. In such cases, both the motive and the means whereby someone implements a decision *not* to experience herself experiencing is also, of necessity, unconscious. This is what is meant by a defense mechanism, and Freud speculated that the various mechanisms that obstruct the entry of certain thoughts, feelings, memories, fantasies, and intentions into consciousness— such as projection, displacement, reaction-formation, repression, sublimation—are first and foremost intrapsychic phenomena. The individual's sense of reality is constricted or distorted by an intrapsychic censor—a part of the ego or, later, the superego—which prevents certain aspects of a person's experience from becoming accessible to reflexive self-awareness.

Laing broadened the scope of analytic inquiry by demonstrating that many of the so-called defense mechanisms are not situated inside the individual, but are distributed throughout the various groups and institutions that claim our allegiance or shape our lives. These he termed "transpersonal defenses." Without denying the existence of the Freudian unconscious, Laing noted that every human collective has implicit rules governing what may or may not be directly experienced or expressed about the group itself, and that any discussion of these rules is also taboo. Adherence to these tacit rules is a collaborative undertaking and, though frequently unconscious, is a decidedly interpersonal process, not a purely intrapsychic affair.[3]

As an illustration of transpersonal defenses, Laing cited Freud's famous case of Dora, "Fragment of an Analysis of a Case of Hysteria" (1905), which he reviewed for his audience at the William Alanson White Institute (January 20, 1967). Dora, aged eighteen, consulted Freud for three months, then left analysis for a year, and returned for a brief period before terminating altogether. She suffered from coughing, aphonia, and *taedium vitae,* which Freud, using free association, connected to several attempted seductions, the last one being at an Alpine lake when she was sixteen. Dora's would-be seducer was Herr K., a family friend who, it turned out, was the husband of her father's mistress—a fact Dora was well aware of on the occasion of his last and most vigorous overture. Though Dora had enjoyed friendly relations with Frau K., she now regarded her with contempt and wanted her father to break off the affair.

On Freud's reading, Dora's physical malaise was the combined product of repressed sexual desire and revulsion. Her horrified response to Herr K.'s advances was a reaction-formation against (1) normal sexual desire, (2) a deep father fixation, and (3) her envy of

Frau K. Freud felt that a healthy girl in Dora's circumstances should have found Herr K.'s proposal "neither tactless nor offensive." Dora balked, and bolted.

After a year she returned, reporting that she had confronted her mother, her father, his mistress, and Herr K. about the concealment of their affairs. Freud regarded this confrontation as an act of spite, but said he would forgive her for depriving him of a more "radical" cure. After a brief but unsuccessful effort to get the analysis back on track, Dora left again, this time with more dignity and resolve.

In his gloss on the case, Laing noted that Dora's father wanted Freud to make her "see reason." And though Laing doesn't say so expressly, Freud evidently sensed that Dora's father really wanted to stop her from making accusations that would mortify her mother and allow him to protect his (steadily dwindling) opportunities for clandestine meetings with his mistress. Furthermore, as Freud freely confessed—and as Laing neglected to note, curiously enough— Freud himself was an old friend of Dora's father. His notion that Dora should have found Herr K.'s advances "neither tactless nor offensive" suggests a singular lack of empathy for the patient, if not indeed collusion with her father.

Laing noted that what is going on here was not so much the repression of sexuality on Dora's part, but a kind of collective "bad faith," a slippery evasion of the truth about the sexual conduct and desires of the adults around her—a situation that, by her own account, was sickening her, both emotionally and physically. Even worse, Laing argued, Dora's father seemed quite willing to exchange her sexual favors for Frau K.'s, while steadfastly denying that he had any such intention. To his credit, Freud saw through the father's self-deception and may have communicated this insight to Dora. But as Laing correctly observed, she was still in a strange and unnerving position, where uttering the simple truth was considered symptomatic of a mental disturbance by her elders and betters, one that rendered her in need of "treatment."

In other contexts, Laing termed this kind of collective denial and disavowal "invalidation," because it depicted a person's attitudes and ideas as depraved or distorted and therefore untrue. By attributing Dora's anguish to an underlying psychological disability, the adults around her could maintain appearances, rendering her an "invalid"—a "hysteric"—in the process.

Looking at Freud's interventions from a Laingian perspective, it is apparent that Freud was sending Dora a very mixed message. As her father and mother and the K.s put up a united front against her, Freud validated Dora's experience, up to a point, by acknowledging the existence of the collective duplicity that, by Dora's own reckoning, was driving her mad. Moreover, he emphatically did *not* accuse Dora of paranoia, though many of his contemporaries doubtless would have. Yet Freud also maintained that the real cause of her malaise lay not in her family situation but in a hidden disability, as her father and Herr K. insisted. Like her father, Freud experienced Dora's need to puncture pretenses as evidence of vindictiveness rather than of justifiable anger at being manipulated and lied to. Judging from Laing's reading here, Freud's diagnosis of hysteria, and his selective emphasis on (real or alleged) intrapsychic factors, relegated the disturbing qualities of Dora's current life to a factor of secondary or negligible importance in the pathogenesis of her disturbance.

This kind of family duplicity was not new to Laing, of course. He was an old hand at bringing such scenarios to light. *Sanity, Madness and the Family* contained eleven case histories of young women who were devastated by such duplicity. But Dora was merely "hysterical." Laing's and Esterson's subjects were psychotic, or allegedly so. What is the difference? Certainly not in their family discourses. Dora's family was as full of collusion, duplicity, and evasion as the families studied by Laing and Esterson. The main difference seems to be that while Laing and Esterson's subjects were invalidated from early childhood, the deception Dora encountered was relatively unprecedented in her experience, and it was specifically designed to allow her father, Frau K., and Herr K. a measure of covert sexual satisfaction and to spare her mother embarrassment.

Furthermore, it should be noted that the invalidation of Dora's experience by her elders was partly a deliberate stratagem, and she knew it. Indeed, Dora probably attributed a greater measure of deliberate deception to her father and the others than was actually so, which is why her father thought her deranged and Freud thought her malicious. In her adolescent naiveté, she could not bring herself to believe that the bargains her elders evidently struck with themselves and one another could not be conscious, and so she faced them angrily, head on.

Dora may have lost some perspective and sympathy for others in the process. Perhaps someone older, with more savoir-faire, would have been more compassionate and avoided a spirited confrontation, as Freud evidently believed. But to her credit Dora also refused to be victimized by the defenses of those around her, whose shared investment in concealing the truth—from themselves and others— was relatively transparent to her. The Laing and Esterson subjects were not so lucky. Their parents perpetrated mind games on their children successfully from infancy on, rendering their children's experience of their environment extremely opaque and ambiguous. With Dora at least, things were relatively clear-cut, and she was just intact enough to cling to her own sense of reality. To paraphrase Laing in a slightly different context, Dora "trusted her distrust" of others just enough to maintain her grip on reality. Had she had a stronger need to trust others, had her doctor been more threatening, invalidating, or dismissive, she might have become as muddled and helpless as Laing's and Esterson's subjects were.

Though it took a while to develop, by 1967 Laing's theory of transpersonal defenses was well articulated. He discussed it in his lectures and in various publications, including "Family and Individual Structure" (1967), *The Politics of Experience* (1968) and *The Politics of the Family* (1968, 1971). Laing now referred to the various strategies people employ to avoid confronting the truth as operations on experience, a term that covers both intrapsychic (individual) and transpersonal (group or family) defenses. He evidently preferred this to the older "defense mechanisms," because the latter term implies misleadingly that (1) the phenomena in question are psychic automata or, in Sartre's terminology, process, and not praxis, and (2) that they occur inside the individual, rather than between people, when in fact they can be either or both.

Laing's other noteworthy achievement during the 1960s was his theory of unconscious fantasy. In order to put this element in perspective, once again let us recall that what individuals will or will not allow themselves to experience, for whatever reason, is always a matter of critical importance in clinical work. This is because certain features of patients' experience—of their therapists, themselves, their families, loved ones, and the world at large—are so different from what other people take to be true, that they call for some sort of explanation. You may think, for example, that your parents are conspiring against you or that you are really female even though you have male organs. Or you may think that you are a worthless, evil person, who is doomed to failure in love, or that your analyst actively dislikes you or means to seduce and humiliate you, without ever convincing the analyst that your grounds for believing this have the slightest justification.

Freud's explanations for experiences that lack consensual validation tended to emphasize intrapsychic factors and the person's past experience, at the expense of latent or hidden features of the person's current situation. And a great deal hinged on what Freud and his followers termed "reality testing." In the ideal case, our sense of reality and personal identity is enhanced as we grow in memory, judgment, and cognitive complexity, and as the ego becomes strong and stable. But if, owing to neurotic or psychotic disturbances, our judgment is impaired by the return of the repressed, we hear talk of regression to earlier "levels," of primary and secondary processes, and of various pregenital attitudes and orientations. Or, after Freud, we hear of the paranoid and depressive positions (Klein), of prototaxic, parataxic, and syntactic experience (Sullivan), of autocentric and allocentric perception (Schactel), and of experience in the imaginary, the symbolic, and the real (Lacan).

According to analytic theory, then, these various modes of experience, and their corresponding forms of cognition, emerge in an orderly maturational sequence, with some transitional overlapping between stages or regression to earlier stages in adverse circumstances. When a person's judgment seems radically unbalanced, the disorder is explained by recourse to repression, regression, and unconscious fantasy. On this reading, *unconscious fantasy is essentially a process whereby the person's grasp of reality is distorted or impaired by unresolved infantile needs and conflicts, which presumably underlie the conscious experience.*

Take the concept of transference. Transference was originally defined by Freud as a defense, since it enables patients to continue repressing the memory of certain episodes in their lives. But the fantasy element is also unmistakable. In the transference, a patient experiences the analyst as having certain qualities or certain attitudes toward the patient that the analyst presumably does not have.

As the analysis unfolds, it emerges that the attitudes, feelings, and qualities the patient experienced in the analyst are really those possessed by a parent, sibling, or significant other, which have been superimposed onto the person of the analyst. The patient has been gripped by a fantasy emanating from earlier experiences and conflicts, but is not conscious of doing so until it is called to his attention repeatedly through the methodical observations of the therapist.

Prior to Laing, the dominant conception of unconscious fantasy in analytic circles was essentially Freudian. It emphasized the role of fantasy in distorting interpersonal perception. According to this rationalist reading, *unconscious fantasy is a device to avoid the experience of something real.* Thus if a patient dreams that her analyst prepared a sumptuous meal and watched with maternal solicitude as she ate it, the presumption is that this oneiric interlude has little or nothing to do with the therapist per se, and speaks solely to the nature of the patient's unconscious desire.

But some dissenting voices—notably Jung, Georg Groddeck, and Melanie Klein—attempted to correct this view, by crediting the unconscious mind with constructive capabilities that Freud typically found lacking. Citing a wealth of clinical material, Jung argued that an individual's dreams and fantasies often bespeak greater insights than the waking ego has yet achieved, and that some unconscious fantasies derive from sources that precede or transcend the individual's experience and development. As often as not, these archetypal fantasies intrude on our waking, adult lives in ways that are disruptive or frankly destructive. But in certain circumstances, if integrated into the self, unconscious fantasies compensate for the blind spots or one-sided development of our adult personalities, and they foster wisdom, integration, and differentiation of the psyche.

Though Groddeck did not use the language of archetypes, he noted the wisdom of the unconscious as it is experienced and expressed in the language of the body. Our bodies "know" a great deal more about ourselves and others than we allow ourselves to acknowledge, and if we take the requisite care to listen, we will grow in wisdom and maturity. According to Groddeck, all our bodily symptoms conceal fantasies that harbor important truths we ignore or dismiss as irrational, for fear of confronting our real selves directly.

Finally, Klein argued that unconscious fantasies are basically of two kinds. Fantasies based on splitting in the "paranoid schizoid position" invariably impair our judgment, while reparative fantasies, in the "depressive position," counteract the earlier, schizoid tendency toward splitting, rendering our interpersonal judgment deeper, more veridical, reliable, and intact. In Klein, as in Jung and Groddeck, the argument is that unconscious fantasy is not invariably a way of avoiding contact with reality. In many instances, the discovery and elucidation of unconscious fantasies gives us a deeper and more direct understanding of existential actualities than we consciously recognized before.

Laing's notion of unconscious fantasy, set forth in his own inimitable style, followed in this heterodox tradition. He readily conceded that our first (and in some sense, primary) way of experiencing the world is through fantasy. But he insisted with equal vigor that fantasy

> has its own validity, its own rationality. Infantile phantasy may become a closed enclave, a dissociated undeveloped "unconscious," but this need not be so. This eventuality is another form of alienation. Phantasy as encountered in many people today is split off from what the person regards as his mature, sane, rational adult experience. We do not then see phantasy in its true function but experienced merely as an intrusive, sabotaging infantile nuisance. (1967, p. 27)

What, then, is fantasy's true function? According to Laing, it is to express the truth of lived experience in symbols and metaphors, whose intuitive and poetic insights often exceed our conscious ratiocination in depth and acuity. If fantasy in this sense is allied to our conscious adult selves, we become more, and not less, in touch with reality. If not, we are alienated from a large part of our experience—in a chronic, low-grade state of schizoid dissociation from the wellsprings of our inner life.

Laing's refusal to denigrate fantasy had vivid antecedents in psychoanalysis, as we have seen, but it also owed a large debt to existential phenomenology. Unlike psychodynamic approaches to psychology, existential phenomenology generally lacks a developmental or ontogenetic dimension, to both good and bad effect. It understands fantasy—conscious or unconscious—as a symbolic codification of the person's experience of the present, of needs, values, and conflicts, and last but not least of his "project," the way he sees his future unfolding. In general, the existential-phenomenological approach to fantasy has a deeper affinity with Jung's notion of the "prospective function" and with Adler's "fictional finalism" than with Freud's determinism.

As a result, existential phenomenologists expect little more from stage theories of experience than a set of useful heuristic concepts. (In view of the never-ending stream of new stage theories, they are seldom disappointed.) Like most phenomenologists, Laing was not enamored of developmental theories of experience, though he did not dismiss them out of hand. But when he did discuss such matters, it was usually to point out their problems and shortcomings, their lack of fidelity to the patient's experience, and their refusal to acknowledge the role of individual life situations in the psychogenesis of their complaints. Transposing the ostensible meaning of symptoms from past to present, from the intrapsychic to the interpersonal sphere, and then demonstrating the hidden but *adaptive* aspect of seemingly maladaptive behaviors—this was the hallmark of Laing's best case histories and clinical vignettes. It also characterized his approach to Freud's Dora. The point was not to interpret symptoms as the lingering residues of a forgotten past, but to demystify the person's enveloping social matrix (which includes the psychiatrist or therapist, who can never be neutral) and to discover the symptom's social intelligibility.

In Laing's opinion, then, many bizarre symptoms and beliefs reflect ongoing conflicts within the family that the others prefer to disavow. Alternatively, conflicts that bedevil the adult personality are the residue of conflictual patterns between one's parents and the compliant or rebellious parts of one's self. So it is no longer a question of a patient's having simply introjected "good" or "bad" objects in early childhood. A disturbed individual frequently incarnates the whole ensemble of social relations that prevail in his family of origin, and many varieties of inner conflict are best construed as the lingering reverberations of these, rather than as conflicts between physiological drives or competing "agencies" in the psyche (Lomas, 1967). Thus introjection is a process of internalizing patterns of relation between various presences at various points in the ontogenetic sequence. But these patterns have a provenance that may stretch back several generations.

Though he was certainly a more eloquent and forceful writer on this point, Laing was not the first to draw attention to the intergenerational context of mental disorder. In a chapter called "Family Scenarios" in *Politics of the Family,* Laing noted that Freud noticed this phenomenon too, albeit without realizing its full implications. For example, Freud related the case of a mother so struck by the resemblance between her young son and her own mad brother that she became convinced her child would follow in his uncle's footsteps. But it is apparent from Freud's narrative that the steps she took to avert this dreaded outcome (in fantasy) promoted the likelihood of its actually occurring (in reality). In other words, her fear of hereditary taint engendered a self-fulfilling prophesy, which left her boy no room to discover his own sense of self apart from the mother's waking nightmare (Laing, 1971, pp. 83–85).

Although Freud touched on these issues only in passing, Jung thematized them explicitly and used association experiments and EEG charts to demonstrate that parents and children often have eerily identical "complexes," indicating a strong mutual identification or a lack of individuation, as the case may be. The sins of the father and mother are visited on their offspring and are literally reincarnated in successive generations through a kind of unconscious emotional contagion that infants are particularly susceptible to (Jung, 1935; Perry, 1961).

Erik Erikson took a different approach. Where Freud and Jung were interested in pathogenesis, Erikson was more concerned about health. He said that some degree of transgenerational identification must take place among grandparents, parents, and children, and it is a natural and necessary process to ensure cultural continuity and a stable sense of identity. Many neurotic and psychotic symptoms attest to the breakdown of transgenerational identification, not to its strength or efficacy (Erikson, 1964).

Whatever else we may wish to say about it, Laing's approach to intergenerational phenomena was essentially the opposite of Erikson's. As Laing understood it, transgenerational identification is not a spontaneous, sustaining process that enables people to define themselves as autonomous beings, or to plot their own destinies within the boundaries of a viable culture. On the contrary, many sensitive souls lapse into psychosis, often never to return, because of the usually unwitting identities that are imposed by one generation on another, which prescribe a life in which an authentic sense of self, and of relationship to others, is sometimes permanently out of reach, wrapped in a fog of projection, misattribution, hidden injunction, and pervasive mystification.[4]

Some of Laing's critics consider this vision of family life ghoulish. But surely there is evidence for both views, and Laing's line of theorizing is no less valid in its methods or conclusions than Erikson's. Scientific merit aside, it is intriguing that Laing's and Erikson's theses are intelligible in light of their own experiences of growing up and of consolidating their own sense of identity. By virtue of his absent father and the difficulties he experienced identifying with his stepfather, Theodor Homberger, Erikson's sense of generational continuity was disrupted, and his adolescent psychosis forced him to compensate by creating a new identity of his own, which is why he eventually changed his name from Erik Homberger to Erik H. Erikson—"Erik, son of Erik" (Monte, 1991, chap. 5).

Laing's approach, by contrast, was rooted in his relationship to his mother. As we have seen, Amelia Laing insisted that Ronald took after her own father, whom she regarded as a wicked man. As Laing experienced it, the strength of this misguided conviction dominated his youth and prevented him from developing a viable relationship with his parent.

Incidentally, I am not arguing that Erikson's attitude toward transgenerational identification was a derivative manifestation of a "father complex" or that Laing's resulted from a "mother complex." The point I do make is that during his childhood and adolescence, Erikson evidently experienced the thread of intergenerational continuity as sorely absent; he spent much of his life trying to recover it for himself, and then thematized this issue for (and with) his patients and the various cultures he studied. Indeed, it is possible to regard Erikson's mature clinical work as creative extensions of his attempt at self-healing, not unlike Freud's self-analysis.

Laing, by contrast, experienced continuity as something manufactured and imposed, a form of mental servitude that precluded self-definition and self-discovery. The result was that, as an adult, his clinical constructs and reflections reflected his struggle for emancipation, autonomy, and wholeness as well.

Despite the bleak, haunting elegance of it all—and the alienating abstractness of his algebraic notations, which he later dropped—

Laing's best work during the 1960s is impressive. Though it may have been one-sided, there was a remarkable clarity and fearlessness in his view of human affairs, with little patience for conventional pieties. But Laing's work did conceal some problems and contradictions. Perhaps the most radical and perplexing was his shifting concept of normality. In *The Divided Self* Laing equated normality with a state of ontological security. The normal person Laing suggested, enjoys a stable sense of identity and autonomy that confers an ability to relate deeply and authentically with others, circumstances permitting. Given the nature of modernity, Laing continued, the normal individual inevitably develops a false self (or selves) adapted to the exigencies of institutionalized living. But as long as the person is sane, more or less, the false self is deployed in the interests of the real self and does not become a dreaded tyrant that threatens to destroy the person through its linkage to the body and the external world.

At this point in his work, Laing used the words "sanity" and "normality" interchangeably, and he defined sanity in terms of the quality of connectedness that obtains in a person's relationship to his own body and to his close friends. In *Self and Others,* however, Laing defined normality in terms of a person's embeddedness in the culture at large and, more specifically, in the belief systems and definitions of reality obtaining within it. Though ontological security had sounded quite balanced and reassuring, considering the torment and loneliness of schizoid experience, the state of normality Laing described in *Self and Others,* just one year later, was frightening:

> To shake one's self out of a false sense of reality entails a derealization of what one falsely takes to be unreality. Only then is one able to apperceive the social phantasy system in which one is. The normal state of affairs is to be so immersed in one's immersion in social phantasy systems that one takes them to be real. Many images have been used to remind us of this condition. We are dead, but think we are alive. We are asleep, but think we are awake. We are dreaming, but take out dreams to be reality. We are the halt, the lame, the blind, the sick . . . We are mad, but have no insight. (1961, p. 38)

From this point on, Laing used the term normality in this pejorative fashion. As far as I know, he never paused to ponder the implications of this radical shift in perspective, much less explain it to his readers—many of whom seemed to take it in stride. But if we approach the matter logically, we can only suppose that the two senses of "normality" are either compatible, as Laing evidently thought,'or irreconcilable. If the former is true, there is no real problem. If the latter is true, all kinds of consequences follow.

Judging from *Politics of Experience,* Laing himself did not see any contradiction between these two views of normality. "Normal" people can be both ontologically secure *and* enveloped in social fantasy systems. They can be relatively sane with respect to their dealings with other individuals and their attitudes toward their own bodies, but quite deluded in their deeper grasp of existential actualities, although their beliefs, socially sanctioned, cause no anxiety. Meanwhile, mad people, who have lost the conventional social filters, may be perplexing or intolerable to most of us, but they do sometimes apperceive truths about social reality that are glimpsed only by poets and prophets in moments of *derealization,* when the scales fall from their eyes and the wretched truth is laid bare.

That Laing saw no contradiction between these definitions of normality raises two troubling issues. One is that in *The Divided Self* a state of ontological security is equated with sanity, while in *Self and Others* normality is described as a state of *pseudo-sanity,* which is invisible because it is so widely shared—Fromm's "socially patterned defect." If we treat these two definitions of normality as consistent, we may no longer be willing or able to discriminate between sanity and pseudo-sanity. Something is amiss.

Another problem with Laing's shift in emphasis has to do with the status of fantasy when normality is defined (1) by reference to one's connectedness to one's own body and intimate relations *(The Divided Self),* or by (2) one's relationship to prevailing false consciousness *(Self and Others).* Though he never brought it out directly, in the first book Laing treated fantasy as a mode of experience in which truths denied entry into consciousness are sometimes symbolically apperceived amid the chronic confusion and deliberate self-concealment of an alienated and disordered mind. In *Self and Others,* by contrast, fantasy is treated variously as (1) a legitimate mode of experience, in which important truths are poetically or symbolically expressed, and (2) as a collective flight from reality.

These divergent possibilities emerge because Laing introduces a new idea, that of *social* fantasy systems as opposed to purely individual ones.

As Laing intimated in *Politics of Experience,* the person who is estranged from fantasy is alienated from the wellsprings of inner life. But what of group fantasies or collective fantasy systems? Laing's characterization of the latter are consistently negative. Rather than enhancing our grasp of existential actualities, the true function of social fantasy systems is to estrange us from reality, to envelop us in a dense, obstructive sense of pseudo-reality that preempts contact with reality through multiple layers of deep epistemological error.

On the face of it, this characterization implies a double standard. To put matters crudely, Laing was saying that individual fantasy, if it is rooted in and related to individual experience, is actually or potentially good, because it can enhance our grasp of reality. Social fantasy systems, by contrast, estrange us from reality and the ground of our being. Now Laing never argued his position in these exact words. But the burden of emphasis throughout his work makes such a conclusion inevitable, so the attribution is fair. Furthermore, we should acknowledge that this way of looking at things—which strikes many as counterintuitive and quite terrifying—may be true, at least in some instances. Anyone who has given thought to the psychology of racism can recognize that. At a bare minimum, this attitude faithfully reflects the experience of many visionary and tormented souls, such as William Blake, Nietzsche, and Antonin Artaud—men whose art and ideas Laing admired and understood far, far better than most.

Still there are no compelling *logical* grounds to justify this invidious comparison between individual and social fantasy. But it does have a respectable pedigree, even in the history of the mental health disciplines. To trace its lineage, we can begin by remembering that Laing's idea of social fantasy systems, while derived proximately from the work of Eliot Jaques, is quite consistent with ideas expressed in Freud's *Group Psychology and the Analysis of the Ego.* There collective fantasies are said to consolidate bonds between men (at the expense of their reason and awareness of reality) through the repression and sublimation of homosexual tendencies. As a matter of historical interest, we should also note that Freud's book opened with a glowing appreciation of Gustav Le Bon, who regarded unconscious group dynamics as collective hypnoid states inimical to reason and self-restraint.

In addition to its Freudian cast, Laing's theory of collective fantasy as shared hypnoid states had a decidedly Platonic and Gnostic inflection. Plato's myth of the cave sums up Laing's approach to collective fantasy systems rather well. And the governing idea of the Gnostic creeds, which invoked Plato's idea of the ignorant demiurge (in *Timaeus*), was that most men are helplessly mired in collective delusions but are so sadly deficient in awareness of their condition that they are hostile to any glimmerings of true knowledge (or "gnosis") that periodically intrude on their slumbers. In short, from the Gnostic perspective, most people exist in an adversarial relationship to the truth, but are so oblivious they think the opposite is true.

Whether Freudian or Gnostic, true or false, Laing's double standard regarding individual and collective fantasy calls for comment. One potential source of difficulty here is that as soon as the individual acquires language, her fantasy life is no longer private. For purposes of discussion or decorum, we may prefer to think otherwise, but in fact, as we mature, our unconscious mental activity is progressively infused with collective myths and symbols (Burston, 1986). Once you realize this, any attempt to create a strict dichotomy between private and social fantasy would seem to promote an undesirable dualism—the very kind Laing preferred to avoid in other contexts.

This does not mean, incidentally, that Laing's notions of social fantasy systems is wrong or without merit. To take that position would be to throw out the proverbial baby with the bath water. It would also reject much of the Platonic tradition with its distinctive concept of collective false consciousness. What the preceding analysis suggests is that we require a more complex, dialectical, and less dichotomous discussion of fantasy and the social unconscious to put Laing's riveting observations on group psychology into deeper and more balanced perspective.

Furthermore, it should be noted that Laing's characterization of normality and of social fantasy systems after *The Divided Self* more or less dictated that his attitude to socialization and education would be negative as well. Throughout *Politics of Experience,* he hammered away at the notion that the processes of socialization and education involve a methodical erosion of one's true possibilities, a training in inauthenticity, a secular version of the Fall. Is this grim characterization always or necessarily the case, as Laing appeared to believe?

If taken to its logical extreme, this line of reasoning suggests that the presocialized person is the only true self, or that the rediscovery of authentic selfhood requires that we unlearn whatever beliefs, identities, and cognitive constructs have been acquired, including the fiction of the autonomous ego:

> Human beings seem to have an almost unlimited capacity to deceive themselves, and to deceive themselves into taking their own lies for truth. By such mystification, we achieve and sustain our adjustment, adaptation, socialization. But the result of such adjustment to society is that, having been tricked and having tricked ourselves out of our minds, that is to say, out of our own personal world of experience, out of that unique meaning with which potentially we may endow the external world, simultaneously we have been conned into the illusion that we are separate "skin encapsulated egos." Having at one and the same time lost our *selves,* and developed the illusion that we are autonomous *egos,* we are expected to comply by inner consent with external constraints, to an almost unbelievable extent. (1967, p. 61)

This remarkable statement bears close scrutiny. Here Laing is drawing a distinction between the real self and the ego, which by definition—as he notes elsewhere—is the "agent" of adaptation to society. The real self, by contrast, is characterized as being "our own personal world of experience" or, alternatively, "that unique meaning with which potentially we may endow the external world." Whether we agree or not, the fact remains that Laing characterized the relationship between the real self and the adapted ego as adversarial, and that his use of the term "ego" is not consistent with conventional Freudian usage, where "self" and "ego" are often used interchangeably.

With terms like "self" and "ego," as in many other instances, Freudian usage is not clear or consistent and leaves itself open to multiple interpretations. Even so, it is apparent that Freud never saw the development of the ego as being inimical to a person's interests, in the sense that Laing evidently intended. The best analogue to Laing's presocialized self in Freud's system—as Laing observed elsewhere (1967e)—is the id. And as Freud was fond of stressing, despite elements of antagonism toward the id's insistent pressures, the ego is largely the servant and protector of the id, and frequently does the id's bidding without knowing it.

By contrast, Laing's usage implies a tacit equation between the ego and the false self. As such, it is also much closer to Jung's terminology, which makes a similar differentiation between the self and the ego. That being so, we might ask what Laing made of the Freudian id. The answer is not easy to find. We get some inkling of his thoughts in the paper "Transcendental Experience in Relation to Religion and Psychosis," where he wrote:

> What both Freud and Jung called "the unconscious" is simply what we, in our historically conditioned estrangement, are unconscious of. It is not necessarily or essentially unconscious.
>
> I am not simply spinning senseless paradoxes when I say that we, the sane ones, are out of our minds. We are unconscious of our minds. Our minds are not unconscious. Our minds are conscious of us. Ask yourself who and what it is that dreams our dreams. Our unconscious minds? The Dreamer who dreams our dreams knows far more of us than we know of it. It is only from a remarkable position of alienation that the source of life, the fountain of life, is experienced as the It. The mind of which we are unaware is aware of us. (1965, p. 57)

These utterances would have certainly gladdened the heart of Georg Groddeck. The emphasis on the superior wisdom of the It, the unconscious, and the assertion that our limited, egoic consciousness is a form of alienation from our fundamental being, which is aware of "us" even though we are unaware of "it" is in keeping with Groddeck's view of human affairs. (It is also congruent with the more philosophical musings of the novelist Henry Miller, whom Laing admired.) Laing doesn't mention Groddeck here, but he told Michael Thompson he read *The Book of the It* at least a dozen times. Again, right or wrong, this is not the Freudian view. Were Freud alive, he probably would have chided Laing for confounding the unconscious with the id as such, and neglecting to note that large portions of the ego's activities are also removed from consciousness as well.

To nonanalysts, controversies like this may sound like so much academic disputation, a mere wrangling over words. But I think we should take up these matters in order to discover the faint lines of cleavage that separate Laing from Freud. Whatever one may think about the nature of the unconscious, there is no denying a marked difference of opinion between Laing and Freud on the vital topic of socialization. Unlike Heinz Hartmann, for one, Freud did not believe that individuals actively seek to adapt to their surroundings or that successful adaptation is intrinsically satisfying. On the contrary, he saw the process of adaptation to reality as a hardship imposed on the id, a source of unending difficulty for the maturing ego, whose distress often enough leads to neurotic disability or to outright psychosis.

At the same time, Freud saw socialization as a necessary evil, which was developed to constrain our instinctive predilections to envy, lack of discipline, and violence. Laing makes no mention of this. Despite Freud's appreciation of the costs of adaptation and his criticism of civilized sexual mores, *Civilization and Its Discontents* is a glowing endorsement of the benefits of civic order, personal hygiene, and the restraint of one's sexual appetites (though not of their repression or disavowal). None of these would be possible without socialization. And without them, Freud reflected, life would not be worth living.

Laing was wrongheaded when he wrote, for example: "The relevance of Freud to our time is largely his insight and, to a very considerable extent, his demonstration, that the ordinary person is a shrivelled, desiccated fragment of what a person can be" (1967, p. 22). On the contrary, Freud thought that, despite the ravages of repression and the frustrations of "everyday unhappiness," most of us are about all we can be, given the pervasiveness of the death instinct in our lives. Admittedly, Freud was no ego psychologist. His view of the human condition was essentially tragic, premised on the inevitability of conflict and compromise both within and between human beings. But though he never made a fetish of adaptation for its own sake, his Hobbesian view of human character dictated a qualified but hearty endorsement of the socialization process.

Laing, by contrast, was a visionary, romantic humanist with deep Gnostic leanings who—like Fromm, from a messianic standpoint— argued that the roots of human violence lie in the disappointment of our existential needs, in our "unlived life," our unrealized potential, our self-estrangement, and not in a basic biological endowment.

This is not a quarrel over words, but a fundamental clash in cultural sensibilities.

In any case, I would venture that the relevance of Freud to our time—indeed, to Laing himself—was his forceful demonstration that the human capacity for self-deception is prodigious. The belief that self-deception is a constitutive feature of the human mind is not a logical (or an illogical) proposition, nor does it lend itself to being tested or refuted experimentally. It is, quite simply, an ineluctable fact of life, whose reality can be established by reference to personal experience and immediately understood by those who have encountered and relinquished many deeply cherished illusions.

In fairness to Freud's predecessors, the idea that self-deception is an integral part of being human was not original to him. Thinkers as diverse as Augustine, Montaigne, Kant, Schopenhauer, and especially Nietzsche had already expressed the same insight with great eloquence and conviction. Similarly, novelists and playwrights— Dickens, Thackeray, Balzac, Flaubert, Tolstoy, Ibsen, Strindberg, Shaw, Lawrence, Pirandello—treated this problem with a psychological acumen that should be the envy of any thoughtful psychoanalyst. In this sense, then, Freud was not unusual. He was a product of his times, riding a wave of cultural consciousness that began to gather force in the late eighteenth century and peaked toward the end of ours, when the very idea of the self is taken to be an illusion, rendering the whole notion of "self-deception" moot.

Still, though rooted in a certain cultural-historical period, Freud also took a decisive step beyond the philosophers and playwrights, by demonstrating that the truths people avoid are frequently concealed in the structure of their symptoms, and that a thoughtful and sympathetic attempt to decipher them may bring the forgotten truths to light, with patience and struggle. Moreover, he showed how a person's symptoms may encode or express more than one meaning or motive ("overdetermination").

So, too, the relevance of Laing to our time is largely in his demonstration that many varieties of self-deception are not purely private or intrapsychic affairs. We share many of our cherished illusions with our family, our clan, or our guild, and collude with others in the perpetuation of our personal and collective mythologies. In instances where we deceive ourselves, it is often not sufficient to fool ourselves alone. If others do not share our opinions of ourselves and

our motives, do not share our memory and interpretation of events,
we will obscure their experience through mystification, or persuade
them to collude with us and to mistake our inflated or distorted images of ourselves for the real thing.

Accordingly, despite their differences on socialization, Laing was
following in Freud's footsteps, without shouldering the formidable
encumbrances of Freud's obsolete and untenable biologism. Without dismissing the vagaries of unconscious conflicts and repressing
forces, Laing showed that the intelligibility of symptoms often re-
sides in the person's social context and in the tangled web of social
relations within the family.

Finally, we should note that Laing's overwhelmingly negative view
of socialization contributed to his essentially positive concept of regression, to both good and bad effect. Freud had thought of regression as involving a progressive loss of reason and contact with
reality, as an abdication of the active, rational, independent self in
favor of passivity, dependence, and indiscipline. Regression had no
redeeming characteristics. But like Jung, Ferenczi, Balint, and Winnicott before him, Laing thought that many instances of psychotic
regression were abortive attempts at self-cure and the rejection of a
socially adapted false self.

Laing observed that adults habitually employ all kinds of cognitive schemata in the interpretation of experience, in order to define
the contents and boundaries of inner and outer, self and other, the
real and imaginary, memory, dream, perception, and so on. He
maintained that these schemata, and the various rules governing
their application to experience and events, are not ontological truths
but are learned through socialization. Experiences that do not conform to the contours of these schemata (as society defines them) will
not get a seal of approval, or consensual validation. In the process of
acquiring the cultural templates for experience, and the more idio-
syncratic rules (and metarules) governing communication in the
family, the person may be come radically estranged from his own experience. In certain circumstances—such as chronic double binds or
"untenable positions"—regression may be a desperate attempt to re-
capture the wholeness and immediacy of experience by *unlearning*
the conventional rules and distinctions. But the result, in practical
terms, is that the person who loses the conventional social filters becomes temporarily disabled and dependent on others—though they

typically loathe this dependence (see Laing, 1967b, lecture of January 11).

According to Laing, the body plays a unique role in this regressive process, often heralding the return of the repressed and of domains of experience that have been effectively cut off from awareness. His interest in the body as a living repository of repressed experience— which again owes much to Groddeck—led to his interest in rebirthing. Instead of stressing the meaning and rootedness of symptoms in the patient's social context, which used to be his trademark, by 1972 Laing was beginning to construe unconscious fantasy as a symbolic codification of the birth trauma and intrauterine experience.

There is a certain irony in all this. Laing's preoccupation with intrauterine experience might also be taken as a belated acknowledgment of "psychic reality," of unconscious but specifically internal factors that give rise to inexplicable feelings and behavior, to anxiety and depression that cannot be accounted for in terms of social context. In his own words:

> Without diminishing anything that Freud said about later development, it seems plausible to me that the intrauterine experience, from *conception,* before implantation, and all the way to implantation, to birth and afterbirth experiences are mapped into our system in some way or another, and stored to express themselves later, especially surfacing after physical growth ends, and . . . adult life begins. One discovers as one gets older that the present situation, whatever it happens to be, doesn't seem to account for one's present behavior. (Evans, 1976, p. 5)

Laing was oblivious of the radical shift in perspective entailed in this departure. In *The Divided Self* he had stated that biological birth is a definitive event, but that the emergence of the self as a subject, the shift from organism to person, occurs afterward, as a consequence of the emergent awareness of oneself as an object of other people's intentions. Admittedly, in this book, he also urged his readers not to judge people whose conception of the boundaries of selfhood did not coincide with his avowedly existential conception of the human condition, as beginning at birth and ending in death.

But in *Facts of Life* and again in *Voice of Experience,* Laing argued that many of the constitutive elements of individual subjectivity precede the moment of birth. In effect, a mother's feelings or intentions toward her child register—somewhere, somehow—shortly after conception and color its experience of the world subsequently. The shift backward to conception as the definitive event vastly expands the domain of personal experience. Physiological processes that were previously designated as prepersonal—in a more Hegelian and existential mode—were now subsumed under the heading of *interpersonal*. Laing did not stop there: ever the Platonist, he now began to entertain conjectures about memories of life before conception, raising the possibility of reincarnation.

Laing's initial attempt to elucidate a science of persons was predicated on a very different conception of the human being. But if it distanced him from his original ground and estranged him from the analytic profession, Laing's growing interest in intrauterine themes did not stop his interest in analytic theory. Laing's sense of kinship with Freud actually deepened during the 1970s. In *Voice of Experience,* for example, Laing reviewed Freud's ideas on birth and intrauterine symbolism in dreams, and discussed the debate between Freud and Rank with considerable insight. I mention this because rebirthing therapists can be divided roughly into two groups—those who reject or belittle Freud and those who see themselves as correcting his work. Along with his friend Stanislav Grof, Laing was a rebirther who continued Freud's effort. In his own estimation at least, this phase of his work was squarely in the analytic tradition.

In fact, however, the idea of therapeutic regression to intrauterine states or previous lives preceded psychoanalysis by a decade or so, and was actively explored in the world of hypnosis that Freud was anxious to escape. As Henri Ellenberger notes in *The Discovery of the Unconscious:*

One of the most controversial issues of hypnotism was the subject of age regression recognized by some hypnotists, and subject to scrutiny in the 1880's and 1890's. The hypnotized subject is told that he is going backward in time, for instance to adolescence or childhood at a given moment in the past. His behavior, movement and voice change accordingly. He seems to have forgotten everything that happened to him since the first moment that he is reenacting, and he gives a detailed account of happenings at this period of his life. Is this "true regression," that is, reviviscence of what the subject actually experienced at that given age, or is it only an excellent histrionic imitation of what he believes to have experienced then? This was a much discussed problem. Colonel de Rochas, a once famous hypnotist, conducted these experiments to their extreme limits and even *ad absurdum*. He thus obtained from his subjects an age regression not merely of an ordinary kind but also the reenactment of their babyhood, their birth, their fetal period. Then came a blackout, followed by the picture of the person's previous life, going backward from old age to childhood, infancy, birth and fetal period, followed by a new blackout and the revival of the second and previous life. De Rochas' subjects thus re-enacted several previous lives, always alternating the life of a man with the life of a woman. Descriptions of these previous lives were often plausible, but marred by anachronisms. Some believed that Colonel de Rochas had found an experimental confirmation of the doctrine of reincarnation. (1970, p. 117)

Though some of his loyal followers would argue otherwise no doubt, there are uncanny parallels between Colonel de Rochas' hypnotic procedures and the kind of group encounters Laing orchestrated in the late 1970s and 1980s. Clearly Laing failed to recognize just how much his new frontier lent itself to theatricality, suggestibility, and outright fraud.

Still, as John Heaton points out, a rigorous assessment of rebirthing therapy should discriminate between the epistemic claims attached to the process, which are dubious at best, and the therapeutic benefits, which are quite robust in some cases. In "The Self, the Divided Self and the Other" (1994), Heaton notes that rebirthing is essentially a mimetic process, in the spirit of ancient healing rituals practiced by shamans the world over. If good and intelligent people say they have benefited by the experience, who are we to argue with them? That said, however, Heaton continues:

it is meaningless to reconstruct what is was like to be born, let alone describe what is was like to be in the womb as Laing tried to do. What possible evidence can be produced that our constructions are true? As shamans knew, all we can do is to give our selves over to mime when it is appropriate, or in the case of the psychotic person, miming takes him over. But it is meaningless to translate the experience of miming into the discourse of the real.

Science grew in opposition to mimesis. For science seeks the "real," and discards what it sees as mere appearance. But as has become clearer in this century, one cannot get rid of mimesis . . . The political and social power of make-believe increases with communication technology; modern man only believes in science, but at the same time is terribly vulnerable to mimesis—slogans, advertisements, mass movements, etc.

And of course psychiatry and psychotherapy are particularly sensitive to the science-mimesis conflict. For neurotic and psychotic people are the victims of mimesis, and the cure, especially in psychotherapy, depends on the therapist's understanding of mimetic power. And yet psychiatry and psychotherapy are supposed to be scientific. Many of Laing's difficulties stem from this conflict; he was particularly sensitive to the power of mimesis, yet lived in a scientific age. He was never able to reconcile the two. (pp. 30–31)

This assessment gets right to the heart of the matter. Laing's fascination with mimesis dates back to his 1950s army research on Ganser's syndrome, in which the patient, "though mentally deranged, not realizing this, wishes to appear so" (Laing, 1985a, p. 137). This interest resurfaced again in *Self and Others*. Take the following passage:

Elusion is a relation in which one pretends oneself away from one's original self; then pretends oneself back from this pretence so as to appear to have arrived back at the starting point. A double pretence simulates no pretense. The only way to "realize" one's original state is to forgo the first pretence, but once one adds a second pretence to it, as far as I can see, there is no end to the series of possible pretences. I am. I pretend I am not. I pretend I am. I pretend I am not pretending to be pretending . . .

Jill is married to Jack. She does not want to be married to Jack. She is frightened to leave Jack. So she stays with Jack but imagines that she is not married to him. Eventually she does not feel married to him. So she has to imagine she is. "I have to remind myself that he is my husband."

A common manoeuvre. Elusion is a way of getting round conflict without direct confrontation, or its resolution. It eludes conflict by playing off one modality of experience against another. She imagines she is *not* married and then imagines she is. Elusive spirals go on and on. (p. 45–47)

Whether we give this scenario of Jack and Jill a comic or a tragic inflection, there is no denying that the plotline is worthy of Pirandello or Kundera. Like them, Laing saw pretense and elusion as integral dimensions of our everyday existence, as well as of aggravated inner conflict and florid psychosis. It may begin as make-believe, as an antidote to boredom or as a way of managing one's responses to a drama that is all too real. Either way, it can miscarry. After all, elusion is a relation to oneself where one pretends, and then pretends that one is not pretending, or not pretending to pretend that one is pretending . . . . .

But what happens when two people forget they are pretending and get transported by the power of their own performances? The demented dance, the *folie à deux* that invariably ensues as they become progressively enmeshed in one another's pretenses, mistaking the appearance for the real thing—in themselves and the other simultaneously—has never been fully described, much less explained, by mental health professionals. But as Laing tried to show, it can have its own weird logic and syntax, a strange kind of music that is alternately amusing, terrifying, and sad. And that, perhaps, is the essence of *Knots:* "Jill believes Jack. She now thinks she sees what Jack thinks Jack sees and that Jack sees it too. They may now both be completely wrong" (1970, p. 64).

Poets and dramatists generally have a much deeper appreciation of the role of pretense and elusion in our attitudes toward the expression of sexual needs and feelings, in matters of faith, in the invisible constraints on our truthfulness and sincerity with friends, and our attitudes toward deviance in all its forms. As Laing and a handful of others knew, mental health professionals had much to learn from art about everyday hypocrisy and self-deception. No wonder, then, that Laing the therapist became fed up and attempted to transport himself and his talents into poetic, musical, and theatrical idioms. When he failed there, he compensated by making his clinical work more theatrical. Metanoia for the masses is not what the earlier Laing was all about, however, and giant rebirthing marathons were a recipe for elusion on a grand scale, and only eroded his waning credibility further.

Heaton's remarks raise another important issue. Laing the therapist was really two people. On the one hand, he was a passionate skeptic who criticized Freud and his followers for multiplying hypothetical entities unnecessarily, and for lacking a genuinely scientific method—a lapse they attempted to conceal by a dedicated misapplication of natural science models to the study of the mind. On the other hand, Laing was also an intuitive healer who made ample use of his mimetic powers in the manner of a modern-day shaman, often with startling and dramatic results.

Surveying Laing's work as a whole, one is tempted to speculate that, during the first half of his career, the skeptical and visionary tendencies in his character existed side by side, resulting in a creative tension that enabled him to play both roles brilliantly. But as his later writings attest, Laing the shaman came to eclipse the rigorous intellectual and led him to blend the symbolic and the real in a strange synthesis that was emotionally and intellectually compelling for him, but lacked a solid theoretical foundation.

This line of conjecture opens up several interpretive possibilities. One might say, in a Jungian vein, that after 1971 Laing was gripped increasingly by the numinous power of the archetypes of death and rebirth, but he lacked the critical distance to make sense of the process. Alternatively, one might say that he was attempting to heal an inner split between aspects of himself that he was weary of trying to keep apart. And again one might note that the shaman and the showman are often kindred spirits, that his attempts to dramatize the issue in his group encounters were simultaneous expressions and evasions of these "inner" processes.

Finally, one might accept all of these explanations, which are by no means antagonistic. In any case, it is true that Laing lost much of his original readership in his turn to mimesis and discredited himself in the eyes of many people who had once taken him seriously. But Laing, for all his faults, was unique. There is surely no one else in the history of ideas who has embodied the skeptical and visionary modes of thought with equal zeal. Ordinarily these attitudes or temperaments are radically antithetical, and it may be inevitable that, in someone so well endowed with both, one sensibility would eventually dominate the other. Yet the fact that the marriage miscarried toward the end does not make the attempt itself any less remarkable. Few people are blessed (or cursed) with Laing's degree of psychological complexity, which renders any attempt to fit a type or diagnostic category to his character, finally, impossible.

11

PSYCHIATRY
THEN AND ℕOW

Laing's attitude toward the psychiatric profession went through several transformations. In the late 1940s, while in the army in Scotland, he tried hard to persuade himself that the insulin comas he was obliged to administer actually did the patients good. By the time he left, he had given up that delusion. His experiences of civilian psychiatry did not improve his opinion of the profession much, and by the mid to late 1950s, he evidently felt that the epistemic foundations of psychiatric discourse were radically unsound.

After his analytic training in the early 1960s, Laing found himself basically opposed to all forms of standard psychiatric care save one-to-one therapy. And though he still made allowance for involuntary hospitalization in some instances and rejected the label of "antipsychiatrist" later, his opposition to most of what psychiatry stood for was unequivocal.

Laing's views of psychiatry followed a pattern of deepening disenchantment. But by the late 1960s he began to soften his opposition. Though his antipathy to lobotomy and electroshock continued unabated, he began to say that he had no objection to people using psychiatric drugs, provided they were not coerced and were informed of all the risks involved (Sedgwick, 1982). In a 1976 interview, Laing mused on the problems confronting psychiatry, psychology, and social work, where the political economy of service delivery appears to necessitate, first, treating psychotherapy (and the therapist's personality and skills) as commodities for sale and, second, an increasing obsession with measurable results. The problem, Laing observed, is that subjective experience and the whole interpersonal field resist quantification and standardization. In the end, human emotions, human empathy, and human relationships are not quantifiable, even if we perversely insist on treating them as such. Yet he hastened to add,

> I am not putting forward . . . a blanket condemnation of the system, or just saying the easy thing—that the system is entirely self-serving, or that the individuals comprising it are self-serving. Our interdigitated plurality of systems is the product of the individuals who compose it, so I am not talking about the system itself as some entirely alien, malevolent, paranoid-persecution machine that is devouring everyone in it, though some of us no doubt sometimes feel that way. (Evans, 1976, p. 37)

Looking back at the fifties and sixties, Laing acknowledged that he had felt "more desperately and unreconciledly negative about . . . the whole thing" (p. 39) than he did in 1976. Now he was resigned, seeing the growing hegemony of the measurers, and marketers, and technocrats in the mental health field as inevitable. (And he was right.)

Obviously this is not a glowing endorsement of psychiatry or the other therapeutic disciplines. But neither is it the flaming denunciation many of his admirers had come to expect. This was the paradox of Laing in the 1970s. As his preoccupation with birth and intrauterine experience deepened, driving him farther and farther toward the edges of the profession, his attitude to psychiatry became less adversarial. But this did not stop his eloquent campaign against the heartlessness and stupidity of the narrow methodologies so many of his psychiatric colleagues espoused. Indeed, *The Facts of Life* and *The Voice of Experience,* which are principally concerned with birth-oriented themes, are punctuated with long, impassioned denunciations of reification in psychiatry. The sharpness of these jeremiads ensured that, despite a palpable shift in position, most psychiatrists would continue to dismiss Laing as the notorious anti-psychiatrist of the past.

As a result, most of Laing's readers—friends and critics alike—are unaware that in *Wisdom, Madness and Folly,* published in 1985,

Laing sounded a new note in his assessment of the psychiatric profession. As Sidney Briskin attests, in so doing he was expressing convictions from the late 1960s, which he was reluctant to put into print
then. Now Laing noted that psychiatry does play a useful role in society: it segregates people whom the rest of us can no longer abide,
those who cannot or will not take care of themselves (or others) in
fairly normal fashion.

Moreover, despite profound misgivings about the profession,
Laing declared that it was hypocritical to reproach psychiatrists with
attempting to perform the very functions that most of us, in dire circumstances, demand them to perform, for lack of an alternative.
The question is not whether there should be a psychiatric profession, but how therapists are discharging their responsibilities, how
they exercise the powers vested in them by civil society. Finally, why
are there no real alternatives to the depersonalizing and bureaucratic
protocols of hospitalization for people in acute mental and emotional turmoil?

Is this the voice of an anti-psychiatrist? When David Cooper first
coined the term, "anti-psychiatrist" meant a psychiatrist who had
come to perceive his field as a tool of capitalist or state-capitalist
(Soviet) imperialism and was therefore committed to the abolition of
the profession. But now the term has broadened to include almost
anyone who advocates either the abolition or the radical reform of
psychiatry, regardless of their professional status. This semantic shift
was inevitable, since so few psychiatrists aligned themselves with the
anti-psychiatry movement (and many former mental patients did).

If prevailing usage is any indication, then "anti-psychiatrist" is little more than a term used by people on opposite sides of an ideological debate who are anxious to differentiate crudely between the
good guys and the bad guys, and who oversimplify some very complex issues in the process. Thus psychiatrists often dismiss and
abuse their critics with this epithet, while those who favor abolition
or radical reform use it to commend those they regard as politically
correct.

To his credit, Laing anticipated these developments, and sought
to circumvent these partisan semantics, though he did lean toward
the anti-psychiatric side of the debate and inspired many of its current advocates in the psychiatric survivor movement. Even so, I
don't think that the anti-psychiatry label fits Laing. Nor would I tax

him, as critics on both left and right have done, with the subtle and not-so-subtle contradictions that crop up between his public and private pronouncements around 1964 and those after 1968. On the whole, the retreat from his more extreme pronouncements of the earlier sixties was wise, whatever his motives may have been. Also, despite the excesses of his birth-centered and prenatal preoccupations during the seventies and eighties, many of his critical reflections on contemporary psychiatry and the mental health field after 1970 are still quite sound.

Laing's legacy to psychiatry and the mental health professions is both vast and ambiguous. Nowhere is its scope and complexity more evident than in his approach to schizophrenia. In a recent article in the *British Journal of Psychiatry* (1994), Lawrence Ratna observes that Laing proposed not one but several theories of schizophrenia. My discussion of Laing's four theses is heavily indebted to Ratna's paper. So, according to Laing:

(1) Schizophrenia is a symptom of extreme ontological insecurity, with its attendant fears of engulfment, petrification, and implosion; the consequent defense mechanisms are designed to maintain the person's precarious sense of identity, such as the flight into fantasy and the deliberate cultivation of the rupture between the so-called real and false selves. Because of its emphasis on issues of authenticity, self-disclosure, and the fear of nonbeing elucidated in *The Divided Self,* this thesis is existentialist, even though Laing borrowed extensively from the psychoanalytic literature when it served his purpose.

(2) Schizophrenia is an adaptation to profound and prolonged communication deviance within the family. Though inspired by the work of Bateson, this approach, in *Sanity, Madness and the Family,* also owed much to Sartre. The painstaking care devoted to articulating the profound miscommunication between family members, and the deliberate bracketing of all psychoanalytic interpretations in the analysis of the data, render it convenient to label this a phenomenological thesis, though strictly speaking it was his method of study, rather than his conclusions, that were phenomenological.

(3) Schizophrenia is metanoia, or an interior journey in which the individual attempts to heal the splits in his psyche by regressing to

the point in his development prior to the emergence of a false self.
Though Laing persuaded himself that this was his idea, it was prefigured in the work of Winnicott and Balint. Moreover, many features of the metanoia concept were introduced by Jung, and since Laing often described this inner journey in archetypal terms, I call this Laing's neo-Jungian interpretation of schizophrenia.

(4) Schizophrenia is an attribution made by some people to others in instances of profound experiential disjuncture, where the attribution serves a political function by invalidating or disempowering the individual, and treating all her experiences as symptoms of disease that warrant the suspension of their ordinary rights and liberties. This is Laing's social-constructivist interpretation of the schizophrenic process.

Unfortunately for posterity, Laing and his followers did not differentiate between these various theories of schizophrenia and treated them as compatible. Indeed, uncritical admirers seemed to think that the endorsement of any one of these theories necessitates acceptance of them all. But, on careful inspection, many find themselves able to give a full or partial endorsement to some of Laing's approaches, but not to the others. Thus they may endorse Laing's existential and phenomenological theses, while rejecting the neo-Jungian and constructivist ones on clinical grounds. Alternatively, they may embrace the phenomenological and constructivist theses, but reject the existential and neo-Jungian ones for political or ideological reasons.

Though Laing may have wished us to do otherwise, it is much wiser to discriminate between Laing's various theses and to assess their merits individually. If we comply with the demand to treat these theses as all of a piece, we are just as likely to reject as to accept them all, and that would be foolishly shortsighted. So it is best to dispense with the polemics of yesteryear and to take them one at a time.

Laing's existentialist thesis, as propounded in *The Divided Self,* is a clear and empathic description of the inner world of schizophrenia—one that many schizophrenics have emphatically endorsed. Unless one is given to an unqualified endorsement of the medical model, it is not one that can be casually dismissed. Significantly, however, this approach entails the assumption that madness is not merely a label affixed by some to others, as Laing later said, but a real and disturbing state of affairs brought about in part by the afflicted person, who attempts to develop an identity, being-for-one-self, that is completely disengaged from the exigencies of being-for-others. Indeed, the flight from the communal and corporeal aspects of life defines the schizoid attitude, whose intensification results in madness.

By contrast, Laing's phenomenological approach, which emerged in 1964, treats schizophrenia as an anguished adaptation to communicational deviance and duplicity in the family, but stipulates no intrinsic features to the process of going mad. In the introduction to *Sanity, Madness and the Family,* Laing and Esterson dismiss all manner of existentialist interpretations that might apply to the testimony of their subjects, just as they bracket the psychodynamic ones. They even deny that there is an entity that corresponds to "schizophrenia" and attempt to show—quite successfully, as a rule—how the so-called signs of schizophrenia often become intelligible once the veil of mystification around them is pierced.

Though this approach to the study of schizophrenia is potentially fruitful and illuminating, it is hard to endorse Laing's conclusions wholeheartedly. Some families of diagnosed schizophrenics do resemble the disquieting profiles sketched so incisively by Laing and Esterson, but others do not. And as Elliot Mishler observed (1973), the manifest irrationality of family discourse may be partially attributable to the family's attempts to adapt to the patient's inner disturbance, and not only the other way around.

Meanwhile, even if we search for the social intelligibility of symptoms, as we should, it seems obstinate to rule out the possible contribution of early brain trauma and infection, acute toxicity, chronic malnutrition, or reduced immuno-competence as potent predisposing factors. Traumatic and complicated births, early childhood sexual abuse, and sheer physical brutality may also play a significant role in many cases. In the present climate of opinion, however, it is impossible to determine what portion of the families of diagnosed schizophrenics conform to Laing's characterizations. If we could do that, even approximately, we might begin to discover how much etiological weight to assign to these microsocial processes in any given case. But the ideological and fiscal obstacles to carrying out such research seem insurmountable. Though they were on to something extremely important, indeed central in many cases, Laing and Esterson have been dismissed, by and large, and are not likely to get their due until the current enthusiasm for biological psychiatry has run its course, and its inherent limitations are palpably felt once again.

Laing's third, neo-Jungian thesis also emerged in 1964: the schizophrenic process was construed as an attempt at self-healing through regression, metanoia. In outline, I think, it is broadly compatible with his first approach. And in some sense it may be compatible with the second one too, since it was also endorsed by Bateson. Even so, there is nothing that compels us to adopt it. Indeed, one could very well endorse parts of his first and second theses while dismissing the third as romantic (and perhaps dangerous) nonsense.

Though many find Laing's metanoia thesis radically implausible, we should remember how much it is caricatured by its critics, who make it seem outlandish. As he stated quite soberly many times, both in lectures and in print, Laing thought that the self-healing potentialities inherent in psychosis can come to fruition only in appropriately supportive surroundings. Even then, there are no guarantees of success, just a much greater probability of spontaneous remission.

In addition, it bears remembering that Laing distinguished between true and false madness, the latter being an abortive attempt to achieve the real thing. While many people are capable of distinguishing between sanity and pseudo-sanity in some fashion, the idea that there is such a thing as a pseudo-psychosis requires an imaginative leap that many clinicians and most laymen are incapable of. (Surely madness is madness, isn't it?) Though Laing did not develop this line of thought after 1967, as far as I know, it would seem that in instances of counterfeit madness, the likelihood of achieving the desired dissolution and renewal of the person is rather slim.

Finally, as Andrew Scull points out, in early Victorian times it was commonplace for asylums to release 25–30 percent of their inmates after stays of one or two years because they had recovered sufficiently to resume a normal life. And Laing said that this was the consensus among senior psychiatrists when he began his professional training (Evans, 1976). Just how many of these early cases actually conformed to a pattern of metanoia is impossible to determine, of course, but probably some of them did, if only because the literature of the time makes reference to such recoveries.[1]

As asylum populations increased, however, living conditions

worsened, and so the did rates of chronicity, so that the chances of spontaneous recovery—conservatively estimated at about one in four at midcentury—fell sharply (Scull, 1979, 1981). The introduction of lobotomies and, later in this century, shock and drug therapies was initially intended to make this increasingly refractory inmate population more manageable and docile, and only gradually was such treatment adapted to outpatient services (Valenstein, 1986). Even at their best, however, these methods seldom enable patients to live without continued reliance on medication or repeated hospital visits—the so-called revolving-door syndrome (Cohen et al., 1990; Breggin, 1991).

On the face of it at least, a case can be made for the argument that if spontaneous remission started to disappear in the late nineteenth century, there must have been something profoundly unhelpful or even unhealthy about the changing hospital environment. Through the clarity and force of his prose, Laing helped to draw attention to this fact; as Elliot Mishler observed, by the late sixties many mainstream practitioners and administrators began to agree with him here (Mishler, 1973). In 1970, for example, two eminent British psychiatrists, J. K. Wing and G. W. Brown, concluded that "a substantial portion, though by no means all, of the morbidity shown by long-stay schizophrenics is a product of their environment" (1970, p. 177).

Unfortunately, the psychiatric response to this situation was a concerted effort to reduce inpatient populations by creating more outside services, using maintenance doses of drugs and electroshock to keep outpatients functioning. As a result, the average length of a hospital stay was reduced to two months, while rates of recidivism climbed concurrently. Today many patients complain that they are being turned out of the hospital too soon, before they are ready to cope with the outside world. The length and quality of a patient's hospital stay are now frequently determined by an overarching administrative and economic agenda that is impersonally enforced, which continues to nullify the person's express needs under the guise of omniscience and benign professionalism. And as Laing frequently observed, administering drugs and electroshock usually precludes self-healing, particularly when the vulnerable person has no sanctuary. No wonder Laing was reluctant to claim credit for his powerful (but indirect) contribution to changes in hospital policies (Mishler, 1973).

One way of approaching Laing's metanoia thesis and the experiments that followed from it is to regard them as an attempt to restore the conditions necessary for spontaneous remission, and to cull whatever wisdom and experience can be gained from studying it systematically, and then applying this knowledge more generally, in the hope that increasing numbers of people can put their shattered minds back together without resorting to intrusive and debilitating treatments. Despite Laing's early left-wing affiliations, there is nothing intrinsically radical or revolutionary about such a project. On the contrary, one could view it equally as a conservative measure—an attempt to revive and to modify the less heroic methods of the past.

Today, when spontaneous remission is increasingly rare—and illegal, for all intents and purposes—evidence in favor of Laing's metanoia is basically of two kinds: narrative accounts of psychotics who eluded hospitalization and recovered their sanity, and who construe their madness retrospectively in this manner; and the actual success rate of therapeutic households specifically designed to foster the process. Sorting out this evidence is a tricky business, though. On the one hand, many chronicles of madness and spontaneous recovery that fit the metanoia pattern predate Laing's efforts, and these specimens, if you like, cannot be dismissed as the artifacts of suggestion. (Laing himself was partial to Barbara O'Brien's *Operators and Things,* which appeared in 1958.) On the other hand, if one is inclined to dismiss such accounts, as Karl Jaspers did, these chronicles of suffering and transcendence do not count for much, leaving us to ponder the degree of success attainable by putting this theory into practice. And how we assess this evidence, in turn, may depend on what we mean by cure or improvement and how we go about measuring it.

Speaking for myself, I am not inclined to dismiss the recollections of people who have recovered from madness without standard psychiatric care as being irrelevant, inconsequential, or "merely anecdotal." Indeed, I admire Laing for having the courage to oppose conventional wisdom on this score. One of his great strengths, and those of all good therapists who treat psychosis, is that they are willing to be instructed by their patients or by people who have been through an acute psychotic episode. To his credit, I think, Laing made a strong case for treating cursory dismissals as instances of scientistic hubris, which indicate a lack of respect for the patient as a person whose experiences, however unusual, merit attention.

At the same time, however, one should not forget the dangers of credulity and suggestion. If people do not achieve Laing's metanoia on the basis of their own experience, but assume its validity a priori, they may be apt to contrive experiences that confirm the theory and to make vastly inflated claims as a result. And without knowing it, they may injure themselves (and others) in the process.

Accordingly, and with all due respect to Laing and his patients, it may be wise temporarily to set aside the whole issue of personal experience and recovery, and to examine the other evidence available to us. If this evidence inspires confidence, then the testimony of people who have recovered from madness is likely to be more compelling and potentially instructive.

Despite all the fanfare and enthusiasm it engendered, Kingsley Hall had a dreadful record when it came to documenting therapeutic successes. The whole ethos of the experiment was against documentation, and despite the ideals that informed its creation, the anarchic atmosphere of the place was not conducive to full recovery. At the end, even Laing conceded as much (A. Laing, 1994, p. 149).

More promising, in my view, are the reports from the Archway and Portland Road communities, the Arbors Association, and Diabasis House, a therapeutic community in San Francisco during the 1970s. Diabasis House was run by John Weir Perry, a Jungian analyst with an impressive record in treating psychoses, whose writings no doubt inspired Laing (Perry, 1961, 1966, 1980).

Even more impressive, from an empirical standpoint, are the efforts of Loren Mosher, a friend of Laing's and Perry's and a former director of schizophrenia research at the National Institutes of Mental Health. Mosher implemented a rigorous research program, the Soteria Project, with two therapeutic households: Soteria, the original facility (1971–1983), and Emanon, an offshoot (1974–1980). Using standard quantitative methods and measures, Mosher demonstrated that therapeutic households that make minimal use of medication and extensive use of suitably trained paraprofessionals are just as effective as standard psychiatric facilities—sometimes more effec-

tive—and can circumvent the toxic side effects of neuroleptic drugs
or electroshock. (Mosher's writings, listed in my references, extend
from 1973 to 1992.)

If those results are any indication, therapeutic households that
manage psychotic regression effectively can operate as relatively
free-standing entities, which in their daily operation do little to enhance the status or financial fortunes of psychiatrists. In fact, reading over the literature on the subject, one gets the sharp impression
that if facilities like these were to proliferate, the demand for the services of psychiatrists could fall sharply, and the pharmaceutical industry would be adversely affected as well.

Mosher's experiment was inspired by his brief stay at Kingsley
Hall and is well documented elsewhere. But I will note here that it
has been studiously ignored by the psychiatric community. Until
Mosher's work is acknowledged in the psychiatric mainstream, little
progress can be made in this area. To many thoughtful people, the
conspiracy of silence that surrounds the Soteria Project has a decidedly ominous feel to it. If Mosher is right about the efficacy of such
households—and I think he is—then it is hard to account for psychiatry's refusal to consider his findings, except by reference to a
covert economic agenda, one that is not even admitted by psychiatrists to themselves.

This conjecture is neither paranoid or Marxist. The political economy of science and medicine, here and abroad, is full of instances of
special-interest groups that rationalize their hegemony or market
share as indisputably integral to the public interest, and feel amply
entitled to discredit innovators who would provide alternative methods and services. If our fears and prejudices prompt us to believe
the medical establishment, then the real truth of the matter will remain obscure.

This brings us, finally, to Laing's fourth theory of schizophrenia,
the social-constructivist approach, which emerged sometime in 1966.
Though anticipated in part by Goffman, Foucault, and Szasz,
Laing's articulation of the theory was highly original, and elements
of it can be traced back to *Sanity, Madness and the Family*. The
essence of this theory is that there is no such thing as schizophrenia
and that the label "schizophrenia" is affixed by some people to others in what is essentially a political power struggle in which psychiatrists intervene on behalf of "normal" family members (or the state).

The diagnosis of schizophrenia, in turn, empowers the psychiatrist to suspend patients' ordinary rights and civil liberties, subjecting them to various treatments against their will.

The problem with this thesis is that it is invariably right in some respects and frequently wrong in others. Any attribution that empowers one person to deprive others of their civil liberties or to impose medical treatments against their will is a political act. Whether or in what circumstances or to what extent this attribution is *warranted* is another matter. And so is the question of what remedial interventions appear to follow from the attribution of schizophrenia.

Many psychiatrists preempt critical reflection on these problems by attacking Laing for politicizing the process of diagnosis. The standard response is that diagnosis is a value-free judgment rendered by a physician for the patient's benefit, and therefore no political act. But how can any action or utterance that results in the suspension of civil rights, and a person's normal rights as a medical patient, *not* be political in character? The stubborn refusal of many psychiatrists to face up to this simple fact is a product of evasion or self-deception that does their profession no credit.

Nonetheless, there are other aspects of the social-constructivist position that are problematic. Among other things, it implies that the recipients of diagnostic labels are simply innocent victims of collective duplicity and aggression, which is sanctioned through the power of the psychiatrist, and that there is no such thing as madness or mental disorder, only different varieties of protest against the family or society that seeks to enforce conformity to its own oppressive norms of conduct and belief.

If we take the social-constructivist position entirely at face value, then, the resulting portrait is of the average mental patient as a helpless victim. Admittedly, in many cases this characterization is apt. At the same time, the notion that there is no such thing as mental disorder runs contrary to Laing's insistence that there are sane and insane ways of living, of being-in-the-world. There is, in short, an insurmountable tension between the existentialist and the social-constructivist approaches on this particular point. Furthermore, the characterization of mental patients as mere victims of aggression or dishonesty is singularly inappropriate in many cases. People who are given psychiatric diagnoses, rightly or wrongly, are as capable of

malice, duplicity and self-deception as anybody else, and to explain
their conduct or motivations invariably as reactions to socially invisible injustices is simply another form of reductionism (Kirsner, 1976; Sass, 1993). If many patients appear to lack insight, decency, or self-restraint, it seems foolish to attribute their attitudes and actions solely to a *lack* of agency brought about through the connivance of others, particularly when so many of their acts and utterances have a strongly purposive character. We might as well suppose that their apparent lack of agency, or of any responsibility for their actions, is strictly a product of neurochemical defects.

In other words, in articulating a social-constructivist theory of schizophrenia, Laing was justified in drawing attention to the political dimension of diagnosis. Though it is rationalized in the name of science or of humanitarian concern, the widespread tendency to condemn him on these grounds is symptomatic of a lack of realism and sensitivity among psychiatrists, who refuse to grapple with the issue. But it is also true that Laing's attempt to construe the mental patient as the victim of the machinations of others—while patently true in many cases—fails miserably as an overall characterization of madness. In his more disenchanted moods, Laing seemed to forget that an oppressed person may be an oppressor and victimizer in turn.

What prompted Laing to espouse this position? There is no simple answer. I suspect that Laing's tendency to idealize the schizophrenic was a product of the perennial temptation to idealize the oppressed and downtrodden that besets those with a strong oppositional identity, those who are incensed by the smugness, banality, and violence of their era. Though some may fault Laing for lack of consistency, I think it is to his credit that, in sober moods, Laing himself rejected the more extreme implications of this mode of protest as unrealistic.

Another reason Laing opted for the constructivist interpretation of schizophrenia is that it served as a powerful antidote to conventional stereotypes. As Laing demonstrated in *The Divided Self,* the standard psychiatric view of the schizophrenic is often a way of *not* seeing, thereby concealing and denying, the violence done to patients by their families and by psychiatrists themselves, who may unwittingly perpetuate a patient's symptomatology. In so doing, Laing was trying desperately to rouse the world from its slumbers. Perhaps untenable in the end, the social-constructivist thesis as he expressed it a generation ago was a bold step.

Still, Laing's advocacy for mental patients did have some unfortunate and unforeseen consequences. In retrospect it is clear that the rapid ascendancy of social constructivists during the sixties and seventies led to an equally vehement counterrevolution in the mental health professions, and to the militant denigration of ideas and perspectives that can loosely be termed "Laingian." As a result, current research into schizophrenia is so polarized that there is no middle ground and little chance of mediation. This sterile state of affairs is in no one's best interest, and until the rival orthodoxies relinquish their ideological warfare and focus on the creation of a more integrated approach, Laing's positive contributions will continue to be ignored.

In the meantime, the last two decades have witnessed the rapid marginalization of social and environmentalist approaches to mental disorder within psychiatry, with the result that the social constructivists—who are mostly sociologists, anthropologists, political theorists, and therefore nonpractitioners—seldom find a good foothold in the policy or research arenas. Admittedly, constructivism is making headway in academic psychology, sociology, and social work, but these gains do not translate into tangible power to change the system. So unless psychiatry recovers an interpersonal dimension, little progress will be made.

Finally, no discussion of Laing and psychiatry would be complete without some reflection on his relationship to the psychiatric survivor movement and his expulsion from the medical profession. A psychiatric survivor is someone who by her own reckoning has recovered from her disorder, *despite* the treatments that were offered or imposed, which in her estimation were more of a hindrance than a help in the search for sanity. Psychiatric survivors have created an international network that consists of journalists, advocates, and activists of various kinds, some of whom have become lawyers or mental health workers in an effort to reform the system. Their publications and activities call attention to the abuse and neglect that continue to plague psychiatric facilities, and to the devastating effects of racism, sexism, and poverty on mental patients.

Contrary to expectation, Laing was not very receptive to the psychiatric survivor movement until quite late in the day. As he frequently remarked, he was interested in engaging people before they were drugged and shocked, not afterward. Once people have received standard psychiatric treatment, he claimed, their chances of achieving a metanoia-like transformation are slim indeed. Also Laing was skeptical of efforts to reform psychiatry; he was more interested in creating alternatives to the system than in trying to abolish it or change it from within.

Laing's unwillingness to engage with the survivor movement puzzled many of its members who, rightly or wrongly, regarded him as a hero. Yet the fact remains that he steadfastly refused involvement until 1986 when, in an interview with Lyn Bigwood, he reluctantly agreed to begin doing some grassroots political work. There was no time for him to make good on this promise, but I doubt that he ever intended to. Depending on your point of view, Laing's attitude toward the psychiatric survivor movement could be construed as prudent or cowardly, honest or insincere. What is beyond dispute is that he was just as ambivalent about anti-psychiatry as he was about psychiatry itself.

Laing's expulsion from the medical profession is a different matter. Admittedly, when he was forced to resign by the General Medical Council, his conduct with patients was not always exemplary. To that extent, the disciplinary action may have been in the public interest. Nonetheless, whatever damage Laing did to a handful of patients around that time is minuscule in comparison to the damage done by more respectable psychiatrists who were never disciplined by their peers—who, on the contrary, received honors and accolades.

An instructive case in point is Laing's older compatriot, Ewan Cameron, who was born in 1901 in Bridge of Allan, a few miles north of Glasgow. Like Laing, he had a strict Presbyterian upbringing and was a very ambitious man, who read widely in psychology, philosophy, and religion as a teenager and became a protegé of Ferguson Rodger in his twenties. There the resemblance ends. Cameron was an ardent advocate of insulin-coma therapy and a great admirer of

Julius Wagner von Jauregg, whom Laing detested. Whereas Laing was something of a technophobe, Cameron had a passionate enthusiasm for gadgets and an utterly uncritical faith in the ability of science and technology to solve all human problems.

After postgraduate study at the Burgholzli Institute in Zurich and the Phipps Clinic in Baltimore, Cameron took charge of the Brandon Hospital for Mental Diseases in Manitoba, from 1930 to 1938, when he was offered the chair in psychiatry and neurology at the Mosher Memorial Hospital in Albany, New York. Considered a rising star in the psychiatric world, he was offered the directorship of the new Allan Memorial Institute in Montreal in 1943. A decade later, Cameron began experimenting with a technique he called "psychic driving." He wanted to "depattern" and "repattern" patients' behavior by subjecting them to thousands of taped repetitions of their own words and ostensibly benign suggestions intended to alter their attitudes and behavior while they were under heavy sedation—often for weeks and months on end. This intrusive and coarse technique was combined with frequent administrations of electroshock and LSD, in order to induce massive amnesia and a state of deep suggestibility.

Cameron experimented openly with his technique for a decade, hoping to win a Nobel Prize. Having published twelve papers proclaiming an imminent breakthrough as he tried to perfect the technique, in 1963 he evidently realized the error of his ways and, in 1964, went to work for the U.S. Veterans Administration in Albany. He died in September 1967, and it was not until 1992 that the eighty-odd victims of his ill-conceived experiments won some compensation from the Canadian government. But no amount of financial redress could restore the shattered minds of his patients or reverse the suffering caused to them and their families. In short, while he was riding his hobby horse, Cameron practiced medicine in utter disregard of the Hippocratic admonishment, *primum non nocere* (above all, do no harm). The only negative consequence for him personally was disappointed ambition.

Now I am not suggesting that Cameron is representative of the entire psychiatric profession. But he was no mere anomaly either. If he were, he would not have been elected president of the American Psychiatric Association, nor would he have founded the Canadian Psychiatric Association and the World Psychiatric Association.

Cameron trained cohorts of senior psychiatrists, many of whom are
still active in hospitals and research around the world. As Anne
Collins observes (1988), Cameron was cut from the same cloth as
Henry Cotton, Egon Moniz, Walter Freeman, and Ugo Cerletti,
whose fanaticism on behalf of their own implausible techniques
caused unimaginable suffering for countless patients. Instead of
being expelled from the profession, however, they were lionized by
most of their peers.

Despite his charisma, energy, and good intentions—which are not
at issue—Cameron's "psychic driving" is a striking example of the
unspeakable violence, sanctioned by scientism, that Laing loathed in
the profession. Even allowing for its polemical excesses, Laing's critique of psychiatry cannot be dismissed as but one more paranoid
fantasy unless we are also willing to disregard or distort much of the
history of psychiatry itself.

Still, merit aside, the reception of Laing's work in years to come
will probably continue to be influenced by the mixed impression he
made when he was alive and by his strong, enigmatic personality.
On the podium, Laing was sometimes weird, bombastic, and self-
indulgent, punctuating his utterances with lengthy silences whose
source or meaning was lost on most of his audience. In person, he
could be dreamy and inaccessible or rude and uncompromising. But
at his best R. D. Laing was a gentle, courteous, and wonderfully
witty man: a lucid, compassionate theorist of human misery, a genius
of our time, whose work repays close and continuing study.

NOTES

1. BEGINNINGS

1. For a memorable account of a childhood and adolescence spent in the Gorbals, see Boyle (1977).
2. When I spoke with her at her home in Largs, Scotland, Laing's Aunt Ethel insisted that his description of these violent confrontations, described so vividly in *Facts of Life,* was somewhat exaggerated. This should not be taken as an attempt to discredit her nephew. Ethel Laing was the only family member I met with who took obvious and unmixed pleasure in recounting Laing's accomplishments.
3. Further evidence for Laing's resentment at being compared with his grandfather can be found in an unpublished fragment called "What have I got myself into this time?" in "A Sutra on Remembering," a mimeographed leaflet handed out to the audience at Laing's lecture at the White Institute, January 11, 1967.

2. SCHOOLING

1. In a recent letter Marcelle Vincent insists that Laing's description of their week in Paris (see Mullan, 1995, p. 227) is quite fanciful.
2. It was claimed that the mortality rate from insulin-coma therapy was approximately 1 percent. It was probably much higher, and the recovery rates much lower, than reported. For more on this treatment, see Chapter 8.
3. Around 1916, Henry Cotton of the State Hospital in Trenton, New Jersey, invented his bacteriological and focal-infection theory of schizophrenia,

which he used to justify many pointless and wanton surgical procedures on thousands of helpless patients, with a reported death rate of 25 percent. (Phyllis Greenacre, who investigated Cotton's methods at the request of Adolf Meyer, put the death rate at 42 percent.) Between 1917 and 1935, 80 percent of Cotton's female patients lost their cervixes; 25–40 percent of the men underwent a resection of their seminal vesicles. Although there was no solid evidence on behalf of the focal-infection theory, it won considerable support from the British Medical Association and The Royal Medico-Psychological Association, which in 1927 convened a special meeting in Edinburgh to celebrate Cotton's "accomplishments" (Valenstein, 1986, pp. 37–42; Collins, 1988, pp. 77–82). Though I can't prove it, surely it is possible that many of the senior psychiatrists in Scotland during the mid-1950s attended this conference in their younger days.

3. THE TAVISTOCK AND FAMILY RESEARCH

1. See e.g., Laing (1976, p. 150). Still another factor in Laing's estrangement from his analyst may have been Rycroft's lukewarm response to Kierkegaard's *Sickness Unto Death.* One of the striking things about my interviews with Sutherland, Bowlby, and Rycroft is that they all recalled Laing circulating this book among his friends and colleagues, using their responses to it as a means by which to gauge something vital about their intellect or character. Judging from their recollections, they all failed the test, Sutherland in particular claiming that Laing never forgave him for diagnosing Kierkegaard as a typical schizoid character.

2. For a more detailed discussion of the psychotic interlude as repudiation of a false self, see Winnicott's much-cited review of Jung's memoir, *Memories, Dreams and Reflections,* in *International Journal of Psycho-Analysis,* 45 (1964).

4. IN AND OUT OF KINGSLEY HALL

1. Sidney Briskin remembers it differently. According to him, Mosher's characterization of the atmosphere at Kingsley Hall rings true for "some people all or some of the time" but not of "all of the people all of the time," adding that Kingsley Hall "had innumerable facades, and the patterns and rhythms of what went on was very varied" (personal communication, 1994).

5. THE TURN TO MYSTICISM

1. Elliot Mishler has noted that most of Laing's existential heros—Kierkegaard, Nietzsche, Kafka, Beckett, Sartre—were all unmarried and *sans famille* (1973, p. 385), arguing that Laing's identification with them be-

speaks an adolescent fixation, even though he himself was a husband and father, and that this may account for his appeal to the young. In any case, the
fact cannot be dismissed as pure coincidence, particularly when we consider
the dramatic contrast between the earlier material available to Mishler as he
was writing his essay and Laing's more positive pronouncements on the family after 1973. See Chapter 6.

6. BIRTH AND BEFORE

1. For some absorbing accounts of how psychosis was handled in the post-
   Kingsley Hall era of the P.A., see Douglas Kirsner's "The Primacy of Experience" (1976) and "Thomas Szasz Confronts R. D. Laing" (1977); Haya
   Oakley's "Touching and Being Touched" in *Thresholds between Philosophy
   and Psychoanalysis: Papers from the Philadelphia Association,* ed. Robin
   Cooper, (1989); Keith Musgrove's *Philadelphia Stories* (1992).
2. Swartley's collected papers are available at the Scott Library, York University, North York, Ontario.
3. Huxley and Balaskas, probably Laing's closest friends in the next decade,
   make brief appearances in *Conversations with Adam and Natasha* (Laing,
   1977) as Monty and Arthur.

7. FADE TO BLACK

1. For a first-person account of life in an Archway community, see Musgrave
   (1992).
2. Currently the Philadelphia Association runs two therapeutic households in
   London, one in Maida Vale and one in Finsbury Park.
3. For a more detailed discussion of Mosher's work, see Chapter 11.

8. A TOPOGRAPHY OF BABEL

1. For a recent debate on unconscious information processing, see the articles
   in the "Science Watch" section of *American Psychologist,* 47 (June 1992).
2. As Paul Ricoeur points out (1970), Freud's theory of psychic determinism
   was anticipated by rationalist philosophy, and by Spinoza and J. F. Herbart
   in particular. Herbart's conception of psychic determinism was informed by
   a theory of unconscious mental processes that made ample allowance for repression. The man who first blended the psychic determinism of the rationalist school with the mechanistic materialism of Helmholtz was Wilhelm
   Greisinger (1817–1869). Freud probably studied Greisinger, who was
   Theodor Meynert's instructor, while training as a neurologist.
3. In "The Birth of Client-Centered Therapy: Rogers, Rank and 'The Beyond'"

(unpublished paper), Robert Kramer traces the roots of Carl Rogers' theory of self-actualization to Otto Rank, whose work Rogers studied in the forties. From Kramer's discussion we see once more the porous boundaries between psychoanalysis and other nonbehaviorist, nonpositivist approaches. For more on Rogers, see the end of this chapter.

9. PHILOSOPHICAL ANTHROPOLOGY

1. As a careful reading of his earliest work discloses, Foucault did not start out from this position—he was very close to Binswanger's existentialism in the mid-1950s. See, for instance, Foucault's brilliant "Dream, Imagination and Existence" in *Dream and Existence* (1986).

2. Although Laing freely concedes that a sense of personal identity utterly detached from consensual validation is an ultimately insane project, there is nothing in his work to suggest that a perfect identity or complementarity between being-for-oneself and being-for-others is either possible or desirable. Still, in *Psychoanalysis and Feminism,* Juliet Mitchell charges Laing with attempting to define ontological security or basic sanity as a supposedly Hegelian unity of objectivity and subjectivity. Though Laing was indebted to Hegel, this is a serious misreading. Laing was also a student of Kierkegaard. He always assumed that even in sane or secure individuals there would always be an element of tension (or conflict) between these two modes of "being for." Besides, the tacit equation between objectivity and being-for-others, on the one hand, and subjectivity and being-for-oneself, on the other, is untenable phenomenologically, and Laing surely knew it. If someone is born black or female or left-handed in a racist, sexist, or superstitious milieu, their being-for-others will be tinted by a collective appraisal of them as defective, irrational, or potentially dangerous. Thus their being-for-themselves will have to come to grips with social stereotypes, whether they embrace or repudiate them. So it is simply wrong to elevate collective subjectivity to the status of objective fact. In most circumstances, being for-oneself is never purely subjective, in Mitchell's sense, but is affected by the appraisals of others. Being-for-oneself and being-for-others are states of mind that inevitably conflict, rendering this kind of dichotomization pointless.

3. For a similar perspective on the pursuit of disembodied existence, see Stolorow and Atwood (1991).

4. For an illuminating discussion of Sartre on human relationships, see Alisdair MacIntyre's "Existentialism" in *Sartre: A Collection of Critical Essays,* ed. M. Warnock, (1971), and Douglas Kirsner's neglected but remarkable *The Schizoid World of Jean-Paul Sartre and R. D. Laing* (1976).

1. Given the strong convergence in their aims and ideas, Roy Schafer's gloss on Laing, "Heart of Darkness: Review of *The Divided Self* and *Self and Others*" (1970), is surprisingly unsympathetic. For more useful critiques from analytic practitioners, see Mishler (1973) and Muir (1982).

2. This statement is a broad generalization and requires immediate qualification. Though Anna Freud and her followers focused chiefly on ego defenses, they had to take unconscious fantasies into account in their treatment of the transference. Melanie Klein and her group, focusing on fantasy, elucidated some defensive strategies of their own, notably splitting and projective identification.

3. John Bowlby addressed many of the same issues in lecture 6 of *A Secure Base* (1988), entitled, "On knowing what you are not supposed to know and feeling what you are not supposed to feel." Laing is not mentioned, but Bowlby acknowledged his influence here when we spoke in London in 1990.

4. Another theorist concerned with intergenerational transmission is Robert Stoller, whose work focuses on gender identity. Unlike most Freudian analysts, who construe it in oedipal or two-generational terms, Stoller traces the development of gender identity over three generations or more. See e.g. Stoller (1985).

11. PSYCHIATRY THEN AND NOW

1. For example, in Charles Kingsley's novel *Alton Locke* (1851), a disenchanted radical undergoes a brief psychotic interlude that fits the metanoia pattern. I don't know whether Laing knew of this or other nineteenth-century examples, but I strongly suspect he did.

REFERENCES

Asch, S. 1952. *Social Psychology*. Rprt. Oxford University Press, 1987.

Bakan, D. *Slaughter of the Innocents*. Toronto: Hunter Rose (CBC).

Barnes, M., and J. Berke. 1971. *Mary Barnes: Two Accounts of a Journey Through Madness*. New York: Harcourt, Brace, Jovanovich.

Bateson, G. 1972. *Steps Toward an Ecology of Mind*. New York: Ballantine Books.

—— ed. 1974. *Perceval's Narrative: A Patient's Account of His Psychosis*. New York: Morrow.

—— 1980. *Mind and Nature: A Necessary Unity*. New York: Bantam Books.

Bateson, G., and D. Jackson, J. Haley, and J. Weakland. 1968a. "Toward a Theory of Schizophrenia," in Jackson, 1968a.

Berke, J., ed. 1969. *Counter Culture*. London: Peter Owen.

—— 1990. "R. D. Laing: An Appreciation," *British Journal of Psychotherapy*, 7.2.

Bigwood, L. 1986. "Sanity, Madness and the Psychiatric Profession: Lyn Bigwood, RMN, Talks with R. D. Laing," *Asylum: A Magazine for Democratic Psychiatry*, 4.2 (1990).

Binswanger, L. 1936a. "Freud's Concept of Man in the Light of Anthropology," *Nederlandsch Tijdschrift voor Psychologie*, 4.5–6.

—— 1936b. "Sigmund Freud and the Magna Charta of Psychiatry," *Schweitzer Archives for Neurology and Psychology*, 37.2.

Bloch, E. 1972. *Atheism in Christianity*. New York: Herder.

Bowlby, J. 1969. *Attachment and Loss*, vol. 1. London: Hogarth Press.

—— 1988. *A Secure Base*. London: Routledge.

—— 1990. Personal communication, London.

Boyle, J. 1977. *A Sense of Freedom.* London: Pan Books.

Breggin, P. 1991. *Toxic Psychiatry: A Psychiatrist Speaks Out.* New York: St. Martin's Press.

———1993. "Psychiatry's Role in the Holocaust," *International Journal of Risk and Safety in Medicine,* 4.

Brierley, M. 1961. "Review of *The Divided Self*" *International Journal of Psycho-Analysis,* 42.

Briskin, S. 1973. Letter of resignation from Philadelphia Association, March 21. Courtesy Sydney Briskin, London.

———1990. "Ronnie Laing—Foundations," *Asylum: A Magazine for Democratic Psychiatry,* 4.2.

———1993. Personal communication, London.

Brown, P. 1990. "The Name Game: Toward a Sociology of Diagnosis," in Cohen, 1990.

Buber, M. 1951. "Distance and Relation." Rprt. in *Knowledge of Man.* New York: Harper and Row, 1966.

Bultmann, R. 1956. *Primitive Christianity in Its Contemporary Setting.* London: Thames and Hudson.

Burchard, E. 1966. "Dr. Laing to Inaugurate New Lecture Series," *William Alanson White Newsletter,* 1.1.

Burston, D. 1986. "The Cognitive and Dynamic Unconscious: A Critical and Historical Perspective," *Contemporary Psychoanalysis,* 22.1.

———1991. *The Legacy of Erich Fromm.* Cambridge: Harvard University Press.

———1992. "Psychiatric Sophistry: A Review of Lawrie Reznek's *The Philosophical Defense of Psychiatry,*" *Contemporary Psychology,* 37.9.

———1996. "Freud, Fromm and the Pathology of Normalcy: Clinical, Social and Historical Perspectives," in M. Cortina, and M. Maccoby, eds., *A Prophetic Analyst: Reclaiming Fromm's Legacy.* New York: Aronson.

Canguilhem, G. 1966. *The Normal and the Pathological.* trans. C. Fawcett, intro. M. Foucault. New York: Zone Books, 1989.

Churchill, B. 1990. Personal communication, London.

———1994. Letter to the author.

Clare, A. 1976. *Psychiatry in Dissent.* London: Tavistock Publications.

Cohen, D. 1990. "Challenging the Therapeutic State: Critical Perspectives on Psychiatry and the Mental Health System," *Journal of Mind and Behavior,* 11.

Cohen, I. ed. 1966. *Family Structure, Dynamics and Therapy.* Psychiatric Research Report 20, American Psychiatric Association, Washington, D.C.

Collier, A. 1977. *R. D. Laing: The Philosophy and Politics of Psychotherapy.* New York: Pantheon Books.

Collins, A. 1988. *In the Sleep Room: The Story of the CIA Brainwashing Experiments in Canada.* Toronto: Lester, Orpen and Dennys.

Cooper, D. 1967a. *Psychiatry and Anti-Psychiatry.* London: Tavistock. New York:
Ballantine Books.

———ed. 1967b. *The Dialectics of Liberation.* Harmondsworth: Penguin Books.

———1971. *The Death of the Family.* New York: Vintage Books.

———1974. *The Grammar of Living.* Harmondsworth: Penguin Books.

———1980. *The Language of Madness.* Harmondsworth: Penguin Books.

Cooper, R., et al. 1989. *Thresholds between Philosophy and Psychoanalysis.* London: Free Association.

Delueuze, G. and E. Guatari. 1977. *Anti-Oedipus: Capitalism and Schizophrenia.* New York: Viking.

Diethelm, O. 1939. "An Historical View of Somatic Treatment in Psychiatry," *American Journal of Psychiatry,* March.

Eccles, J. 1989. *Evolution of the Brain: Creation of the Self.* London: Routledge.

Ellenberger, H. 1970. *The Discovery of the Unconscious.* New York: Basic Books.

Erikson, E. 1964. *Insight and Responsibility.* New York: Norton.

Esterson, A. 1970. *The Leaves of Spring: A Study in the Dialectics of Madness.* Harmondsworth: Pelican Books.

Evans, R. 1976. *R. D. Laing: The Man and His Ideas.* New York: Dutton.

Feyerabend, P. 1975. *Against Method.* London: Verso Books.

Foucault, M. 1954a. "Dream, Imagination and Existence," *Review of Existential Psychology and Psychiatry,* 19.1 (1986).

———1954b. *Mental Illness and Psychology.* Berkeley: University of California Press, 1976.

Freeman, T. 1961. "Review of *The Divided Self*" *British Journal of Medical Psychology,* 34.

Freud, S. 1905. *Fragment of an Analysis of a Case of Hysteria,* vol. 7 in *The Standard Edition of the Complete Psychological Works of Sigmund Freud,* ed. James Strachey, 24 vols. London: Hogarth Press, 1953–1974.

———1916. "Some Character Types Met with in Psychoanalytic Work." *Standard Edition,* vol. 14.

———1920. *Beyond the Pleasure Principle. Standard Edition,* vol. 15.

———1921. *Group Psychology and the Analysis of the Ego. Standard Edition,* vol. 18.

———1923. *The Ego and the Id. Standard Edition,* vol. 19.

———1927. *The Future of an Illusion. Standard Edition,* vol. 27.

———1930. *Civilization and Its Discontents. Standard Edition,* vol. 21.

Friedenberg, E. 1973. *R. D. Laing.* Modern Masters Series. New York: Viking.

Friedman, M. 1984. *Contemporary Psychology: Revealing and Obscuring the Human.* Pittsburgh: Duquesne University Press.

Fromm, E. 1941. *Escape from Freedom.* New York: Holt, Rinehart and Winston.

———1955. *The Sane Society.* Greenwich: Fawcett Premier Books.

———1956. *The Art of Loving.* New York: Harper and Row.

———— 1961. *Marx's Concept of Man.* New York: Frederick Ungar.

———— 1968. Correspondence with R. D. Laing. Erich Fromm Archive, Tübingen.

———— 1970. *The Crisis of Psychoanalysis.* New York: Holt, Rinehart and Winston.

———— 1992. *The Revision of Psychoanalysis.* Boulder, Colorado: Westview Press.

Gardner, H. 1987. *The Mind's New Science: A History of the Cognitive Revolution.* New York: Basic Books.

Goffman, E. 1961. *Asylums: Essays on the Social Situation of Asylum Patients and Other Inmates.* Chicago: Aldine.

Goldblatt, D. 1986. "The Practical Application of Existential Phenomenological Psychotherapy in a Residential Setting." Paper at 5th Annual Human Science Research Conference, Berkeley.

———— 1989. "In Search of True Psychiatry." Memorial address for R. D. Laing, New School for Social Research, New York, October.

Goldman, A. 1971. "Meeting R. D. Laing," *Modern Occasions,* Spring.

Gordon, J. 1990. "Visionary Who Always Saw the Individual: R. D. Laing Remembered," *Psychiatric Times,* April.

Greenwood, M. 1993. "In Defense of Law 180—The Story That Isn't Being Told," *Asylum: A Magazine For Democratic Psychiatry,* 7.3.

Groddeck, G. 1950. *Exploring the Unconscious.* New York: Funk and Wagnall.

———— 1977. *The Meaning of Illness.* London: Hogarth Press.

———— 1979. *The Book of the It.* London: Vision Press.

Grof, S. 1975. *Realms of the Unconscious.* New York: Viking.

———— and C. Grof. 1980. *Beyond Death.* New York: Thames and Hudson.

Grosskurth, P. 1986. *Melanie Klein: Her World and Her Work.* New York: Knopf.

Hacking, I. 1990. *The Taming of Chance.* Cambridge: Cambridge University Press.

Heaton, J. 1994. "The Self, The Divided Self and the Other." Paper at 12th Annual Conference, Simon Silverman Phenomenology Center, Duquesne University, Pittsburgh, March 10–12.

Henry, J. 1963. *Culture Against Man.* New York: Random House.

Home, H. 1966. "The Concept of Mind," *International Journal of Psycho-Analysis,* 47.

Howe, E. G. 1931. *Motives and Mechanisms of the Mind.* London: *The Lancet.*

———— 1937. *The War Dance: A Study in the Psychology of War.* London: Faber and Faber.

———— 1949. *Mysterious Marriage.* London: Faber and Faber.

———— 1965. *Cure or Heal?,* intro. by R. D. Laing. London: Allen and Unwin.

Hood, J. 1989. "R. D. Laing," *Independent,* August 24.

Huxley, F. 1989. "Liberating Shaman of Kingsley Hall," *Guardian,* August 25.

Ingelby, D. ed. 1980. *Critical Psychiatry.* New York: Pantheon Books.

Jackson, D. ed. 1968a. *Communication, Family and Marriage.* Palo Alto: Science and Behavior Books.

———— 1968b. *Therapy, Communication and Change.* Palo Alto: Science and Behavior Books.

———— and P. Watzlawick. 1968. "The Acute Psychosis as a Manifestation of Growth Experience," in Jackson, 1968b.

Janov, A. 1970. *The Primal Scream.* New York: Delta Books.

Jones, M. 1953. *The Therapeutic Community.* New York: Basic Books.

Jung, C. G. 1935. *Analytical Psychology: Its Theory and Practice.* New York: Vintage Books, 1968.

———— 1952. *Symbols of Transformation: An Analysis of a Prelude to a Case of Schizophrenia,* in *Collected Works,* vol. 20. Princeton: Princeton University Press, 1976.

———— 1953. *Two Essays on Analytical Psychology.* New York: Meridian Books, 1971.

———— 1954. "On the Psychology of the Trickster-Figure," in *Collected Works,* vol. 9.

Kahr, B. 1994. "R. D. Laing's Missing Tooth: Schizophrenia and Bodily Disintegration," *Journal of the Society for Existential Psychology,* 5.

Karon, B. and A. Widener. 1994. "Is There Really a Schizophrenogenic Parent?" *Psychoanalytic Psychology,* 11.1.

Kirsner, D. 1976. *The Schizoid World of Jean-Paul Sartre and R. D. Laing.* Brisbane: University of Queensland Press.

———— 1976. "The Primacy of Experience: R. D. Laing and the Philadelphia Association," *Meanjin Quarterly,* 3.

———— 1977. "Thomas Szasz Confronts R. D. Laing." Unpublished paper.

———— 1980. Interview with R. D. Laing. London, February, later broadcast on Australian National Radio.

———— 1994. "Books Reconsidered: *The Divided Self,*" *Australian and New Zealand Journal of Psychiatry,* 28.1.

———— 1994. "R. D. Laing's Existential Quest: From *The Divided Self* to *The Politics of Experience.*" 5th Annual R. D. Laing Memorial Lecture, Free Association, London, June 22.

Kolakowski, L. 1981. *Main Currents in Marxism,* 3 vols. London: Oxford University Press.

Kovel, J. 1980. "The American Mental Health Industry," in Ingelby, 1980.

Kuhn, T. 1970. *The Structure of Scientific Revolutions,* 2nd ed. Chicago: University of Chicago Press.

Laing, A. 1994. *R. D. Laing: A Biography.* London: Peter Owen.

Laing, R. D. 1953. "An Instance of the Ganser Syndrome," *Journal of the Royal Army Medical Corps,* 99.4:169–72.

———— 1960. *The Divided Self: An Existential Study in Sanity and Madness.* London: Tavistock Publications. Harmondsworth: Pelican Books, 1965. Penguin Books, 1990.

——— 1961. *Self and Others.* London: Tavistock Publications. Harmondsworth: Pelican Books, 1971.

——— 1962. "Series and Nexus in the Family." *New Left Review,* 15 (May–June). Rprt. in *Politics of Experience.*

——— 1963a. "Minkowski and Schizophrenia," *Review of Existential Psychology and Psychiatry,* 3.3.

——— 1963b. "Review of *Schizophrenia as a Human Process* by H. S. Sullivan," *International Journal of Psycho-Analysis,* 44.3.

——— and A. Esterson. 1963. "The London Centre for the Study of Schizophrenia." Brochure.

——— 1964. *Sanity, Madness and the Family.* London: Tavistock Publications. Harmondsworth: Penguin Books, 1990.

——— and D. Cooper. 1964. *Reason and Violence: A Decade of Sartre's Philosophy, 1950–1960.* New York: Pantheon Books.

——— 1964a. "Review of *General Psychopathology* by Karl Jaspers," *International Journal of Psycho-Analysis,* 45.4.

——— 1964b. "Practice and Theory: The Present Situation." Paper at 6th International Congress of Psychotherapy, London. Rprt. in *Politics of Experience.*

——— 1964c. "Violence and Love." Lecture at Institute of Contemporary Arts, London. Rprt. in *Politics of Experience.*

——— 1964d. "What Is Schizophrenia?" Paper at 1st International Congress of Social Psychiatry, London. Rprt. in *Politics of Experience.*

——— 1964e. "Transcendental Experience in Relation to Religion and Psychosis." Paper at 1st International Congress of Social Psychiatry, London. Rprt. in *Politics of Experience.*

——— 1965a. "A Ten-Day Voyage," *Views,* 8. Rprt. in *Politics of Experience.*

——— 1965b. "Mystification, Confusion and Conflict," in I. Boszormenyi-Nagy, and J. Framo, eds., *Intensive Family Therapy.* New York: Harper and Row.

——— H. Phillipson, and R. Lee. 1966a. *Interpersonal Perception: A Theory of Method and Research.* London: Tavistock Publications.

——— 1966. "Ritualization and Abnormal Behavior," *Philosophical Transactions of the Royal Society of London,* 13.251.

——— 1967a–e. William Alanson White Lectures 1–5. New York Academy of Medicine, January 9–20. Transcripts at William Alanson White Institute, New York.

——— 1967f. "Sutra on Remembering." Leaflet. William Alanson White Institute, January 11.

——— 1967g. Psychotherapy Seminar conducted by R. D. Laing. William Alanson White Institute, January 14.

—— 1967h. Fellows Seminar on Kingsley Hall. William Alanson White Institute, January 16.

—— 1967i. *The Politics of Experience*. London: Tavistock Publications. New York: Pantheon Books and Ballantine Books, 1968. Includes "The Bird of Paradise."

—— 1967j. "Family and Individual Structure," in Lomas, 1967.

—— 1967k. "The Study of the Family and Social Contexts in Relation to the Origin of Schizophrenia," *Excerpta Medica International Congress Series,* 151. Proceedings of 1st Rochester International Conference, March 29–31.

—— 1968. "The Obvious," in Cooper, 1967b.

—— 1969a. *The Politics of the Family*. Toronto: CBC Publications.

—— 1969b. "Intervention in Social Situations." Foreword by Eileen Youngshusband. London: Association of Family Caseworkers and Philadelphia Association.

—— 1969c. *The Politics of the Family and Other Essays*. London: Tavistock Publications. New York: Pantheon Books.

—— 1970. *Knots*. London: Tavistock Publications. New York: Pantheon Books.

—— 1973a. "Counter Culture," *William Alanson White Newsletter,* 7.3.

—— 1973b. "On Neurosis," *William Alanson White Newsletter,* 7.4.

—— 1976. *The Facts of Life*. New York: Pantheon Books.

—— 1976b. *Do You Love Me?* New York: Pantheon and Ballantine Books.

—— 1977. *Conversations with Adam and Natasha*. New York: Pantheon Books.

—— 1979. *Sonnets*. Harmondsworth: Penguin Books.

—— 1982. *The Voice of Experience*. New York: Pantheon Books.

—— 1983. "Sparks of Light," interview with George Feuerstein in *Laughing Man,* 5.12.

—— 1985a. *Wisdom, Madness and Folly: The Making of a Psychiatrist*. New York: McGraw-Hill.

—— et al. 1985b. "Oran's Trust: A Description and Outline." Courtesy Stephen Ticktin, London.

—— 1985c. "Review of *Psychoanalysis and Beyond* by Charles Rycroft," *New Scientist,* November 28.

—— 1986. "Sanity, Madness and the Psychiatric Profession: Lyn Bigwood, RMN, Talks with R. D. Laing," *Asylum: A Magazine for Democratic Psychiatry,* 4.2 (1990).

—— A. Feldmar, P. Wilensky, and G. Marcuse. 1989. "The Lies of Love," transcript of CBC radio series *Ideas,* broadcast on May 18 and 25, June 1, Toronto.

Lester, M. 1937. *It Occurred to Me*. New York: Harper.

Lewontin, R., S. Rose, and L. Kamin. 1984. *Not in Our Genes: Biology, Ideology and Human Nature*. New York: Pantheon Books.

Lidz, T. 1964. *The Family and Human Adaptation.* London: Hogarth Press.

Lomas, P. 1967. *The Predicament of the Family.* London: Hogarth Press.

Matthews, S., M. Roper, L. Mosher, and A. Menn. 1979. "A Non-Neuroleptic Treatment for Schizophrenia: Analysis of the Two Year Post-Discharge Risk of Relapse," *Schizophrenia Bulletin* (NIMH), 5.2.

May, R., E. Angel, and H. Ellenberger. 1958. *Existence.* New York: Simon and Schuster.

Merton, T. 1973. *The Asian Journal of Thomas Merton.* New York: New Directions.

Mezan, P. 1972. "After Freud and Jung, Now Comes R. D. Laing," *Esquire,* January.

—— 1976. "R. D. Laing: Portrait of a Twentieth Century Skeptic," in Evans, 1976.

Milgram, S. 1974. *Obedience to Authority.* New York: Harper and Row.

Miller, A. 1986. *Thou Shalt Not Be Aware.* New York: Meridian.

Miller, H. 1939. *The Cosmological Eye.* Norfolk: New Directions.

Milner, M. 1960. "Supervision Report on R. D. Laing." Courtesy Marion Milner, London.

Mirowsky, J. 1990. "Subjective Boundaries and Combinations in Psychiatric Diagnoses," in Cohen, 1990.

Mishler, E. 1973. "Man, Morality and Madness: Critical Perspectives on the Work of R. D. Laing," in B. Rubinstein, ed., *Psychoanalysis and Contemporary Science,* vol. 2. New York: Macmillan.

Mitchell, J. 1975. *Psychoanalysis and Feminism.* New York: Vintage Books.

Monte, C. 1991. *Beneath the Mask.* New York: Harcourt Brace Jovanovich.

Mosher, L. 1970. "Kingsley Hall as Experienced by a Member of the American Establishment." Courtesy Loren Mosher, Washington, D.C.

—— A. Reifman, and A. Menn. 1973. "Characteristics of Nonprofessionals Serving as Primary Therapists for Acute Schizophrenics," *Hospital and Community Psychiatry,* 24.6.

—— and A. Menn. 1978. "Community Residential Treatment for Schizophrenia: Two-Year Follow Up," *Hospital and Community Psychiatry,* 29.11.

—— 1979. "Soteria: An Alternative to Hospitalization for Schizophrenia," *New Directions for Mental Health Services,* 1.1.

—— and L. Burti. 1989. *Community Mental Health: Principles and Practice.* New York: Norton.

—— 1991. "Soteria: A Therapeutic Community for Psychotic Persons," *International Journal of Therapeutic Communities,* 12.

—— and R. Vallone. 1992. "Soteria Project: Final Progress Report." Courtesy Loren Mosher, Washington, D.C.

Mott, F. 1959. *The Nature of the Self.* London: Allen Wingate.

—— 1960. *Mythology of Prenatal Life.* London: Integration Publishing.

Muir, R. 1982. "The Family, the Group, Transpersonal Processes and the Individual," *International Review of Psycho-Analysis,* 9.317.

Mullan, B. 1995. *Mad To Be Normal: Conversations with R. D. Laing.* London: Free Association.

Musgrove, K. 1992. *Philadelphia Stories.* Sutton Mandeville, Wiltshire: Spineless Books.

O'Brien, B. 1958. *Operators and Things: The Inner Life of a Schizophrenic.* Cambridge, Mass.: Arlington Books.

Parkin, A. 1987. *A History of Psychoanalysis in Canada.* Toronto: Toronto Psychoanalytic Society.

Perry, J. W. 1961. "Image, Complex and Transference in Schizophrenia," in A. Burton, ed., *Psychotherapy of the Psychoses.* New York: Basic Books.

———— 1966. *Lord of the Four Quarters: Myths of the Royal Father.* New York: Braziller.

———— 1980. "Psychosis as a Visionary State," in I. Baker, ed., *Methods of Treatment in Analytical Psychology.* Dallas: Spring Publications.

Philadelphia Association. "Report: 1965–1969." London.

"Philadelphia Association Limited: A Registered National Charity." Pamphlet, May 1, 1969. London.

Porter, R. 1989. *A Social History of Madness.* New York: Dutton.

Ratna, L. 1994. "Books Reconsidered: *The Divided Self* by R. D. Laing," *British Journal of Psychiatry,* 165.

Redler, L. 1990. "Obituary: Ronald David Laing, 1927–1989." *Journal of the Society for Existential Analysis,* 1.1.

———— P. Seal, and M. Yockum. 1970. "Kingsley Hall and the Philadelphia Association," *Network Newsletter,* London (November).

Resnick, J. 1990. "R. D. Laing Remembered," *Asylum: A Magazine for Democratic Psychiatry,* 4.2.

Rosenhan, D. 1973. "On Being Sane in Insane Places," *Science,* 179.

Roy, J. 1991. Personal communication.

Ruesch, J., and G. Bateson. 1968. *Communication: The Social Matrix of Psychiatry.* New York: Norton.

Russell, R. 1981. *Report on Effective Psychotherapy: Legislative Testimony.* Lake Placid: Hillgarth Press.

———— 1992. *R. D. Laing and Me: Lessons in Love.* Lake Placid: Hillgarth Press.

Rycroft, C. 1960. Letter to Dr. Frances Wride. Courtesy Charles Rycroft, London.

———— 1968a. *A Critical Dictionary of Psychoanalysis.* London: Penguin Books, 1972.

———— 1968b. *Imagination and Reality.* London: Karnac Press, 1987.

———— 1968c. *Anxiety and Neurosis.* London: Karnac Press, 1988.

———— 1981. *The Innocence of Dreams.* London: Oxford University Press.

—— 1985. *Psychoanalysis and Beyond,* ed. P. Fuller. Chicago: University of Chicago Press.

—— 1990. Personal communication, London.

—— 1991. *Viewpoints.* London: Hogarth Press.

—— 1993. "Why Analysts Need Their Patient's Transference," *British Journal of Psychotherapy,* 10.1.

—— 1994. "Psychoanalysis, 1937–1993: Reminiscences of a Survivor." Address to graduating class, School of Psychotherapy and Counselling, Regent's College, London.

Sacks, O. 1993. "To See and Not to See: A Neurologist's Notebook," *New Yorker,* May 10.

Sarbin, T. 1990. "Toward the Obsolescence of the Schizophrenia Hypothesis," in Cohen, 1990.

Sass, L. A. 1992. *Madness and Modernism.* New York: Basic Books.

Schafer, R. 1970. "Heart of Darkness: Review of *The Divided Self* and *Self and Others,*" *Contemporary Psychology,* 15.9.

Schatzman, M. 1968. "Madness and Morals," in Berke, 1969.

—— 1973. *Soul Murder: Persecution and the Family.* New York: Random House.

—— 1989. "Obituary: R. D. Laing," *Independent,* August 25.

—— 1990. Personal communication, London.

—— 1995. Letter to the author.

Scheff, T. 1976. *Labelling Madness.* New York: Prentice-Hall.

Schimel, J. 1990. Letter to the author, March 20.

—— and P. Schimel. 1991. Personal communication, New York.

Scull, A. 1979. *Museums of Madness.* London: Allen Lane.

—— ed. 1981. *Madhouses, Mad-Doctors and Madmen: The Social History of Victorian Psychiatry.* Philadelphia: University of Pennsylvania Press.

Sedgwick, P. 1982. *Psycho Politics.* London: Pluto Press.

Shenker, I. 1972, "R. D. Laing: 'Pure as the Driven Slush,'" *International Herald Tribune,* October 14–15.

Showalter, E. 1985. *The Female Malady: Women, Madness and English Culture, 1830–1980.* New York: Viking Penguin.

—— 1990. *Sexual Anarchy.* New York: Viking Penguin.

Sigal, C. 1976. *Zone of the Interior.* New York: Crowell.

—— 1989. "The Rebellious Games of a Divided Self," *Independent,* August 30.

Silverstein, B. 1985. "Freud's Psychology and Its Organic Foundation: Sexuality and Mind-Body Interaction," *Psychoanalytic Review,* 72.2.

Simon, R. 1983. "Still R. D. Laing after All These Years," *Family Therapy Networker,* 7.3.

Singer, M. T., and L. Wynne. 1966. "Communication Styles in Parents of Normals, Neurotics and Schizophrenics Using a New Rorschach Scoring Manual," in Cohen, 1966.

Stoller, R. J. 1985. *Presentations of Gender.* New Haven: Yale University Press.

Stolorow, R., and G. Atwood. 1991. "The Mind and the Body," *Psychoanalytic Dialogues,* 1.2.

Storr, A. 1989. "The Divided Legacy of R. D. Laing," *Observer,* August 27.

Sutherland, J. 1970. *Language and Psychodynamic Appraisal: A Development of the Word Association Method.* London: Tavistock Institute of Human Relations.

———— 1980. *The Psychodynamic Image of Man: A Philosophy for the Caring Professions.* Aberdeen: University Press.

———— 1989. *Fairbairn's Journey into the Interior.* London: Free Association.

———— 1994. *The Autonomous Self: The Work of John D. Sutherland.* New York: Aronson.

Suttie, I. 1935. *The Origins of Love and Hate.* Harmondsworth: Pelican Books.

Swartley, W. 1975. "Report on the State of Primal in Europe, Fall, 1975," *Newsletter,* Center for the Whole Person, Toronto.

———— 1978. "Major Categories of Early Traumas," in *The Undivided Self.* London: Churchill Center.

Szasz, T. 1976a. "Anti Psychiatry and the Paradigm of the Plundered Mind," *New Review,* 3.29 (August).

———— 1976b. *Schizophrenia: The Sacred Symbol of Psychiatry.* Syracuse: Syracuse University Press.

———— 1990. *Anti-Freud: Karl Kraus's Criticism of Psychoanalysis and Psychiatry.* Syracuse: Syracuse University Press.

Temerlin, M. K. 1968. "Suggestion Effects in Psychiatric Diagnosis," *Journal of Nervous and Mental Diseases,* 147.

Thompson, M. G. 1985. *The Death of Desire: A Study in Psychopathology.* New York: New York University Press.

———— 1994. "Deception, Mystification, Trauma: Laing and Freud." Paper at 12th Annual Conference, Simon Silverman Phenomenology Center, Duquesne University, Pittsburgh.

Ticktin, S. 1986. "Brother Beast: A Personal Memoir of David Cooper," *Asylum: A Magazine for Democratic Psychiatry,* 1.3.

———— 1990. "R. D. Laing: A Personal Tribute," *Asylum,* 4.2.

———— 1994. "R. D. Laing's Divided Tooth," *Journal of the Society for Existential Analysis,* 5.

Trist, E., and H. Murray, eds. 1990. *The Social Engagement of Social Science: A Tavistock Anthology,* vol. 1. Philadelphia: University of Pennsylvania Press.

Trist, E. 1992. Personal communication, London.

Tyson, A. 1971. "Review of *The Divided Self* and *Self and Others,*" *New York Review of Books,* February 11.

Valenstein, E. 1986. *Great and Desperate Cures.* New York: Basic Books.

Vincent, M. 1993. Letter to the author.

Watzlawick, P. 1968. "Review of the Double Bind Theory," in Jackson, 1968a.

Wendt, R., L. Mosher, S. Matthews, and A. Menn. 1982. "Comparison of Two Treatment Environments for Schizophrenia," in *Principles and Practices of Milieu Therapy,* ed. J. Gunderson, O. Will, and L. Mosher. New York: Aronson.

Wing, J. K., and G. W. Brown. 1970. *Institutionalism and Schizophrenia.* Cambridge: Cambridge University Press.

Winnicott, D. W. Letters to R. D. Laing. Winnicott Archive, Oscar Diethelm Historical Library, Cornell University Medical Center, New York.

——— Letter to Nicholas Latimer. Winnicott Archive.

——— 1960. Letter to Dr. Frances Wride. Winnicott Archive.

——— 1967. "Mirror Role of Mother and Family in Child Development." Rprt. Winnicott, *Playing and Reality.* London: Routledge, 1991.

Wynne, L. 1970. "Communication Disorders and the Quest for Relatedness in Families of Schizophrenics." 18th Annual Karen Horney Lecture, Cornell University Medical Center, New York, March 25.

INDEX

Abenheimer, Karl, 57
Abraham, Karl, 47
Adler, Alfred, 216
A Group, 48
Alpert, Richard (Ram Dass), 59, 60
anti-psychiatry, 62, 107, 237
Anti-University, The, 107–108, 111
Aquinas, Thomas, 195
Arbors Association, 92, 115, 244
Archway communities, 92, 120, 133, 244
army experience, 35
Artaud, Antonin, 221
Augustine, St., 173, 195, 226
authenticity, 158–159, 180–181

Baba, Gangotri, 119–120
Bakan, David, 13
Balaskas, Arthur, 117, 129, 137, 255
Balint, Michael, 48, 148, 227, 239
Barnes, Mary, 81–83, 116
Basaglia, Franco, 95
Bateson, Gregory, 49, 59, 61, 69, 105,
    108, 154, 159, 169, 238, 241
behaviorism, 152–153, 160, 167
Berke, Joseph, 81, 83, 87, 90, 91–92,
    105, 107, 108, 111, 115, 130, 148
B group, 48
Binswanger, Ludwig, 176–177, 256
Bion, W. R., 47

birth: archetype, 233; biological versus
    existential, 126–127; dreams about,
    229; trauma, 125. *See also* rebirthing
Blake, William, 182, 221
Bloch, Ernst, 108–109
Bowlby, John, 42, 46, 48, 50, 56, 60, 65,
    67, 73, 112, 257
Brentano, Franz, 175, 207
Briskin, Sidney, 70–73, 77, 79, 81, 83,
    85, 120–121, 140, 237, 254
Buber, Martin, 172, 178, 184, 201, 202
Buddhism, 23–24, 95, 111, 118–119, 130
Burch House, 142

Calvinism, 28, 195
Cameron, Ewan, 60, 164, 249–251
Camus, Albert, 189
Carmichael, Stokely, 106
Cerletti, Ugo, 165, 251
Ceylon, trip to, 117–118
Chisholm, Brock, 103–104
Churchill, Ben, 6, 54, 74, 78, 90
Clare, Anthony, 106, 134, 141
cognitive psychology, 153–154, 167–168
Collins, Anne, 251
Cooper, David, 61–62, 77, 80–81, 84,
    94–95, 98, 101, 105, 106, 107, 108,
    111, 117, 130, 143, 177, 198, 237
Cotton, Henry, 251, 253–254

Crawford, Hugh, 92, 110–111, 116–117, 125, 132–134

Davidson, Leonard, 25–26, 27, 140, 142
depression, 28, 106, 141
derealization, 219–220
Diabasis House, 92, 244
Dialectics of Liberation Conference, 81, 96, 105–107, 109
Diethelm, Oscar, 165
Dilthey, Wilhelm, 176, 203, 204
Dionysius the Areopagite, 108, 109, 194
"Dora," the case of, 209–212
Duffy, John, 25, 140, 142

ego, and socialization, 155–156, 222–225
electroshock therapy, 35, 43
Eliade, Mircea, 108
elusion, 231–233
Ellenberger, Henri, 229–230
Elzey, Roberta, 108
embodiment, 185–188, 256
Erikson, Erik, 184, 217–218
Esterson, Aaron, 26, 58, 61, 63–64, 67–74, 81, 90, 115, 130, 211, 240
existential needs, 182–184
existential phenomenology, 32, 40, 46, 61, 84, 147, 157–159, 177–178, 215–216

Fairbairn, W. R. D., 42, 49, 114
false self, 3, 41–42, 64, 65–66, 97, 193–195, 224
Fehr, Elizabeth, 121, 125. See also rebirthing
Ferenczi, Sandor, 47–49, 227
Foucault, Michel, 159, 163, 169, 177, 199, 245, 246
Freeman, Tom, 54
Freeman, Walter, 251
Freidenberg, E. Z., 67, 73
Freud, Anna, 47, 48, 50, 56, 82, 205, 257
Freud, Sigmund, 8, 24, 30, 48–49, 50, 55–56, 87–88, 96, 102, 115, 125, 127, 154–156, 170, 175–176, 180–181, 188, 198–201, 203–205, 209–217, 221–229, 255
Fromm, Erich, 56, 93, 96, 110, 118, 155–156, 158, 172, 180–182, 205, 206, 220, 225
Fromm-Reichmann, Frieda, 32, 93

Gandhi, Mohandas (Mahatma), 16, 78, 86
Ganser syndrome, 32, 231
Gartnavel Mental Hospital, 35–38, 42, 80
Gelfer, Richard, 12, 26, 51, 59
General Medical Council, 141, 142, 143, 249
Gide, André, 198, 200
Ginsburg, Allen, 106
Glasgow, 9, 23, 28, 35, 253
Glasgow University, 8, 24–28, 107
Gnosticism, 95, 108, 187–188, 194–195, 222, 225
Goffman, Erving, 3, 41, 59, 63, 102, 159, 167, 169, 245
Goldblatt, David, 142
Gordon, James, 147–149
Graves, Robert, 108
Groddeck, Georg, 54, 214–215, 224, 228
Grof, Stanislav, 60, 229
Guatari, Felix, 95
Guntrip, Harry, 114
Gurdjieff, G. I., 194

Hartmann, Eduard von, 175, 198–199
Hartmann, Heinz, 155–156, 225
Hearne, Anne. See Laing, Anne
Heaton, John, 7, 54, 57, 87, 92, 117, 120, 121, 124, 136, 230–233
Hegel, G. W. F., 29, 178, 200, 229, 256
Heidegger, Martin, 26, 29, 114, 157, 159, 176–177, 196
Herbart, J. F., 175, 255
Hinduism, 23–24, 95, 119
Home, James, 204–205
Hood, James, 7, 25, 146
Howe, Eric Graham, 57, 60, 65, 118, 125
humanistic psychology, 157–158, 171–173
Husserl, Edmund, 26, 29, 157, 175, 176, 178, 203–204, 207
Hutchinson, Douglas, 25, 54, 140
Huxley, Francis, 84, 108, 110, 117, 124, 128–129, 137, 255
hysteria, 34, 209–212

identity: personal, 40, 178–179; collective, 189–196; and madness, 184–185
India, 1971–1972 visit to, 117, 118–120
Institute of Psycho-Analysis (London), 47–57
insulin coma therapy, 32, 164–165, 235, 249
intergenerational transmission, 216–218
interpersonal defenses, 209–211
Itten, Theodor, 7, 143–144, 169

Janov, Arthur, 125
Jaques, Eliot, 221
Jaspers, Karl, 31, 65–67, 243
Jones, Ernest, 47–49
Jones, Maxwell, 78, 80, 81, 86
Jung, C. G., 3, 8, 17, 22, 57–58, 102, 108, 188, 214, 215–216, 217, 224, 227, 239, 254

Kahr, Brett, 137
Kali, cult of, 119–120
Kallman, Franz Josef, 166
Kanduboda Meditation Center, 118
Kant, Immanuel, 29, 152, 194, 226
Kierkegaard, Søren, 29, 157, 170, 173, 254, 256
Killearn, neurosurgical unit at, 29
Kingsley, Charles, 78, 257, 139, 144
Kingsley Hall, 78–92, 115–117, 193, 195, 244
Kirsner, Douglas, 107, 114, 143, 255, 256
Klein, Melanie, 47–50, 56, 127, 137, 155, 181, 188, 201, 205–206, 213–215, 257
Kohut, Heinz, 200
Kuhn, Thomas, 161–162

Lacanian theory, 160, 196, 213
Laing, Adam (son), 101, 106, 117–118
Laing, Adrian (son), 10, 27, 65, 74, 100, 102, 111, 121, 123, 130, 138, 140, 142
Laing, Amelia (mother), 9–19, 25, 27, 100, 110, 126, 140, 142, 218
Laing, Anne (wife), 34–35, 42, 45, 54, 74–75, 100, 125, 140
Laing, Benjamin (son), 136
Laing, Charles (son), 139, 144
Laing, David (father), 9–11, 13–19, 20,
110, 140
Laing, Ethel (aunt), 9–13, 16–17, 145, 253
Laing, John (paternal grandfather), 9, 16–17
Laing, Jutta (wife), 6, 74, 75, 86, 101, 117, 120, 123, 124, 134–138, 143
Laing, Karen (daughter), 100, 145
Laing, Max (son), 101, 123
Laing, Natasha (daughter), 101, 116, 117
Laing, Paul (son), 45
Laing, Susan (daughter), 11, 14, 75, 100, 125
Langham Clinic, 57–58, 60
Leary, Timothy, 60, 86
Le Bon, Gustav, 222
Lester, Muriel, 78, 79, 91
Lidz, Theodor, 99–100
lobotomy, 29, 235
LSD, 59–61, 89, 94, 250
Luther, Martin, 195

MacDiarmid, Hugh, 107
MacNiven, Angus, 35, 37, 43
Mahathera, Nyanaponika, 57, 118
Marcuse Herbert, 98, 102, 104, 105
Marx, Karl, 24, 26, 122, 159, 170, 192–194
Marxism, 30, 61, 80–81, 94–95, 107–109, 123, 169–170, 192–194, 198
Maslow, Abraham, 171, 184
maternal deprivation, 199–200
May, Rollo, 142–143
Mead, G. H., 2, 159
Merleau–Ponty, Maurice, 27, 111, 157, 178
metanoia, 41, 65–67, 97, 238–239, 241–245
Meynert, Theodor, 175, 225
Mezan, Peter, 22, 23, 108–109, 121–122
Middle Group, 48–49, 50
Miller, Alice, 13
Milner, Maron, 26, 48, 50–53
Mishler, Eliot, 67, 73, 240, 242, 254
Mitchell, Juliet, 123, 206, 256
Mosher, Loren, 84, 86, 92, 244–245
Mott, Francis, 125
Mullan, Bob, 45, 92, 144–145, 172
music, 11, 18–19

mysticism: and psychotherapy, 89; and politics, 108–109

"Nan," case of, 39–40
Neoplatonism, 22–23, 38–41, 194
Netley (British Army Psychiatric Unit), 31–34
neurology, 28–31, 38–41, 68, 127, 152, 163–164, 198
Nietzsche, Friedrich, 24, 26, 29, 170, 179, 198–199, 221, 226, 254
normality, 219–224

object relations theory, 49, 114
ontological security (and insecurity), 12, 183–189, 219–220
operations on experience, 208–212
Oran's Trust, 139–140

Payne, Silvia, 48, 50
Perry, John Weir, 92, 244
personality formation: the case of "Nan," 39–40; the case of "Julie," 168
Philadelphia Association, 6, 64, 71–83, 88–92, 110–111, 128–131, 137, 170, 193–196
phrenology, 159–160
Piaget, Jean, 153
Pirandello, Luigi, 2, 3, 226, 232
Plato, 2, 22, 108, 222, 229
psychiatric survivor movement, 248–249
psychopathology: individual, 200–201, 216; familial, 72, 159, 209–212, 217–219

Rajneesh, Bhagwan Shree, 138
Ram Dass. See Alpert, Richard
Rank, Otto, 48, 125, 127, 255
Ratna, Lawrence, 238. See also schizophrenia
rebirthing, 125, 126–130, 228–231
Redler, Leon, 2, 87, 92, 105, 107, 115–116, 133, 138–139
regression, 41, 97, 227–228
Reich, Wilhelm, 98
Rodger, Ferguson, 35, 42
Rogers, Carl, 129, 142, 171–172, 201, 255
Romayne-Kendon, Marguerite, 139, 143

Rosenfeld, Herbert, 47, 52
Rumpus Room, 37–38
Russell, Roberta, 74, 134–136, 138, 198
Rycroft, Charles, 42, 48, 50, 52–57, 206, 256

Sakel, Manfred Joshua, 164–165. See also insulin coma therapy
Sanctuary. See Oran's Trust
Sartre, Jean Paul, 8, 27, 61–62, 69, 72, 104–105, 167, 169, 193, 212, 238, 254, 256
Schatzman, Morton, 13, 84–85, 87, 90–92, 93, 110, 115–116, 130, 147
Schimel, John, 93, 94, 122
schizophrenia: as capitalist artifact, 94–95; definitions of, 238–239; diagnosis of, 97–98, 166, 245–247; and evil, 172–173; and families, 67–74, 98–99, 211–212, 238, 240–241
Schopenhauer, Arthur, 175, 198–199, 226
Schorstein, Joseph, 29–31, 43, 59
Sedgwick, Peter, 123, 170
shamanism, 129, 231–233
Shenley Hospital. See Villa 21
Showalter, Elaine, 82–83
Sigal, Clancy, 60–61, 81, 87–90, 92, 143, 145–146
Slater, Eliot, 166
social constructivism, 39–40, 109–110, 168–171, 190, 246–248
Soteria House. See Mosher, Loren
Southern General Hospital, 35
Stobhill Hospital, 28
Stoicism, 194–195
Storr, Anthony, 146–147
Strachey, James, 48
Sullivan, Harry Stack, 32, 62–63, 213
Sunkel, Susan, 136, 138
Sutherland, John D., 42, 48, 256
Suttie, Ian, 49
Swartley, William, 125–127, 255
Szasz, Thomas, 82, 159, 170–171, 245

Tavistock Clinic, 42, 45–46, 49, 82
Tavistock Institute of Human Relations, 46, 58–59
Templeton, James, 23, 145
Thompson, Michael, 125, 129, 135, 142, 143, 170, 224

Ticktin, Stephen, 138–139
transpersonal defenses, 209, 210, 212
Trist, Eric, 42, 86

unconscious defenses. *See* operations on
    experience
unconscious experience, 197–198,
    202–205, 207–212, 224
unconscious fantasy theory: individual,
    205–206, 212–216; collective, 221–224
unconscious information processing,
    154, 255

Villa 21, 61, 77, 80
Vincent, Marcelle, 26, 31, 34, 74, 140,
    189, 197, 253

Wagner-Jauregg, Julius von, 30, 250
Werner, Jutta. *See* Laing, Jutta
William Alanson White Institute, 78,
    93–96, 209
Winnicott, D. W., 48, 50, 51–54, 64–65,
    200, 227, 239
Wittgenstein, Ludwig, 8, 27
Wride, Francis, 52–54

Yockum, Michael, 116, 133

Zeal, Paul, 116, 133